FISHING IN
HARTLEPOOL

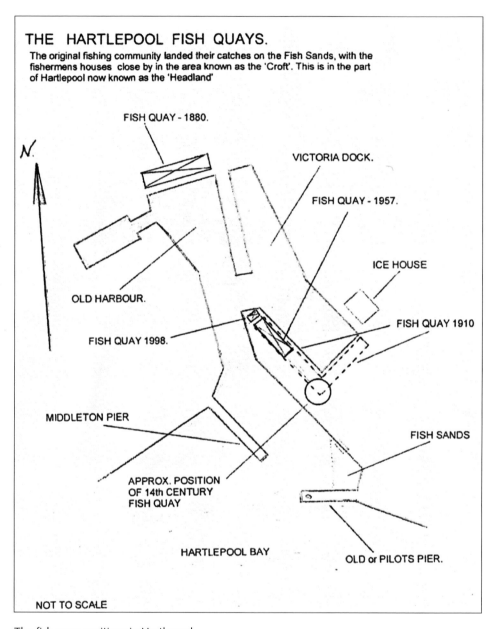

THE HARTLEPOOL FISH QUAYS.

The original fishing community landed their catches on the Fish Sands, with the fishermens houses close by in the area known as the 'Croft'. This is in the part of Hartlepool now known as the 'Headland'

FISH QUAY - 1880.

VICTORIA DOCK.

FISH QUAY - 1957.

N.

ICE HOUSE

OLD HARBOUR.

FISH QUAY 1910

FISH QUAY 1998.

MIDDLETON PIER

FISH SANDS

APPROX. POSITION
OF 14th CENTURY
FISH QUAY

HARTLEPOOL BAY

OLD or PILOTS PIER.

NOT TO SCALE

The fish quay positions in Hartlepool.

FISHING IN
HARTLEPOOL

MALCOLM COOK

The
History
Press

Longscar (HL 16) with a deckful of coal.

First published 2011

The History Press
The Mill, Brimscombe Port
Stroud, Gloucestershire, GL5 2QG
www.thehistorypress.co.uk

British Library Cataloguing in Publication Data.
A catalogue record for this book is available from the British Library.

ISBN 978 0 7524 5893 9

Typesetting and origination by The History Press
Printed in Great Britain

CONTENTS

PREFACE

I was encouraged to write about the Hartlepool fishing history after reading Bert Spaldin's book *Maritime Hartlepool* where a brief reference is made. After talking to Bert and realising that no one had written a complete history of this once-important local industry, I decided to give it a go – never thinking that it would take so long to complete and never having written articles of more than a couple of pages for magazines. My qualifications for writing this book perhaps come from my family history: my great-grandfather started going to sea in sailing trawlers out of Lowestoft; he was followed by various members of the family in both the catching and processing sides of the industry from then on. I worked on the fish quay in Hartlepool for over twenty years, running the family business which was started by my grandfather in 1919 after he came ashore as a chief skipper of a trawler minesweeping flotilla, which followed a successful career fishing out of Aberdeen. The fishing industry of Hartlepool and around the whole of the British Isles is now disappearing, and unfortunately no UK Government, of any colour, appears to have any interest. So perhaps by putting pen to paper I may help to preserve some memories of a once-thriving industry. What may be confusing for some readers is the reference to Hartlepool and West Hartlepool; these were two separate towns once upon a time prior to their amalgamation in 1967. 'West' began during the Industrial Revolution, when docks were built on the other side of the bay to rival the expanding docklands of Hartlepool so all listings of shops etc. refer to 'Old' Hartlepool or the area that is now referred to as the 'Headland'.

ACKNOWLEDGEMENTS

My grateful thanks must go to numerous people who have helped me with the production of this book. Bert Spaldin for his initial encouragement and for reading through my manuscript, various members of the local fishing community who kept me right with facts, figures and photographs, my brother Alan, Steve Horsley, Keith Williams and others too numerous to mention. My thanks must also go to the staff at The Teesside Archives in Middlesbrough for putting up with my visits over several months as I plodded my way through the Fishing Vessel Registers.

I would also like to thank the following who provided photographs for this book:

Bert Spaldin, Hartlepool; Bob Slimmings, Hartlepool; David & Graham King; Peter Watt, Hartlepool; Robbie Wray, Hartlepool; Stephen Horsley, Hartlepool; Sonny Ray, Hartlepool; Jenny Hillier, Hartlepool; Hartlepool Headland History Group; Port of Lowestoft Research Society; Alan Cook; Hartlepool Museums and Heritage Services.

Abbreviations

APV	armed patrol vessel
m/s	minesweeper
BDV	boom defence vessel
6pdr	6-pounder gun
AA	anti-aircraft
HL	Hartlepool
SH	Scarborough
SN	North Shields
SSS	South Shields
GY	Grimsby
H	Hull
A	Aberdeen
LT	Lowestoft
S.T. Co.	Steam Trawler Company
S.F. Co.	Steam Fishing Company
r/n	renamed
3cyl	3-cylinder engine
2cyl	2-cylinder engine
A/deen	Aberdeen
H/pool	Hartlepool
NER	North Eastern Railway
LNER	London & North Eastern Railway
40+ FBA	40+ Fishing Boat Association

1

THE BEGINNING

The origins of Hartlepool in the dim and distant past must have had something to do with the natural harbour enclosed by the Headland and the availability of fish stocks off the coast. Together with the cultivation of fields on the Headland, these two occupations would have provided the local population with an income. This lifestyle would have been similar to that carried on all round the coast of these islands in medieval times and which lasted, in some corners of the Scottish Highlands and Islands, into the twentieth century. People working the land and the sea are known as 'crofters' and that is where the local name for residents of the Headland must have come from. If it was not for the original fishermen forming a settlement on the Headland, perhaps the present town of Hartlepool may never have existed.

Over time the town became more important with the building of a monastery, and having the advantage of a sheltered harbour Hartlepool became a staging post for numerous monarchs assembling fleets on the stormy east coast. By the 1300s a wall was

Cobles ashore at low water on the fish sands.

The Town Wall and Sandwell Chare.

built around the town to keep out the marauding Scots. This wall started on the cliffs at the base of the Old Pier and extended down to the ferry steps before turning across the dock to pass near where the present-day Co-op store is situated and continued to the cliff edge on Marine Drive. The wall traversed the sheltered harbour with a gateway left in the wall so that ships could enter and leave, a chain being suspended between two towers which formed the entrance to keep out unwanted intruders. The harbour was bounded by the wall and the curved route of Northgate, round to the 'dock head'.

The area known as the Fish Sands gets its name from its use as the landing area for the cobles where the fish was brought ashore. Evidence of a second gateway can be seen in the present wall next to the Sandwell Chare opening; this had to be provided because of congestion due to so many horses and carts wanting to be on the sands to collect fish for delivery to local towns and villages. The Fish Sands lie in the shelter of the Old Pier or Pilots Pier, one of the oldest piers in the country, dating from the 1470s. However, archaeologists discovered a substantial quayside during excavations in Southgate in the 1980s. There was evidence that this quay was used for the landing of fish in the fourteenth century; this would put the fish dock in the area of Friendship Lane, not too far from the present Fisherman's Arms pub and close to the boundary wall of the current fish quay. The local fishing fleet declined in the 1560s with the loss of the fish trade to the local religious houses, including Monkwearmouth, due to the Reformation. The Prior of Durham, in the fourteenth century, bought 3,500 salt herring in 1353, sixty-two cod in 1357, eighty cod in 1370, 2,000 salt herring in 1373 and 140 cod in 1380.

'Long lines' appear to have been the most common form of fishing, together with beam trawls and drift netting for both salmon and herring. Crabs and lobsters were also caught from boats or gathered from the local rocks at low water. Apparently this fishing was left to the older fishermen who perhaps could no longer stand the rigours of longer trips at sea.

Winter fishing in medieval times would be up to 8 or 10 miles offshore, but in the summer, with longer spells of fine weather, 10 to 20 miles out to sea, or 'offing' as it was known. This later developed into 'offside', the term for fishing farther out to sea and staying for a number of days. Fishing grounds would be found by local knowledge, a certain amount of instinct and experience passed down from your forebears. The only navigation equipment would be a compass and a line to sound the bottom, with a weight on the end which would be dipped in tallow so the nature of the seabed could be sampled.

While the men were at sea their wives would be selling fish round the doors of the local villages or baiting lines ready for the next day at sea. Before they could bait the lines the women would have to gather mussels or limpets from the rocks, 'skein' them and bait up to 400 hooks per line. Lines were then coiled carefully onto a rip, a flat oval board, for carrying down to the boat. Different bait was used according to the seasons: mussels, limpets, herring, or, as in old writings, tentails (or squid).

In between trips, boats and fishing gear would have to be maintained, boats painted and caulked, and nets and sails dipped in 'cutch' to preserve them from salt water. Old photographs show nets hung over the length of the Town Wall, drying out after being treated.

It is noted in Cuthbert Sharp's *History of Hartlepool* that a great number of live turbot were exported to London by 'well smacks' calling at the port. A well smack was a sailing

Evidence can still be seen of the second opening in the wall.

vessel where the fish room, or hold, had holes drilled through to let sea water in so that fish could be kept alive with a constant flow of fresh sea water. A good price was obtained for live fish in Billingsgate, and in one week 1,050 live fish were sent to the London market. Also from Sharp's book, Richard Hunter, fisherman, caught a skate of 16st. 4lb (103kg). It is also recorded that John Scott paid the Mayor 12p per year to lay his oysters in the Old Harbour.

In times of good catches, fish would be salted or pickled and exported to the Mediterranean or the West Indies, where the large Catholic populations of the area would need fish for consumption on Fridays.

Regulations

Prior to 1883, there were no regulations applied to the fishing industry; it was a free-for-all. A Royal Commission was set by the Government of the day and took evidence from around the coast, including from Hartlepool skipper Thomas Hood. He complained about trawlers damaging grounds and sweeping the seas, while local driftermen also complained that their nets were being towed away. Eventually trawling was banned inside 3 miles but even in 1909 it was alleged that eleven Hartlepool cobles were trawling illegally. And with regulation came paperwork; skippers would have to pass examinations and be required to fill in logbooks – unfortunately many skippers, at that time, could not read or write.

Opposite: **THE COD END**
A *Norwood,* B *Golden Boy,* C *Cleveland,*
D *Cleveland,* E *Lady Patricia,* F *Margit.*

2

THE QUAYS

By the early 1800s, with the coming of the Industrial Revolution, coal mines were being sunk in all areas of County Durham and the mine owners were looking for ports from which to export their coal to the south of England. Hartlepool was a prime candidate. When the Hartlepool Dock & Railway Co. was formed in 1832, the geography of the whole area changed completely as it was transformed into a major coal-exporting port. In 1865 the docks were taken over by the North Eastern Railway Co. (NER). With these changes came a new fish quay situated in the area we know as the deep water berth at the northern end of the Old Harbour. This quay paved the way for bigger fishing boats to use Hartlepool; whereas previously boats landing on the Fish Sands were cobles of 20–30ft in length, the new quay could accommodate any size of drifter or trawler. As this quay was a purpose-built facility, vessels could be accommodated at any state of the tide. Some idea

Steam trawlers landing on the fish quay in the Old Harbour.

of the expansion of the fisheries can be gathered from the fact that in 1856 seventy cobles landed fish at Hartlepool to the value of £7,000, and in 1909 over 600 vessels landed fish to the value of £80,000. Instead of dried or salt fish, railway connections to all parts of the country enabled distribution of fresh fish to towns inland that were outside the capacity of supply from the Fish Sands landing point. Ice now had to be imported from Norway to keep the fish in good condition.

As can be seen from the table below, the town's growth in population was rapid over a comparatively short time:

1801	993
1811	1,074
1821	1,247
1831	1,330
1832	Hartlepool Dock & Railway Co. formed
1851	9,530
1861	12,245
1880	Fish quay opened
1900	22,613

Local interests purchased larger fishing boats and also introduced steam-powered vessels, thus dependency on the wind was becoming less of a factor. The herring fleet, which

Steam and sail: locals and visitors crowd the quay.

followed the shoals down the east coast, was now able to call and land catches into Hartlepool, increasing the demand for quay space and facilities. Very soon the quay was too small for the amount of fish being landed. Within thirty years of moving from the Fish Sands to the Old Harbour, a new fish quay had to be built.

Greater Expansion

The expansion of the fleet continued alongside the expansion of the docks in general and a new facility was built by the NER in Victoria Dock. The plan was to remove the lock gates from Victoria Dock, which would then become tidal, giving 24-hour access to both the fishing boats and the colliers as the exports of coal continued to rise.

The new quay was officially opened on 5 December 1910 by Lord Wenlock, chairman of the NER Traffic Committee. At the opening auction, Lord Wenlock paid £10 for a large bream, the Mayor, J.T. Graham, paid £5 for a large cod. Skipper Truford was believed to be the master of the first trawler to land.

This 'L'-shaped quay was 1,000ft long and 80ft wide (333m x 27m), with a floor of concrete slabs. Backing onto the quay was a railway line where fish could be loaded directly into trucks for dispatch around the country. Up to three trains a day were leaving Hartlepool at one time. Backing this up was an extensive number of sidings where fish trucks and cattle trucks were stored. Live cattle were offloaded on a ramp just inside the fish quay gates near the Golden Anchor pub (also known as the 'Grill'), these cattle

Work in progress removing the lock gates from Victoria Dock.

The first auction on the new fish quay in Victoria Dock.

were then lead away to the various butchers on the Headland who used to slaughter and cut their own meat. Hence, the name given to this entry to the fish quay was the 'Bull Gates'. A policeman was always on duty on these gates and if you had a 'fry' or had purchased some fish, you needed a pass from the merchant to prove you had bought the fish and not stolen it. You would often purchase a 'bass' to carry your fish home in from the merchant. This was a raffia-type bag about the size of a modern plastic carrier and reusable numerous times at a cost of about 6*d* (2.5p).

With the building of the ice factory at the eastern end of the new quay, stores and offices for the trawler owners such as Graham's and Sutton's were gradually built extending down the 'wood' quay towards the first ice store, later known as 'Graham's store'.

The majority of fish was moved by train after the First World War. Fish stocks had recovered following four years of reduced fishing and with trawlers returning from wartime duties this lead to a major increase in landings. One destination for Hartlepool fish was Aberdeen, where, just after the war had finished, the local fishermen had gone on strike in protest against German trawlers being allowed to land there. Billingsgate, in London, was also an important destination for fish from Hartlepool and other UK ports; taking two particular dates, on 13 October 1928 only 'light' supplies of 500 tons by rail and 49 tons by steamer arrived, and on 15 October supplies into Billingsgate of 660 tons were delivered by rail and 97 tons by steamer from Denmark. The railways were used as the primary means of distributing fish around the country for many years until the expansion of the roads gradually took the business away. The railways' dominance began

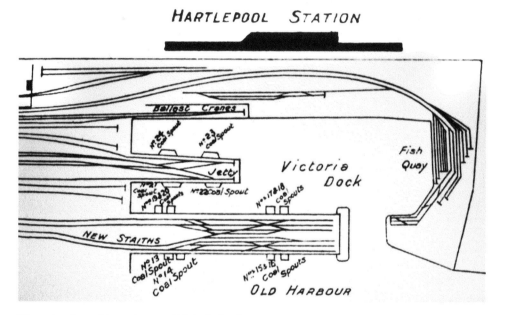

Harrison, Printer Stockton

A pass that had to be checked by the dock 'bobby'.

The extensive rail layout around Victoria Dock.

to be eroded in the 1920s when the Government began to sell off surplus lorries from the First World War. Anyone could buy one for, say, £30, go to the nearest railway station, ask what they charged for haulage to, for example, Manchester, and the stationmaster was obliged to tell them by law, then all they had to do was undercut the rate and they were in business.

Before telephones became commonplace, merchants would obtain orders from their customers by means of telegrams. First, they would have to send a telegram to say what fish was available, with the customer then sending a telegram back with their orders. The telegram office was situated just outside the small gate in the fish quay wall in Friendship Lane. To get there you had to cross the railway lines at the corner of the fish quay by the footbridge, or over the lines themselves. The telephone did not come into general use for quite a number of years, with some still using telegrams until the early 1950s. On old company letterheads there would always be a telegraphic address alongside a telephone number of only three or four digits.

The first fishing boats back from sea would land their catch at the ice house end of the quay and the rest would follow around in order of arrival; they would then be auctioned in that order. In general the crews of the fishing boats would land their own catches, but for the bigger trawlers or the boats with heavy catches 'lumpers' would be available. These were groups of men who turned out overnight to land the fish from the trawler onto the quay, sort it into types and sizes and weigh the boxes ready for the morning auction. Each box of fish would be a 'kit' or 10 stone (67 kilos). A kit of ice, which is how the merchants bought ice, was 8 stone (55 kilos). Later in the day, once the merchants had emptied the market boxes, they were collected and washed ready for the next morning. Before boxes were used for the auction, the fish would be laid directly on the floor of the quay. A hand bell was rung to summon the buyers to the start of sale, with the auctioneers coming from various agents, depending on which office looked after the paperwork for each particular boat. To the outsider, the sometimes unintelligible vocals from the salesmen must have sounded like a foreign language; however, after some time listening, especially if you were a buyer, you could get to grips with what the auctioneer was

Boxed fish laid out ready to be auctioned (1970s).

Buyers gather ready for the morning auction (1950s).

saying. Bids would be given to the salesmen by a discreet nod, a tap on the ankles, raising an eyebrow or by just shouting out loud. In times of low demand and plenty of fish, the auctioneer would have to cajole merchants to buy and the sales would take a long time; however the salesman would have his day when supplies were short and everyone was desperate for supplies.

From the merchants' side, you had to decide whether to buy early in the sales to guarantee you had fish or wait and buy later in the auction, perhaps when the price had dropped. Whichever you did, you could end up paying double or half by the end of the day's auctions: experience and 'reading' the market played a great part in deciding your day's buying tactics. Once the fish was sold and the buyers' tallies placed on the boxes, the fish would then be removed to the merchants' 'stands'. Here it was sorted into various orders packed into wooden, later cardboard, boxes for distribution around the country. Wooden boxes had to have a lid fitted and nailed down and a destination tally fixed on the end before it was loaded onto the appropriate railway truck. Before filleted fish became commonplace, all fish was dispatched whole.

The length of the working day obviously varied with the amount of fish landed. When landings were light or on bad weather days, when there was no fish at all on the quay, time would be spent making or repairing the wooden boxes which were used to dispatch fish to customers, but when times were busy you hardly had time for a break. On many occasions children would go home from school, eat their dinner, then take their father's

Lol Richardson (left) gets help to load fish during the auction (1970s).

meal down to the fish quay to be eaten at work. This had to be carried very carefully, of course, probably in a wicker basket, with another plate on top and wrapped around with tea towels, being careful not to spill any gravy off the plate. An improvised table (fish boxes) was set up and an improvised chair (another fish box) would be sufficient so that the meal could be enjoyed.

These were the days when 'dinner time' was around 12 noon; that was when everyone took their main meal of the day. Many people from the town will be able to remember hearing the 'buzzer' going off at Richardson and Westgarth's Engineering Works, after which the workforce from Richardson's and Gray's shipyards streamed out of the docks area, thousands of workmen on bikes, racing home for their meal, which would be timed by their wives to be on the table as they walked through the door. So many bikes would be at Throston Bridge and Middleton Road junctions that police would be on point duty to control the flow of traffic.

Recruiting new staff for the merchants or crew for the boats never seemed to be a problem; if your family was involved in either side of the industry you were probably expected to go to sea or join the family business on the quay. In the days when the quay was open to members of the public to walk on and watch what was going on, young lads from around the Headland area of Hartlepool, where the fish quay was situated, would get involved in helping merchants or help landing boats before going to school. Gradually they would get a taste of working on shore or perhaps go to sea on a weekend, so that when they left school they were already known to people and a job could be obtained somewhere in the industry.

During the early part of the twentieth century very little filleting of fish took place as most was sold over the counter whole. One of the most popular species was cod, which fishmongers sold by slicing through, so that you obtained a round 'steak' with the bone through the middle. Filleting was introduced after it gained popularity in Scotland and gradually nearly every kind of fish was cut before it left the quay. The waste or offal from this operation in the latter part of the twentieth century was sold for processing into fishmeal fertiliser, pig food or to maggot farms. In the early part of the century the offal was tipped into a barge, taken into the bay and discharged. This would then end up as food for crabs, lobsters and other fish, so helping to maintain stocks in the bay. There was, at one time, a fishmeal plant situated near the kipper houses on Hart Road, where the offal was turned into fertiliser. Even the larger cod heads had the cheeks and tongues removed before disposal; these parts of the fish were disregarded by the general public but 'fought over' by the locals as the best part of a cod to eat.

Before hosepipes became commonplace it was the job of the labourer or the youngest member of staff to fill the filleting bench by carrying buckets of water from the nearest tap. The fish were tipped into the bench, which would be about 5ft long by 4ft wide and 1ft to 1ft 6in deep. Once the hosepipe was introduced water ran through the bench all the time. This kept the water clean and washed the fish in the process. The water overflowed the bench and ran down the quay into the dock. There was no pollution at all, as the only addition to the water came off the fish that came out of the sea in the first place. Each

King Bros' stand and staff around the 1920s.

A quiet day on the quay in the 1970s.

merchant would have one or two benches on their stand, under the shelter of the fish quay roof. However, during the winter, with the quay being an open-sided building, the wind would 'funnel' through, often blowing snow around you as you worked. Improvised shelters were often erected using wooden boxes nailed together to make windbreaks. There was no such thing as factory regulations – minimum temperatures and working conditions – no matter how cold it was, even below zero, work went on with your arms in and out of the cold water until the job was done. Despite these conditions the fish quay was quite a cheerful place to work, with banter or 'insults' flying between the workers on different stands. Sickness levels were very low, with colds and flu quite rare compared to office workers. Before refrigeration, the merchants would keep fish overnight in large insulated boxes, 'ice chests', possibly 8ft long, 4ft wide and 4–5ft high. Fish would have to be re-boxed with ice on the bottom and the top; the boxes were then placed inside the 'chest'. This was known as 'icing back'.

Fish Boxes

During bad weather, when there was no fish landed, the merchants would often make their own wooden boxes and lids. Buying in timber from a local sawmill, the planks would be cut to length and nailed together to form a returnable box. The merchant's name was then marked on the sides of the box using a metal stencil and black marking stain which

A busy day on the quay in the 1970s.

looked like a large tin of boot polish and was applied with a short bristled brush. This box could be reused many times before becoming worn out and probably burned in a barrel on a cold winter's morning on the quay to try and defrost pipes to get the water running after freezing overnight. The sizes of wooden box used were generally 6 stone (38 kilos), 4 stone (27 kilos), 2 stone (13 kilos), 1 stone (6.5 kilos) and a half stone (3.5 kilos). The largest, 8 stone (54 kilos), were known as 'Norways'; they were reused boxes from when fresh headless cod and haddock was imported from Norway. A 3-stone box, also used, was known as a 'margarine'. This name appears to come from when margarine was imported from Denmark, a single block inside a wooden box; once the grocer had finished with the box they were reused for packing fish. When you bought your margarine from the grocer, such as Ernie Herbert in Northgate, he would slice off a portion just as he would when you bought a piece of cheese. The name for this size of box continued well after margarine ceased to be sold in this manner.

Opposite: **SEINE NETTING ON THE *MARGIT*** (Photos courtesy of Alan Cook)
A Taking ice. **B** The Huntersted twin-cylinder engine. **C** After dropping the dan on an anchor, one end of twelve coils of rope is fastened to the dan (each coil equalled 120 fathoms – so twelve amounted to about 1.2 miles). The boat then steams away from the dan in a large circle, shooting the twelve coils, then the net, then another twelve coils on the way back to the dan. (The number of coils used depends on the ground and the depth of water.) **D** Back at the start; pick up the dan and the other end of the rope. **E** Both ends of the ropes are fastened to the winch and hauling begins. **F** The ropes are wide apart, sweeping the seabed, herding the fish towards the net. **G** As the net comes off the seabed, the ropes get closer together and close the net. **H** The cod end comes aboard.

I The catch is emptied into the pound. J A good haul of cod. K Landing back in Hartlepool.
L Lumpers Derek Bradley and Tommy Allen sort the catch ready for the auction.

3

CHANGING TIMES

Gradually, in the 1950s, as the last of the steam trawlers were scrapped and the amount of fish landed reduced, the number of merchants who had offices on the quay also diminished and the last of the trawler owners, Sutton's and Graham's, closed their doors.

The trawler owners also acted as agents for other vessels and auctioneers of fish on the quay, however two new agencies were set up: Bill Grigg and his father started W.K. Grigg & Son and Bob Douglas, Walter Storrer and Pip Mallinson started the Lola Fishing Co.

As the steam trawlers were scrapped, the fish quay went through a quiet period, but there was a revival of crab and lobster fishing during this time. This had always been carried out by cobles and small boats working off the rock edges and around Longscar Rocks, but now keel boats were joining them and working farther offshore. The Picknett family had been working off the beach at Redcar for many years but moved their fishing to Hartlepool when they invested in two keel boats for the crab fishery, the *Pride of Redcar* (HL 70) and *Supreme Endeavour* (HL 109). These were the first new builds to arrive in the port for many years. Other vessels, such as *Three Lads*, *Energy* and *Peggy* from Grimsby, also moved to the port to take advantage of the expanding shell fishery. The Horsley family, which had been fishing from Hartlepool for many generations, also invested in a keel boat about this time when Bill Horsley brought the Scottish ring netter *Embrace* (KY 43) to the port. There was a daily time limit on the crab boats as they had to be back in port so that they could land with enough time for the merchants to weigh and box the

Supreme Endeavour with a deckload of crab pots.

Bill Horsley's *Embrace*, used for crab and lobster fishing.

M.K. Noer, one of the Danish vessels to arrive in the port.

crabs and lobsters as the steam train left the fish quay at 4p.m. This took the boxes to West Hartlepool goods station to catch the connections for the inland markets. Crabs were packed in wooden boxes with lids nailed down, while lobsters were packed in a similar fashion but in rows, carefully, with a layer of wood chippings on the bottom and top. Sometimes, in the summer, a damp newspaper would be placed on top of the chippings to help keep the lobsters cool. It was essential that the lobsters arrived at their destination alive as dead ones were worthless; one weather condition which was not wanted was thunder, as thunderstorms kill off lobsters.

Gradually the fishing fleet was built up again by the purchase of Danish anchor seiners brought in from other ports. The vessels which arrived included *Janet* (HL 6), *Kis* (HL 77), *Sven Knud* (HL 72), *Nordland* (HL 19), *Prince Igor* (HL 61) and *M.K. Noer* (HL 84).

Many Danish anchor seiners were painted in traditional fashion with light blue hulls, and coupled with the 'pom pom' sound of their single-cylinder engines, blowing perfect smoke rings into the air from their wide-diameter exhausts, these were distinctive vessels. New-built vessels were added in the late 1950s to replace some of these older seiners as they left the port, and these included *Fiona Fay* (HL 113), *Castle Eden* (HL 115), *Kristiona* (HL 111), *Scema* (HL 79) and *Dunelm* (HL 89). Danish-style, built in Scottish yards, they were dual purpose, trawling in the winter and anchor seining in the summer.

There were often landings in Hartlepool from Grimsby-based seiners; some vessels which can be remembered are *Clavis* (GY 347), *Emmie* (GY 425), *Tarma* (GY 615), *Grenna Rise* (GY 435), *Grenna Dawn* (GY 532), *Grenna Way* (GY 1375), *Iris Dean* (GY 701) and *Jersey* (GY 262).

The launch of the *Castle Eden*.

Tarma, one of the regular visitors from Grimsby.

Scottish seiners were gradually introduced, such as *Garland* (INS 228), *Acacia* (BF 199) and *Press On* (BF 65), some as replacements and some as additional vessels; all were by now rigged as dual purpose, seining in the summer and trawling in the winter. The port was having something of a revival in the 1960s and '70s; the fleet was increasing due to the lucrative winter prawn fishery. There was a big export market in France and Spain for large whole prawns and it was about the time when pubs started to realise the importance of serving food on their premises and scampi became the nation's favourite. Scampi is made from the long-ignored prawn, *nephrops norvegicus*. This had been caught in the nets of fishing vessels for many years, the fishermen would perhaps eat them on board or take some home, but no market existed for them so any excess were thrown back over the side. This fishery gradually increased and eventually over fifty vessels were working from the port in some winters of the 1980s. About thirty of these were local, with the balance coming from Whitby, Grimsby and other ports. In 1989, the value of fish landed was £566,000, and the value of prawns landed was £360,000.

Another Move

By the 1950s the quay itself was in a bad state of repair, with holes in the roof and many of the concrete slabs rocking underfoot as they rested on rotten wooden piles. About one third of the quay, adjacent to the dock head, was demolished and rebuilt and the remaining merchants moved onto this section in 1957. When the Victoria Dock fish quay was opened in 1910, the merchants' offices were square wooden structures with

Press On brought in to replace *Fiona Fay*.

enough space for two high desks with two high stools, where the office clerks would sit and write out the invoices and keep the accounts in big ledgers, all in neat handwriting, with numerous pens at hand and ink-wells always topped up, and lit with the latest gas lighting. On reflection, a Dickensian scene, but normal for the day, with very little change until the quay was demolished. On the move to the 'new quay' the office provided was a small concrete prefab type with enough space for two desks in the double office and one desk in the single, but with the addition of electric light. Large walk-in fridges replaced the ice chest for 'icing back' and gradually large freezers were being used by merchants as fish supplies became more intermittent and imported frozen fish was substituted.

The new quay was an improvement on the old but it was still basically an open-sided shed where the winter wind and snow blew straight through while you stood and worked. To comply with Government regulations being introduced in the 1970s, the Port Authority built processing bays behind the offices; this did then give some shelter from the winter cold.

The railway had provided two lines of track laid behind the 'new quay' which was never fully used and towards the end of its time only one or two boxes of crabs were being sent by rail to Billingsgate in London each day. Sometimes these were taken to West Hartlepool station either on the guards van or even on the engine itself. The steam engine would often stand for hours waiting for the afternoon run to 'West'. As road transport took over, the railway was withdrawn and the tracks removed. The final day for the withdrawal of the railway was 12 August 1963.

Merchants on the quay still kept their trade with the major inland markets of Leeds, Manchester, Birmingham and Billingsgate. Transport was now all by road with the

The winter prawn fleet alongside the 1957-built quay.

overnight haulage contractor based in North Shields – this meant a daily journey up the A19 and through the Tyne Tunnel, adding another 2 hours to the day's work.

The End of an Era

The 'new' fish quay, which had been in use since 1957, was eventually too large as the stocks of fish diminished and the industry came under the influence of the EU's catching, processing and hygiene rules. One of the two fish selling and vessel agencies remaining, the Lola Fishing Co., went into receivership in early 1984 and this left only W.K. Grigg & Son to manage the boats in the port. On Bill Grigg nearing retirement age, he in turn sold out to Caley Fisheries of North Shields in 1987. The prawn fishing, which had kept the local fleet in business for many years, was showing a reduction in landings and boats were sold or took advantage of Government decommissioning schemes, so eventually another move was on the cards. To enable a new facility to be built, a co-operative was set up to take over the day-to-day running of the fish quay from the Port Authority, known as the Hartlepool Fish Co. Ltd, with members drawn from all sides of the industry. Grants were obtained from various local and national bodies which enabled the project to go ahead.

This time the move was to a single building which would house an auction hall, box store, and offices for the agents (Caleys) and the Fish Co. manager. The fish quay

One of the last auctions before the demolition of the quay.

Fish Co.'s auction hall under construction.

had diminished from its heyday at 1,000ft long (333m), to a building 75ft x 60ft (25m x 20m), the size that one merchant's 'stand' used to be. This was positioned on the site where the dock head office, later Grigg's office, once stood. A pontoon was laid close by as mooring facilities had gone with the demolition of the quay. The new building was opened in 1998. The first vessel to land in the new building was the *Amanda* (RO 23), skipper Alan Cook, on Monday 8 June. The last vessel to have her catch auctioned in this building was the *Norwood* (LH 347), skipper Stephen Horsley, which made £592.53 for 124 stone (787 kilos) of mixed fish. (By coincidence, both vessels were owned by Alan Hodgson, Fish Merchant.) After this, the auction stopped as not enough fish was going across the market and fish was sold direct to each merchant by agreement between the boat and the buyer. By the beginning of the twenty-first century the fishing restrictions were beginning to bite harder. The reduced fishing days allowed for boats and constant cutbacks in the quota of fish make the industry a difficult one to survive in, whether you are catching or processing fish. The dozen or so full-time fishing boats, which are all that's left at a once-major port, have to spend more time tied up than at sea, and the outlook is bleak. Perhaps the warning from ancient times has at last come true: 'A petition was presented to Edward III that the "Wondrychoun" (or beam trawl) … which it is said presses on the bottom so hard it destroys all life, and in taking one good fish they destroy thousands for no real purpose.' The petition to ban this type of fishing was presented in AD 1376.

One of the first auctions in the new hall.

The fish quay in the twenty-first century.

FISHING ON BOARD THE *FRIARAGE* (Photos courtesy of Sonny Ray)
A Sonny Ray and Eddie Wrigley in the wheelhouse. **B** A deckhand mending nets. **C** Crew Sonny Ray, Timmy Reynolds, Bobby Slimmings and Shackles Hanley. **D** Jock Archibald, engineer. **E** Deckie in amongst the cod. **F** Trawl wires across the deck and barrels ready for the cod livers around the mast. **G** Releasing the cod end. **H** Eddie Wrigley's first bag of cod. **I** A deck-full.

4

THE HERRING INDUSTRY

The humble herring provided possibly the most important seasonal fisheries in the history of the British fishing industry. Its capture and processing gave employment to thousands of people over many generations, either directly or indirectly.

The table below gives the landings for 1903 at the thirteen principal ports in England; these ports represent 98 per cent of the herring landed in the country as a whole.

—	Port.	Cwts.
1	Yarmouth	1,227,020
2	Lowestoft	889,900
3	Grimsby ·	342,820
4	Scarborough	159,100
5	North Shields	130,980
6	North Sunderland	67,480
7	Plymouth	49,580
8	Hartlepool	43,900
9	St. Ives	24,260
10	Newlyn	23,560
11	Berwick...	19,920
12	Peel	13,480
13	Whitby	7,920
		2,999,920

Chart of herring landings for 1903.

Down the east coast of the UK from the start of the fishing in the north of Scotland in spring till the season's end in East Anglia in the autumn, thousands of people were involved as the shoals appeared with clockwork regularity until they gradually disappeared in the 1960s, a victim of overfishing and predation by all kinds of other sea creatures. At first it was thought that the same herring shoal was migrating down the coast, but others began to question this theory and argued that each fishery was a different stock. As filter feeders, their predictable appearance was probably governed by the sea temperature and conditions being right in each coastal area for the zooplankton and copepods to multiply. The plankton rises to the surface at night followed by the herring; this is where the drift

Lowestoft drifters landing over their bows onto Hartlepool quay.

nets are set to catch the shoals of fish. It's a hard life being a herring: from being an egg (each female lays 20–50,000 eggs) on the seabed where you are a target for crabs and other shellfish, once hatched virtually any other fish or seabird will eat you. 'Herring whales' used to be a common sight, as were tuna, all chasing this abundant food source. During the summer season at major seaside resorts such as Scarborough, steam drifters, on a Sunday, which was their day off, would take parties out rod and line fishing for 'tunny' as tuna was known in the early part of the twentieth century.

Sailing drifters and herring cobles were used to pursue the herring in season. At the turn of the twentieth century, with the advent of the steam drifter, the chase for the herring intensified. The peak was probably reached in the autumn fisheries of 1913 at Yarmouth where over 820,000 tons of herring were brought ashore. Landings of herring gradually reduced over the years and different methods of catching were tried, including trawling the seabed in daylight when the herring stayed close to the sea floor. Another method brought in by Scottish fishermen was ring netting, an operation using two boats to encircle the shoal. A special type of vessel was developed for this which was broad in the beam and had a very low rail to help get the net on board. Many of these 'ring netters' became adapted for other fisheries after the herring was finished. A local example would be Billy Horsley's *Embrace* (KY 43). When ring netters began landing in Hartlepool, George Cook of W. & G. Cook's kipper house remarked that 'ring netting would be the end of the herring' because it took even the small fish, whereas drifting allowed the small to escape through the net. By the 1960s the herring had all but disappeared.

In Victoria Dock, opposite the fish quay, was an area known as the 'wood quay', a name which stuck until the area was taken over by the oil industry in the 1970s. Located here

Fisher lasses take a break as the coopers seal the barrels of herring.

was the first ice house and stores belonging to the agents, which held nets, ropes and all kinds of materials that kept the fishing vessels working. During the early years of the twentieth century, this area was used by the fisher lasses during July and August to clean and pack the herring caught by visiting and local drifters.

Numerous photographs exist of the Scottish fisher lasses working on this quay packing herring into barrels for export, mainly to Germany, Poland, Russia and other Eastern European states. If you study these photos you can date some of them by where the fisher lasses are working. Some are working on the site that was to become the ice factory, so that would place the photo between 1911 – which would be the first season for herring in Victoria dock – and before 1914, when the ice factory opened.

The fisher lasses followed the herring fleets from Scotland down the east coast as far as Lowestoft. Their lodgings in Hartlepool where mainly in Charles Street and Francis Street, just off Northgate, near to the railway station.

As they worked, the fingers of the girls were bound up with rags to try to keep the salt out of their hands, salt being used to preserve and pickle the herring as they packed them into the barrels. They usually worked in teams of three, with two girls gutting up to fifty or sixty herring a minute and the third packing and salting the herring into the barrels. The barrel makers, or coopers, also travelled down the coast and would make the thousands of barrels required for exporting the catch. The expansion of the herring fleets from the late 1800s in the UK came about because of the vacuum left by the Dutch loosing or withdrawing from the market to supply the Eastern states of Europe with the salted herrings. The Dutch had been dominant in this sector for a number of centuries and no one appears to know the answer to why they withdrew.

Fisher lasses working on the wood quay where the ice factory was later built.

Dutch herring drifters were regular visitors during August in the 1950s and '60s.

The herring drifters would lie bow-on to the quay, packed together, landing their catches over their bows. A sample of herring was taken from each boat to the herring ring on the quay where the buyers could then check the quality of the herring and decide which boat's catch to bid for. An estimate of the catch was also given so the buyers knew how much fish each boat had on board. This estimate was given in 'crans', the measure by which herring was sold (a cran = 28 stone = 177kg). The majority of the herrings would be processed by the fisher lasses and packed into barrels for export and left the port by train. Other herring was used by the local smokehouses.

Along with herring drifters from England and Scotland, the port had regular visits from the Dutch drifters following the same shoals. Often the fish quay was so full of Dutch drifters you could walk across the dock jumping from boat to boat. The crews would come ashore and spend their money in the shops in Northgate and were easily recognised by the wooden yellow clogs they all wore. Many of these drifters were registered at Katwijk (KW), Urk (UK) and Scheveningen (SCH).

The Kipper Houses

The invention of the kipper has been attributed to a John Woodger who produced the first in Seahouses, Northumberland. After a while they became a firm favourite around the country. Local businesses were established in Hartlepool to cater for the local and national demand for kippers. The NER built a number of smokehouses in Hart Road, on the main road leading to the Headland, and nine smokehouses existed at one time. If you had been away from the town, you would always know when you were home as you would be able to smell the smoke from the kipper houses as you approached Throston Bridge.

Well-known names in the kippering business were Cook's, Pattison's, Sutton's and Brown's. Once the local herring landing season had finished, local processors would follow the boats down the coast and bring back herring to Hartlepool; when the east coast was finished a journey to the west coast of Scotland to buy herring would be necessary.

There is a local story about Charlie Cook, who took delivery of a brand new Commer truck, jumped into it, drove to the West of Scotland, picked up a load of herring, returned home, then took the lorry to the garage the next day for its first service, to the amazement of the garage staff.

As the supply of herring diminished, so did the companies which smoked them. The last two smokehouses in Hartlepool were Pattison's, run by Tony and Jamie Pearson, and W.& G. Cook, long since sold out of the Cook family and run by the Clapham family, who previously ran Lear's fishmonger's shop in York Road, West Hartlepool. Alongside the kippers, cod and haddock was also smoked.

One of the last landings of herring in Hartlepool from Scottish drifters in the 1960s.

The Smoking Process

The herring and fish were smoked by what is now known as the 'traditional' method, that is, the fish was smoked overnight in 'kilns'. The kiln was a wide chimney with rails on the sides where the 'sticks' holding the kippers were held. The herring were first split open along the line of the belly so that the fish opened out flat. This was done at first by hand, but a machine was designed to complete this tedious part of the work – with the herring placed on a turntable the machine split the fish and dropped then into a basket ready for washing. After washing, the herring were then placed in a pickle containing salt and a vegetable dye which gave the kipper its distinctive golden colour. After a time in the pickle, the herring were 'pricked on' to hooks on a long wooden bar so that the smoke could circulate all around the herring. After allowing time for draining off, the wooden bars would then be taken and hung in the kiln. Wood chippings from a local sawmill were heaped on the floor of the kiln, fine oak sawdust was then placed on top, and the chippings lit. As the flames took hold, the chippings burnt but the sawdust would smoulder and give off the smoke that cured the herring and turned them into kippers. The kiln would be left to smoke overnight. By the morning when the kiln was 'struck', the herrings would now be kippers and would be packed into wooden boxes

Patterson's kipper house – John Macdonald feeding herring onto the splitting machine.

Keith Harrison checks herring in the brine tub.

Mary Kendal, Ernie Harrison and Les Raper 'pricking on'.

Paul Moore placing the sticks in the kiln for smoking.

Once the herring have been smoked overnight they come out of the kiln as kippers. Charlie Cook, of W. & G. Cook's, packs kippers for distribution.

for transport all over the UK. Also produced in the kipper houses were baked herring. Herring fillets were rolled up and fifteen to twenty placed in a shallow metal tray and cooked in gas ovens. What a wonderful distinctive smell would greet you when you entered the cookhouse!

Now there is no evidence at all that kipper houses existed as the site has been demolished and taken back into the dock estate. The herring has all but disappeared from the North Sea and if they ever reappeared in quantity, would anyone know what to do with them?

Fish Curers

This list has been compiled with the help of Kelly's and Ward's Directory's of 1890, 1896/7, 1910 and 1921 along with other research.

Many fish curers are listed as having premises in Hart Road where new curing houses were added with the expansion of the fish quay in 1910. Hart Road then started at the 'other side' of Throston Bridge and continued to West View:

Albert Sutton, Hart Road
George Cooper, Hart Road
George Wardell, Clifton Street
Guthrie Bros, Hart Road
Harrison, 31 Clifton Street
Henry Wardell, Hart Warren, Hart Road
J. Pattison, Hart Road
Jacob Cox, 31 Clifton Street
King Bros (address unknown)

L.G. Brown, Hart Road
M. Guthrie, Hart Warren, Hart Road
Moody Bros, Hart Road
Mrs Hannah Harrison, 31 Clifton Street
Rickman Cox, Fords Yard, Clifton Street
Robert Stewart, Hart Road
Sutton Bros, Hart Road
W. & G. Cook, Hart Road

A

B

C

D

LAST OF THE STEAMERS
(Photos courtesy of
Robbie Wray)
A *Eileen Wray.*
B *George D. Irvine.*
C *Loch Blair.*
D *Isabella Fowlie.*

E *Gertrude Cappleman.*
F *Respondo.*
G *Kudos.*
H *Calypso.*

I *Ben Tarbet.*
J *Fort Ryan.*
K *Friarage.*
L *Longscar.*

5

THE FISH MERCHANTS ASSOCIATION

With the opening of the new extended fish quay in Victoria Dock in 1910, there was also an increase in the number of merchants establishing themselves to handle the amount of fish being landed. There was a growing need for an association to represent the merchants' side of the industry when speaking to local and national bodies; other merchants around the country were forming similar associations. A meeting was held on Friday 25 May 1925 in the office of Hastings & Stewart, a committee was formed, and the 'Fish Merchants Protection Association' was born. The president was to be the town's MP Sir Wilfred Sugdon, chairman, A. Lancaster, treasurer, I. Webber, and secretary, E. Poskitt. Various other positions were filled by Arthur Sutton, Frank Hastings, H. Stewart, L. Brown, W. Thomas, J. Guthrie, G. Wardell, W. Cook, F. Gardner, W. Hodgson, J. Farrar, F. Gardner, T. Warrand, Geo. Cook and F. Shackles (F. Gardner represented the London company of S. Larkin and A. Lancaster the London company of E. Clark). A dinner to inaugurate the formation was held in the Golden Anchor pub (or the 'Grill' as the locals knew it) on 10 July 1925. Fees for membership were to be 1 guinea (21s or £1.05)

A selection of items extracted from the Association minute book over the years:

1925
- Numerous debates with the railway company took place over many years about the rates charged for carriage.
- Asking the railway company to drop the 1d charge on basses of fish being taken off the quay as they were mainly 'fries' (a bass was a wicker-made, reuseable carrier bag which cost 6d (2.5p) when the last were being sold in the 1960s).
- Discussions with the Postmaster in West Hartlepool to improve the delivery of telegrams in the morning.

1926
- In 1926 the Association had thirty-eight members.

1928
- Abolition of the 'one basket in ten' rule, where, when a catch of herring was purchased, one basket in ten was free.
- Complaints about the smell from the liver barrels worked by Mr Kendal.

1929

– A letter was sent to Buckingham Palace expressing thankfulness at the King's recovery after numerous operations (reply received).

1930

– Letter sent to Amy Johnson (daughter of a Hull fish merchant) on her achievement.

1931

– A letter from the Port Sanitary Authority over the amount of smoke coming from the visiting drifters.

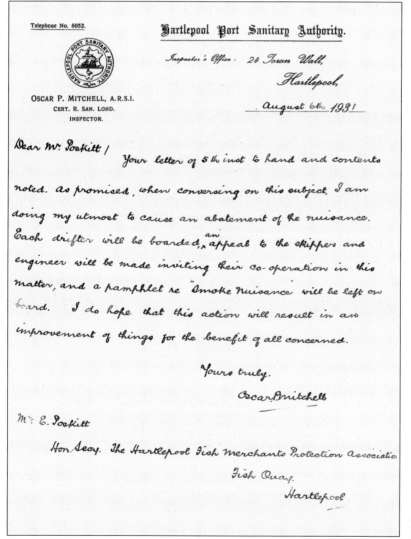

Port Sanitary Authority letter.

1932

- 'In all matters this world would seem to be full of rapid changes, and what is new this year is almost old and obsolete next year'– from the secretary's report 1932.

1934

- Mr Lancaster had to resign as chairman because of his financial position, a collection was carried out and Mr Lancaster was to be paid £1 per week as long as the fund lasted.
- The herring season a 'dismal affair' and 'The general plight of the industry is indeed very grave and drastic efforts will have to be taken to save it from collapse.' Secretary's report, 1934.

1935

- Telegram sent to congratulate the King and Queen on their Silver Jubilee; reply received by telegram and framed.
- The trade welcomed the 'sixpenny wire' (telegrams costing 2.5p) and the fact that you could now phone anywhere in the country for 1s (5p) after 7p.m.
- Opposition to the proposed closure of Bear Isle and White Sea as it would result in Hartlepool trawlers being laid up.
- A typewriter be purchased for the secretary, if a suitable second-hand one could be found.

1936

- Filleting had become widely established.

1937

- Invitation to a town council meeting as the council 'deplored the state of trade done on the fish quay'.
- Donation of five guineas (£5 5s 0d – £5.25) from the Association to the *Jeanie Stewart* trawler fund. Trawler presumed lost in December 1936, fishing from North Shields.

1939

- Request for a telephone kiosk for the use of merchants.
- First train of the day to leave at 10.55a.m. instead of 11.10a.m.
- Fish rationing scheme to be set up, this would be based on the last three years' buying by the merchants and was to run through the war years.

1940

- Request from the Ministry of Food for the names of all employees between the ages of thirty to forty, for exemption from call-up as key workers.

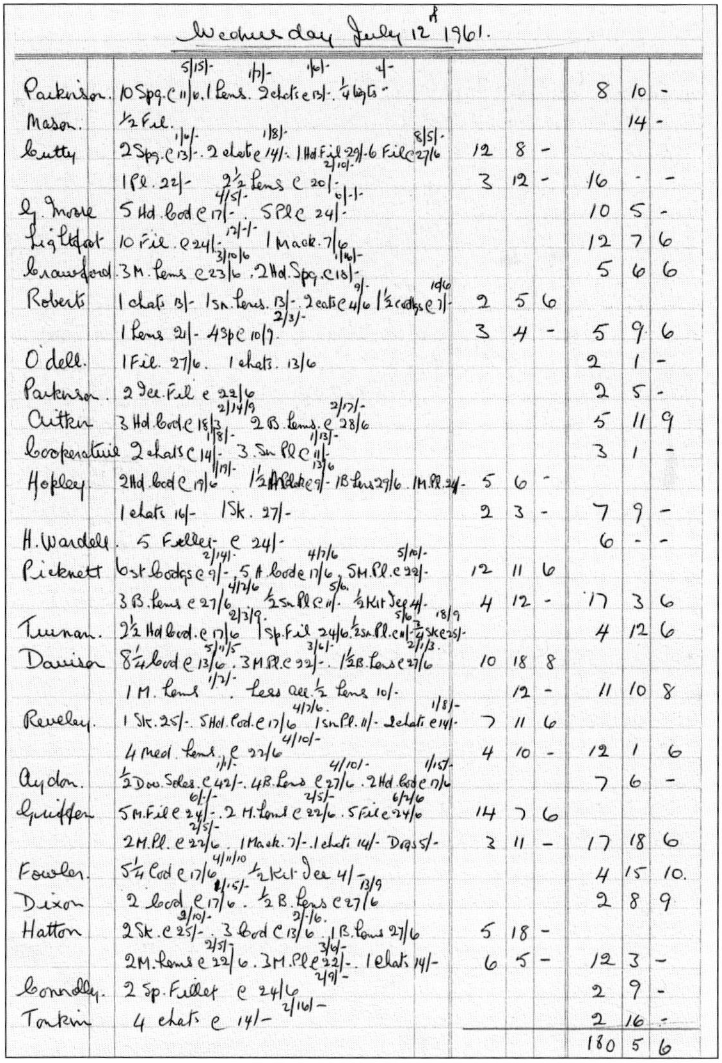

Page from sales book.

1941

- Letter from the A.R.P. Authorities offering tin helmets to Fire Watches for 5s 6d each (27p).
- All fish merchants had to be licensed; licences were issued to: G. Wardell, W. Cook, W. Hodgson, W. Thomas, L. Brown, G. Cook, J. Nash, S. Pibell, A. Roberts, Fillets Ltd, A. Sutton, S. King, J. Pattison, C. Hansellman, E. Kendall.
- Only two trawlers left in the port due to being called up by the Navy for the war, although the seine net boats were still working.

1942

- A zoning scheme was set up by the Government for distribution.

Auctioneer Bob Douglas selling to (from left to right) Jack Firs, Bob Richmond, Tommy Sutton, Laurie Nash, Dave Sangster and Ronnie King.

1943
- Prices fixed and customers of each merchant listed.
- In the first eight months of the year, 240 boxes of fish a day landed.
- Agreement to send 250 cigarettes each to men from the fish trades serving in the war: Tom Hatton, Stan Wilson, S. (Davy?) Henderson & G. Staincliffe.
- A weekly allocation of frozen fillets to the port by the Ministry of Food (A Director of Fish Supplies controlled the allocation of fish throughout the war and for some time after).

1945
- Danish seine netters allocated to Hartlepool had landed 56,000cwt (2,800 tons) of fish in the first ten months of the year.
- An application was made to the Ministry of War Transport to allocate two Danish fishing boats laid up in the docks to Hartlepool.

1947
- A letter was written to the town's MP concerning a proposal by the Parliamentary Labour Party that the fishing industry be concentrated at twelve major ports.

1950
- In the spring, fish would be de-controlled.

1952

– Two Swedish vessels landed herring during November as an experiment, but were not satisfied with prices.

1953

– Request made to the landlords as to the cost of installing electric light in the merchants' offices.
– There was a proposal from a Mr Pailor that Icelandic fish be landed at Hartlepool; further discussions would take place.
– Salesman Mr J. Graham warned that Grimsby seine netters would not land in Hartlepool if Icelandic fish was landed here.

1954

– Merchants agreed not to buy any Icelandic fish if it was landed directly into the port until the dispute between the Icelandic government and the Humber ports was settled.
– Merchants still had to be licensed as in wartime.
– Continuing discussions with the railways about charges made to return empty boxes to Hartlepool.

1955

– Shortage of supplies; merchants were talking about getting together and buying a couple of seine netters, the last of the steam trawlers having been scrapped.

Auctioneer Dave Carroll (left), trying to get bids out of Tony Prearson, Dave Warrand and Malcolm Cook.

Filleting bays being added to the stands.

1956
- Letter from the British Transport Commission, proposing that rents for offices be doubled.
- Increased rents would be £30 for a double office and £16 for a single office per year.

1957
- Disappointment expressed that Graham's new trawler *John O'Heugh* would work from Lowestoft.

1958
- The disposal of offal was up for tender with Mr Warrand bidding 11s 6d (57p), Mr Glenton 10s 6d, and Coastal Food Recovery bidding up from 7s 6d to 10s; these prices were for a 40-gallon drum (180 litres).

1960
- The question of auctioneers taking bids from the public raised its head again; this had been a sore point since the fish quay opened, and persisted until the quay closed.

1963
- A new company was set up to purchase and run the trawler *Fairy Cove* as the present owners, Graham's, were about to go bust.
- British Railways announce that the branch line would close on 12 August, and any fish for the London train would be collected by road transport and taken to West Hartlepool station.

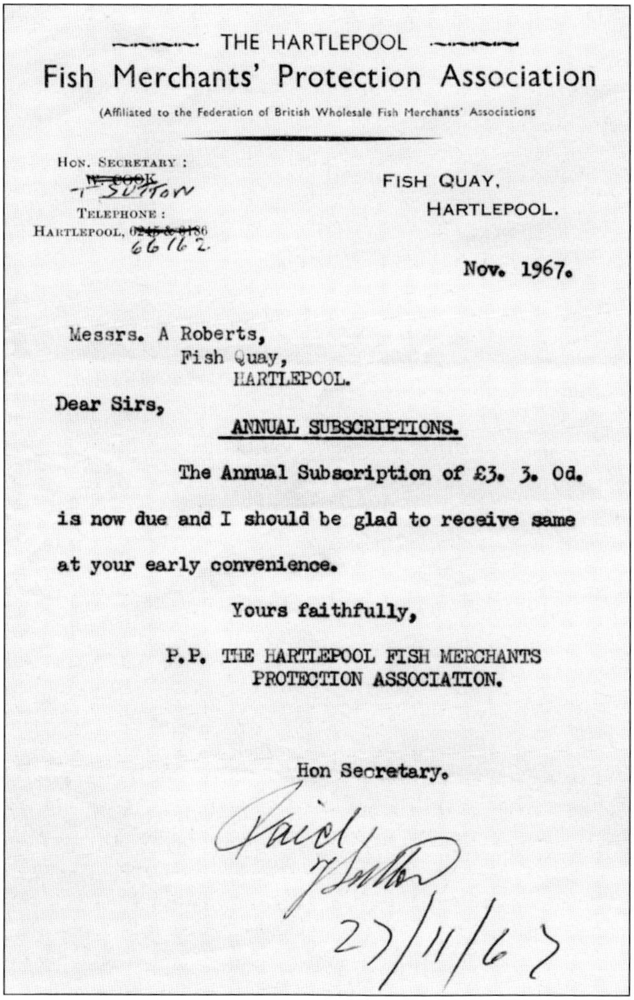

THE HARTLEPOOL
Fish Merchants' Protection Association
(Affiliated to the Federation of British Wholesale Fish Merchants' Associations)

HON. SECRETARY :
T SUTTON
TELEPHONE :
HARTLEPOOL, 66162.

FISH QUAY,
HARTLEPOOL.

Nov. 1967.

Messrs. A Roberts,
Fish Quay,
HARTLEPOOL.

Dear Sirs,

ANNUAL SUBSCRIPTIONS.

The Annual Subscription of £3. 3. 0d.

is now due and I should be glad to receive same

at your early convenience.

Yours faithfully,

P.P. THE HARTLEPOOL FISH MERCHANTS
PROTECTION ASSOCIATION.

Hon Secretary.

Paid
T Sutton
27/11/67

A subscription renewal.

1965
– At a meeting with the White Fish Authority in the Grand Hotel, a scheme was announced that would introduce a minimum price for certain species of fish; the merchants were opposed to this.

1977
– A proposed increase in the rents on the quay from £87 to £180 as processing bays had been built so that filleting and processing could now be carried out under cover.

1978
– An agreement with the Fishermen's Association that each merchant on the quay would contribute towards the newly organised security patrol.

After this date meetings became intermittent and the Fish Merchants Association appeared to fade away.

When first established, the Association's AGMs were given a full-page report in the national newspaper of the industry, the *Fishing News*, for many years.

At the first Annual Dinner in 1927 it was reported that over 2,000 people were employed in the fish trades in the port. The guest speaker, the Mayor, could recall Major Graham's grandfather being one of the salesmen on the Fish Sands, with High Street and Sandwell Chare being busy with horses and carts taking the fish away.

The Social Side

The social side of the Fish Merchants Association was reported by the local newspaper alongside other news from the industry. The first Dance and Whist Drive was held in Hartlepool Town Hall in 1926, while other venues used included the Borough Hall, the Golden Anchor, the Rover's Club and Birk's Café. Whist drives appear to have been popular, with the *Northern Daily Mail* reporting up to 400 people attending some of the events with entry prices 5s 6d for couples and 3s for singles (27p and 15p). A social event known as a 'smoker' was arranged now and again, something which would be unthinkable in the twenty-first century! At one of these 'smokers' a wireless was provided by one of the merchants which brought 'live music from London'. Profits from the majority of these events were donated to Hartlepool's Hospital. Bowls tournaments were arranged during the latter part of the herring season, with locals taking on visitors from Scotland and East Anglia for trophies donated by companies involved the industry.

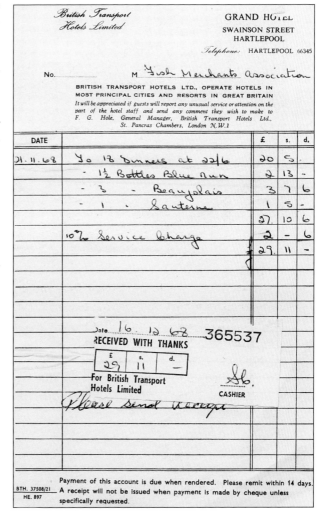

A bill for the annual dinner.

Fish Buyers and Merchants

The list below shows buyers who attended the auctions on the fish quay. Some were based on the quay with an office and a stand and others attended the sales to buy for their own retail outlets. Merchants from North Shields and Whitby would also travel to Hartlepool to buy on the market. Some names have been obtained from Kelly's and Ward's Directory's of 1898/9, 1890, 1910 and 1921:

A. Garforth	Guthrie Bros	Robert Stewart
Alan Gowler	H. Chapman	Sam King
Albert Sutton	Harrison	Samuel Francis
Bob Richmond	Hastings & Stewart	Scarborough Fishing Ind.
Charles Swales	Henry Coser	Scotprime Ltd
Charles Turner	Inshore Fisheries	Sid Clapp
Charlie Hanselman	J. Farrah	Sid Coulson
Colin Tonkin	J. Pattison	Stonehouse
Cornelious Hodgson	J. Wild	S. Pibell
D.B. Osbourne	J. Wren & Co.	Stott Bros
Dave Sangste	Jack Firs	Sudders
Dave & Sid Flower	Jackie Bloom	Sutton Bros
David Miller	Jackson Mills	T. Leak
Dennis Crooks	John Mitchell	T. & G. Warrand
Don King	Joseph Dixon	Thomas Tweddell
E. Clark	King Bros	Thomas Verrill
E.J. Dudley	L.A. Walton	Tommy Hatton
E. & J. Plant	L.G. Brown	Tommy O'Dell
Ernie Poskitt	Laurie Nash	W. & G. Cook
F. Gardner	Lockwood	W.C. Farrow
F. Shackles	Mrs Hannah Harrison	W. Mallet & Son
Fillets (R. King)	Mrs Pricilla Walker	W. Roberts
Flounders	Nick Newrick	Wm. Cook Ltd
Fortune & Peacock	North East Seafoods	Wm. Cooper
Frank Gardner	Peter Liddle	Wm. Cushway
G. Moore	R. Corner	Wm. Hodgson
Geo. W. Crawford	R. Hopper	Wm. Manship
George Bainbridge	Ramus of Harrogate	Wm. Thomas
G. Glenton	Redshaw	Wm. Thorpe
George Wardell	Ringwood	

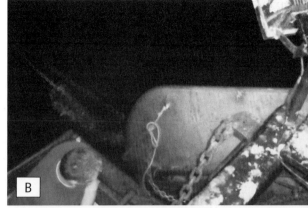

PRAWN TRAWLING ON THE *NORWOOD*
A Shooting the net away. **B** The doors follow on. **C** Towing as dawn breaks. **D** After a number of hours towing the doors come back aboard as hauling starts. **E** After the trawl wires are wound onto the winch, the net is fastened to the drum. **F** The drum does the hard work of getting the net aboard. **G** The cod end is taken aboard and the bag is emptied into the pound.

H Sorting the catch under the shelter deck.
I Fish and prawns boxed-up in the fish room.
J Stephen Horsley guides the boxes out of
the fish room as the catch is landed. K The
Norwood.

6

ICE SUPPLIES

With the move from the Fish Sands to the quay in the Old Harbour, the traditional methods of preserving fish by salting, drying or smoking were changing; the expanding railways provided the means to deliver fish in fresh condition to inland markets. Combined with the increase in the number and size of the fishing boats able to use the new quay, ice supplies became important. To fulfil this need, ice was imported from Norway. Here it was readily available, where Mother Nature supplied the ice in the form of glaciers which ran down to the fjords, or was cut during the winter from frozen lakes. Ice was cut into manageable blocks and loaded onboard sailing vessels for export to the UK and the rest of Europe. Blocks were taken aboard the fishing boats and broken up to spread onto the catch, and merchants packed fish in ice for transport inland.

This method continued when the Victoria Dock lock gates were removed in 1910 and the fish quay moved to an even bigger facility as it had outgrown the Old Harbour site.

Ice blocks which have just been unloaded from the sailing ship alongside the fish quay in the Old Harbour.

The original ice store in Victoria Dock, later known as Graham's store and shown as Hartlepool Marine Services.

A building was provided for the storage of the ice blocks adjacent to the 'wood quay', on the north side of Victoria Dock, with the thick wooden walls packed with sawdust for insulation. This building was later used as 'Graham's' store for many years. However, this method of supply was proving to be inadequate as the fleet was expanding, especially as the steam trawler was now appearing in greater numbers. A group of fish merchants and trawler owners got together and formed The Fish Traders Ice Co. Ltd, which was incorporated on 3 June 1912.

The chairman was J.T. Graham, and the directors J.J. Lister, S. Francis, A. Sutton, W. Cappleman and J.B. Graham, with G. Nicholson and Wm. Gray representing the North Eastern Railway Co., the owners of the dock estate. The company's bankers were to be the London Joint Stock Bank Ltd, Hartlepool, with power supplied by Cleveland & Durham Electric Co. and the Hartlepool Gas and Water Co. the other services. The company's registered office was The North Eastern Railway Buildings, High Street, Hartlepool, where the directors' meetings and any official business would be carried out. After formation, the company negotiated with the North Eastern Railway Co. as to the best position for building an ice factory and agreement was reached for a location at the corner of Victoria Dock, close to the eastern end of the fish quay. The NER initially took 200 shares in the Ice Company, hence their two directors on the company board. The following has been extracted from the minute book of the directors' meetings:

– In July 1912 the Company took over a contract with 'Pontiflex' for the supply of ice-making machinery from J.T. Graham, who must have been in negotiation with the company before the formation of the Ice Co. The value of the contract was £4,594.

– In January 1913 tenders for the building were invited from six leading contractors of the day, with W. Pearson & Son awarded the contract in February for the price of £2,440.

– Mr J. Wood of Scarborough was appointed Clerk of Works to oversee the construction of the building and the installation of the plant at a salary of £2 5s 0d per week (£2.25). A manager was also appointed, a Mr Campbell, who came from the Darlington Ice Co.

– Also, an investigation into the cost of a telephone, to be installed in the office, was set underway.

The ice factory building was placed adjacent to the dock wall, and during the construction, subsidence was experienced as the dock wall was giving way. The NER carried out investigations by drilling with the result that shifting sands underground appeared to be the problem. The main external wall had to be shored up during construction and internal supports provided in the engine room until a solution was found.

The plant started production on Saturday 8 August 1914, with the first deliveries on Monday 10 August. Sales for the first week were £137 2s 11d (£137.15).

Ice was produced by filling moulds with water and placing them in cooled tanks of brine until they were frozen solid. Each block weighed 1cwt (8 stone or 50kg), the blocks were then stored until required. When needed, the block was sent through a crusher to break it up into small pieces and was then sent to either the conveyor for transfer to the boats or the loading gantry for transfer into fish merchants' boxes.

By October 1914 it was realised that the plant was not big enough to meet the demand, even though four trawlers were away on minesweeping duties, but another six trawlers were due to work out of Hartlepool. Output for September was 593 tons, October 629 tons, November 362 tons and December 135 tons. The drop in output was put down to 'the stoppage of fishing' – this was the war starting to take effect on the fishing fleets; trawlers and fishing boats of all sizes were being sunk by German planes and submarines, no vessel of any size was safe.

Sales for the first full year 1915:

The completed ice factory and cold store in the corner of Victoria Dock.

January 223t	February 235t	March 334t
April 258t	May 278t	June 364t
July 541t	August 744t	September 656t
October 521t	November 426t	December 205t

By July 1915 the price of ice, to ice cream makers, was fixed at 1s 3d per cwt (6.5p/50kg).

Ice cream makers, butchers, fishmongers and other traders did not have fridges as we know today, but cold rooms, insulated and chilled down with the addition of a block of ice.

A new manager was also appointed, a Mr Farrow, at a salary of £2 15s 0d a week (£2.75).

Among the monthly bills to be paid for August 1915 were:

Hartlepool Gas & Water Co.	£13 9s 1d (£13.45)
NER Co. (ground rent)	£10 12s 6d (£10.62)
Cleveland & Durham Power Co.	£71 9s 0d (£71.45)

Following increasing overheads, such as the rising cost of electricity and the two engineers having wage increases of 5s (25p) per week, the cost of ice was raised in May 1915 to 17s 6d per ton (75p) for boats and 1s 3d per kit (7p per 50 kilos) for fish merchants.

The First World War had far-reaching effects, the company invested in the War Loan Programme to help the country, and the engineer, Mr Farrow, was called up for the Army. Sadly he never returned from the Front as he was fatally injured in France.

When the war was finally over and the industry was returning to normal, sales in 1919 were increasing rapidly. In August 1919 ice produced was 657 tons and ice bought in from outside suppliers was a further 293 tons.

The ice bought in to make up the stocks came from various places, such as the Hull Ice Co., the Whitby Ice Stores, Darlington Ice Co., the Crystal Ice Factory, the Shields Ice Co., North Shields, and W. Tipple (Ice).

Included in the accounts to be paid in August 1919 is £188 8s 8d for carriage to the North Eastern Railway Co.; from this it would appear that most of the ice was delivered to Hartlepool by rail. In August 1920 a cargo of ice was purchased from Norway to meet the shortfall.

With the increasing demand the question of expanding the output, once again, came to the fore. A tender for the building works was accepted from E.M. Tweddle for £4,930, and the plant was to be installed by 'Pontiflex', the same contractor who installed the original machinery. The new enlarged plant started production on 1 July 1921.

Enquiries had been received in December 1919 as to the prospect of supplying a further 30 to 40 tons of ice a day as a Scarborough trawling company was considering a move to work out of Hartlepool. Another enquiry, from Ellis Bros (Hull) Ltd, asking for an allotment of shares, was received in June 1920. This would then enable them to supply their own trawlers as they would have a share in the business. Unfortunately, this was turned down as the expanded plant would still be unable to keep up with demand. However Scarborough trawlers did call into Hartlepool for ice for a number of years, with demand from these trawlers falling off in 1934.

This and the following five images: Ice production: blocks were stored until required for crushing.

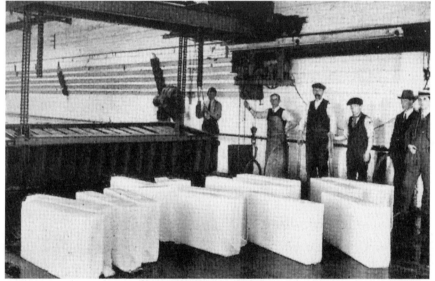

By 1922 sales of ice had progressed to 12,056 tons, and by 1923 to 12,487 tons.

Charges for using the cold store were up for discussion in May 1922, with the following prices agreed:

Kipper boxes	1*d*/week/box (1-stone box = 6.36kg)
Margarine	1.5*d*/week/box (3-stone box = 19kg)
6-stone box	3*d*/week/box (1.5p/38kg)
10-stone box	4*d*/week/box (2p/63kg)

According to the Companies Act of 1929 (section 149), all of the directors had to reveal other companies in which they had a financial interest. The particulars are as follows:

J. T. GRAHAM   J. Graham & Son, Hartness S.F. Co., Heugh S.T. Co.
   Friarage S.T. Co., Fairy Cove S.T. Co.
   Midland Bank Ltd, General Electric Co., J.H. Dunning (?) & Co.
   Whitby Fish Selling Co.

A. SUTTON   A. & T. Sutton Ltd, Sutton Bros Ltd, Sutton S.T. Co.
   Hartlepool Box Factory Ltd, Steam Trawler Supply Stores
   Gt Grimsby Coal Salt & Tanning Co. Ltd, Cerebos Ltd
   Girl Anne S.T. Co.

R. H. DAVISON   R.H. Davison & Co. Ltd, H/Pool S.T. Co., Doris Burton S.T. Co.
   Stranton Drifters, Albion Engineering Co., H/pool Fish Meal Co.
   Gt Grimsby Coal Salt & Tanning Co. Ltd, Cerebos Ltd
   Buntons (Stockton) Ltd

S. FRANCIS   H/pools Haulage Co., Armstrong Whitworths Ltd, Gales Motor & Engineering Co.

W. TIPPLE   Humber Shipwrights Co., Hull Ice Co. Ltd, Shields Manure Co.
   Hull Fish Meal Co., Scarborough Ice Co.

J. B. GRAHAM   J. Graham & Sons, Hartness S.F. Co, Heugh S.T. Co.
   Friarage S.T. Co., Fairy Cove S.T. Co., Dalkins Ltd
   Imperial Chemical Industries,- Whitby Fish Selling Co.
   Gt Grimsby Coal, Salt & Tanning Co., R. Jacob Ltd (?)
   ? Shipbuilding Co. Ltd

This list shows that the interests and investments of the directors were mainly kept to local or fishing-related industries.

In between the two wars the ice sales for 1930 (9,361 tons) and 1931 (9,656 tons), along with the cold storage facilities used for meat and fish products, contributed an income of £1,628 for 1930 and £1,910 for 1931. There were up to fifteen people employed by the Ice Co. during the 1930s.

During 1934 and 1935, negotiations were underway to purchase the West Hartlepool Ice & Cold Storage Co. of Swainson Street and Villiers Street, but the talks came to nothing as the 'West Co.' did not want to sell out. However, during 1936 the directors looked, with a view to conversion, at F. Craven's Liverpool Buildings in Thornton Street, land in Stockton Street, West Hartlepool, and also land near the public slaughterhouse, in Barnard Street, with a view to building another cold storage facility. These moves were taken during a period of great depression in the country, so the directors must have been

Tony Pearson, Sid Flower, Ken Farrar, Derek Bradley and Malcolm Cook in front of the Ice Co-op flake ice machine. (Photo by kind permission *Evening Gazette*)

confident that another cold store was a viable proposition. In the end another store was not built.

During the Second World War, ice production dropped as trawlers were, once again, taken up by the Navy for minesweeping and other duties.

In 1940 the company secretary, J.B. Graham, reported he could no longer carry on in that position, so it was agreed that Miss W. Walker should take up the post at a salary of £26 a year. Miss Walker's name appears in the earliest wage book I have seen, which starts in October 1933. Miss (Winnie) Walker was to continue employment with the Ice Co. until her retirement in the 1960s.

As the war continued, ice production reduced and the Government took charge of all cold storage facilities in the country, and the price of ice was increased in January 1941 from 20s per ton to 30s per ton (£1 to £1.50).

After the war was over the fishing industry got back onto its feet once again with sales for 1946 at 5,462 tons, 1947 at 6,376 tons, and 1948 at 6,172 tons.

With the remaining fleet of steam trawlers reaching the end of their working lives and gradually being scrapped in the 1950s, ice sales fell. Although some motor trawlers were brought in to replace the aging steamers, ice production was never to reach anything like the tonnage seen in previous years. The cold storage facilities were still in use for meat, butter and other foodstuffs so the 'ice house' was still viable.

People who worked on the fish quay can well remember loading a long-handled barrow with three or four 'kit' boxes, walking round the quay to the ice house, passing your ticket for ice through a small window, and exchanging it for a ticket to take round to the loading bay. All you saw of Miss Walker, for many years, was a hand as it passed your ticket through the little window. Passing your ticket over on the loading bay, ice was tipped into your boxes, and then you had to take a run at the ramp leading up to the fish quay and back to your stand.

The massive building, which had dominated the fish quay and the surrounding area for years, was coming to the end of its working life as the 1980s approached. The fish quay itself had been reduced to a quarter of its previous length as merchants and boats disappeared. In 1984 the Ice Co. ceased trading – ice sales and cold storage were no longer viable – and the building was demolished. Everyone thought this was a huge building, but on a site adjacent to the 'ice house corner' was to be erected a shed for oil rig building into which the old ice house would have fitted several times.

For a time there was a void in supplies when ice had to be brought down by road from the nearest facility in North Shields. Merchants would fill their vans after delivering to overnight haulage contractors, and boats would have to steam there if they needed any tonnage of ice before going off-side. Occasionally, boats would land in Shields as the facilities were all on hand, to the loss of the Hartlepool market.

Eventually, local merchants, boat owners and agents began talks with the local council, Cleveland Co-operative Agency and the Port Authority on how best to provide new ice facilities in the port. Taking their advice, Hartlepool Ice Cooperative was set up. The Port Authority agreed to provide foundations for the plant and £1 shares were sold to over sixty merchants, fishermen and buyers, loans were set up, and the £20,000 project started production in early 1988. The new facility was situated under the fish quay itself and consisted of an insulated bunker which could hold 24 tons of ice, on top of which was a flake ice machine which could produce up to 12 tons a day. This machine produced ice by spraying water onto a drum which was filled with refrigerant, the ice then fell away into the bunker below. Doors in the bunker served the merchants and a conveyor delivered ice to the boats lying alongside.

Carolyn (INS 276) takes ice from the 'Fish Co.' ice machine.

The Cooperative succeeded in maintaining ice supplies to the port for a number of years until, once again, fishing boat numbers decreased and merchants closed down. There were also problems with the fish quay structure itself; new Health and Safety regulations could not be met and demolition loomed. With demolition and the formation of the Hartlepool Fish Co. in 1998, all the facilities, auction hall, offices and box store moved into a new, much smaller building where the dock head office once stood. Ice is now provided by the Fish Co. from a similar type of ice machine, producing about 10 tons a day; this is situated on the dock head and ice is fed to the boats through a conveyer.

WAGES
National Insurance Acts

Copyright.—Chas. Knight & Co., Ltd., Tooley Street, S.E. 1—S 819-1932—Form II.—F/cap

| | Week ending 4th June, 1938 | | | | | | Week ending | |
NAME OR NUMBER (2)	Weekly or Monthly Wages (3)	Deductions from Wages on account of Insurance — Health, &c. (4)	Unemploy't (5)	Net Wages Payable (6)	Contribution by Employer — Health, &c., Insurance (7)	Unemploy't Insurance (8)	Weekly or Monthly Wages (3)	Deductions Wages on of In- Health, &c. (4)
	£ s. d.	s. d.	s. d.	£ s. d.	s. d.	s. d.	£ s. d.	s. d.
Emm. W.J.	5 10 ·			5 10 ·			5 10 ·	
Barnes J.	3 12 6	10	9	3 10 11	10	9	3 12 6	10
Caussens N.	3 12 6	10	9	3 10 11	10	9	3 12 6	10
Walker W.	1 10 ·			1 10 ·			1 10 ·	
Torlelson D.	1 5 ·			1 5 ·	1 2	1 4	1 5 ·	
Dixon	3 4 2	10	9	3 2 7	10	9	2 12 11	10
Tweddle	3 12 8	10	9	3 11 1	10	9	2 12 11	10
Robson	3 4 2	10	9	3 2 7	6	9	2 12 11	10
Hunter	3 9 3	10	9	3 7 8	10	9	2 15 2	10
Hood	3 8 7	10	9	3 7 ·	10	9	2 19 ·	10
Stoddart	3 10 10	10	9	3 9 3	10	9	2 19 ·	10
Lund R	3 16 4	10	9	3 14 9	10	9	3 · ·	10
Shadforth	2 5 ·	10	9	2 3 5	10	9	2 5 ·	10
... fard	3 ·			3 ·	1 2		3 ·	
A. Restall								
Totals	44 7 -	8 4	7 6	44 8 2	10 8	8 10	37 9 11	8 4
				1 15 4				

A page from the Ice Company's wage book.

PEOPLE
A Freddie Boagey and Kevin Cook on board *Sanrene*.
B Norman Wallace (the Jewel) on the *Scema*.
C Bobby Slimmings on the *Scema*.

D Bill Horsley mending a crab pot. **E** Frankie Benton and Graham 'Diddy' Watt on board *Embrace*.

F

H

G

F Griggs' storeman, Jackie Ray. **G** Billy Nunn, who spent all his working life on the fish quay. **H** Skipper Peter Watt, with a sturgeon. **I** Tommy O'Dell, who could still handle a knife well into his eighties. **J** Tony Raper, filleting small codling.

I

J

7

7

FISHING BOATS

The predominant boat in use in the 1800s and before was the open coble, many of them built by local craftsmen from the Cambridge or Pounder families. The average length of a fishing boat when the register was opened in 1869 was 18.5ft (6m), with the larger vessels coming in at 25–30ft (8–10m). Powered by sails on one or two masts, they also carried one or two pairs of oars or 'sweeps', as they were sometimes known, for times when the wind died away and they had to row back to shore or for use when manoeuvring back to the beach. The local boats were built on the lines of the 'English' or 'Whitby'-style coble which was evolved through the ages to work from the shallow shelving beaches of the north-east coast. These cobles come ashore stern first, having a flat underwater section at the after end of the hull which keeps the boat steady as she comes onto the beach. The crew for an 18.5ft boat would be three men while the 20–30ft would take three or four men. Many of these fishermen could not swim, and had no intention of learning; if you fell overboard wearing heavy leather sea boots and oilskins, swimming only 'prolonged the agony', a view that persisted into the second half of the twentieth century.

Shooting and hauling of lines and nets was all done by hand, and navigation by compass and local knowledge. This is the way it had been for centuries, however with the Industrial Revolution came improvements which rapidly changed the way fishing was carried out. In the second half of the 1800s, bigger sailing trawlers, of up to 70ft in length, were introduced. Based on the Brixham sailing trawlers' design, these vessels had a good reputation for seaworthiness, and could make up to 12 knots, outpacing the yachts of their day, especially in heavy weather.

In 1887 there were over 3,000 first-class smacks registered in England and Wales. By 1903, with the coming of steam, the number of sailing smacks was down to 920. In some cases nearly new vessels had been scrapped to make way for steam.

The steamers, at first, carried on using the same beam trawl which their sailing predecessors had used, but showed an increase of three to four times the catching power. When the otter trawl was introduced, using doors to keep the mouth of the net open instead of the beam, the catch improvements were eightfold. As the 1800s turned into the 1900s, over 2,000 steam trawlers were built in a ten-year period, the beginning of the end for sail. Many of the early steam trawlers were relatively small, about the same size as the sailing trawlers they replaced – 70–80ft. As signs of overfishing in the North Sea appeared, bigger trawlers of 120ft or so appeared which could fish virtually anywhere.

Cobles

Lots of cobles of 18.5ft were in use in the 1800s, either double-enders or with square sterns. Many of these were built locally to a virtual standard design, with minor modifications to suit each owner and for the type of fishing they would be engaged in. It was reckoned that 'Jonty Punder' (Pounder), could build a 24ft coble for £1/foot. These were built by eye or perhaps with the aid of a half model. The Cambridge Brothers had a very good reputation for their boatbuilding skills, with many of their cobles going to other east coast ports, Staithes fishermen in particular favouring Cambridge-built boats. There is a record of how fast a coble can sail in ideal conditions; when a coble left Hartlepool for Staithes for the wedding of one of her crew, the distance of sixteen sea miles was completed in 1 hour 20 minutes, an average speed of 12 knots.

The building of Whitby cobles 'by eye' was carried on until the end of the twentieth century. Basic design details were worked out between the fisherman and builder – length, beam, depth etc. – the rest was down to the skill and experience of the boat builder. Some keel boats were built virtually the same way, for instance the *Fiona Fay* and the *Castle Eden* of 1958 had no formal drawings done before they were constructed.

The first motor-driven coble is believed to be the *Constance* (HL 52), owned by a local group and registered in November 1914; however there is also a motor-powered coble *Children's Friend* (HL 40) on the register in September 1914.

The English or Whitby coble has survived into the twenty-first century, with many in daily use with some older, sail-powered, restored examples afloat on the east coast. While

Restored Whitby coble *Golden Gleam* with lug rig sail.

the hull design remains basically the same, changes, such as a wheelhouse, trawl winches and greater beam to accommodate new equipment, have been made to make the boat more versatile.

Keel Boats

The term 'keel boat' is used in Hartlepool for any other boat that was not a Whitby coble, or a steel trawler. A coble does not have a keel as such with the shape of the boat being formed by the planks. The keel boat starts from the keel with the frames or ribs being fastened at right angles to this, these then form the shape of the hull. Planking is then added to the frames to complete the hull in the conventional manner.

The keel boats of the 1800s would carry one or two masts and were either lug or ketch rigged. This type of boat would have to lay off the beach at the Fish Sands or alongside a quay as they were not built to 'take the ground' like a coble. The length of a keel boat was generally from 30ft up to 70ft.

The large sailing trawlers reached the peak of their refinement in the late 1800s, just in time for the introduction of steam engines into fishing boats which changed the face of fishing. There are examples of preserved sailing trawlers at various ports around the country.

Ha'burn, one of the smaller keel boats to join the local fleet in the 1980s.

Steam

The steam engine created a world of difference when it was introduced onshore in its various guises, whether it was pumping water out of coal mines or transporting people and goods along the rapidly expanding railways. As the steam engine developed it was adapted to maritime use, being fitted initially to tugs, the earliest of which were powered by paddle wheels. These same paddle tugs were helping sailing trawlers out to sea, often towing a string of sailing trawlers out of harbours so they could catch the wind beyond the piers.

In November 1877, the steam tug *Messenger* towed a sailing trawler out to sea from the River Tyne and because of the flat calm the trawler skipper asked the tug to keep towing while they shot the trawl. When the *Messenger* returned to the river, the tug skipper had alterations made so that the tug could tow the trawl itself. This was apparently the first successful experiment at steam trawling. The idea rapidly caught on and other paddle tugs were adapted in North Shields and various other ports to go fishing. (The last Scarborough paddle trawler, *Constance*, was lost off Hartlepool on 22 March 1910.)

Steam had already been in use in connection with the fishing industry for some years, with capstans on sailing trawlers introduced to haul in the trawl warp and the use of steam carrier vessels. In 1865, Hewett's sailing trawlers of Hull were serviced by Stockton-built iron steam carrier vessels. Sailing trawlers from the same company worked in a group or fleet, all fishing the same area, with the steam carrier collecting the fish and providing ice and stores, leaving the sailing trawlers at sea for weeks at a time. Fish was boxed up as it

Sybil, built as a steam carrier before being converted to trawling.

was caught; when the carrier arrived, the trawler's small rowing boat was launched, boxes transferred into it, and it was then rowed over to the steamer where the boxes were lifted aboard. This was carried out in all weathers. Transferring fish at sea became one of the most hazardous operations and claimed many lives.

The first steam trawler in Hartlepool is believed to be the 1885-built *Tantallon*. This was possibly the first 'purpose-built' trawler in Hartlepool, which was purchased by J.T. Graham in 1897. However, the first steam-powered fishing vessel on the local register, on 4 March 1878, is the *Star o' Tay*, a tug, rigged fore and aft, with fishing lines, with the first steamer listed as a trawler being the *Brilliant*, registered on 10 July 1878, owned by George Wright, and believed to be a paddle tug conversion.

More steam-powered vessels were added to Hartlepool's fleet after 1880 when the fish quay in the tidal harbour (deep water berth) was developed. Although these fishing vessels are listed as steam powered, the register still shows them as 'ketch rigged', or similar, that is carrying a full set of sails – jib, main and mizzen. This practice of listing steam-powered trawlers with sails continued until the 1930s. Fishing vessels of various sizes continued to be built with the addition of sails long after this time, although their use was more for keeping the boat steady or keeping head to wind while drift net fishing, than for propulsion.

Among the local people investing in new or second-hand steam trawlers were Graham's, Cappleman, Pattison, Davison, Peverill, Sutton, Wray, Mason and J.J. Lister, who, along with other owners, also provided bunker coal and stores for visiting and local vessels.

Tantallon, believed to be the first steam trawler in Hartlepool.

St Hilda, built in 1897.

Dozens of shipyards were building steam trawlers from the 1880s, with some yards turning out ten or twelve steam trawlers and drifters a year. There appeared to be an endless supply of fish in the sea and very good returns were being made investing in the increasing trawler fleet. Some well-known builders included Smiths Dock on the Tees and the Tyne; Hall Russell, Duthie, John Lewis and Alexander Hall, of Aberdeen; Cook, Weldon and Gammel and Cochranes of Selby; John Chambers and Colby Bros of Lowestoft; Mackie and Thompson of Govan; and Wood & Skinner, Hepple, and Eltringhams on the Tyne.

Technical advances allowed the steam trawler to increase in length to 100–120ft, engines became more reliable with the triple expansion replacing the two-cylinder units in earlier use and steel replaced iron for the hull construction. Many of the engines were built 'in house' but others were bought in from outside engineering companies such as Edwards, South Shields, McCail & Pollock, Sunderland; Westgarth, English & Co., Middlesbrough; Elliot & Garrard, Beccles; C.D. Holmes, Hull; Abernethie, Aberdeen; and Wood Bros, Sowerby Bridge.

As this building boom took place just before the First World War, it was fortunate that the country had an ample supply of vessels capable of being requisitioned and put to numerous uses in the defence of the nation.

Motor Power

The early motor-powered cobles and small boats used petrol or petrol/paraffin engines, but it was the advent of the diesel engine, which was more economic and reliable, which changed the face of the inshore fishing industry. Many cobles and keel boats were converted to take engines and retained their sail plan but as more engines came onto the market, fishing boats were designed from the keel up to take a power unit. Vessels fitted with engines gradually reduced sail plan and the size of the masts, with only the need for a small steadying sail to be catered for.

Some of the well-known engine producers included Gardner, Kelvin, Thornycroft, Tuxham, Parsons, Gleniffer, Bolinders, Beardmore, Ailsa Craig and Hundersted.

The steam trawlers in Hartlepool, as elsewhere, became increasingly uneconomic after the Second World War, and were gradually sent to the breakers. The last steam trawlers in Hartlepool were *Ben Tarbet, Calypso, Fort Ryan, George D. Irvine, Kudos, Loch Blair* and the last to go to the breakers in 1957 was the *Friarage* (HL 18). Although various diesel trawlers were based in the port, there was a shortage of vessels to supply the fish market.

The boats which were built to replace the out-of-date steamers were a class of dual-purpose seine netter/trawlers, of traditional layout and timber construction, around 50ft length, built mainly in Scotland and powered by Gardner, Kelvin or Lister diesel engines.

A belt drive was used to power the main trawl winch and seine net rope coiler on these vessels but with improvements in hydraulics the power block appeared for hauling the net onboard and, for seine net fishing, rope drums on the deck took away the backbreaking work of lifting the coils of rope from under the winch as they came on board and stacking them on deck.

Castle Eden, one of a number of similar vessels built to replace the steam trawlers.

J.J., typical of the new generation of 'plastic' boats.

The 'Plastic' Boats

Another major change in fishing boat technology took place in 1976 when a new style of inshore fishing boat appeared in Hartlepool with the arrival of the 32ft-long *Cygnus* (HL 107). Built in Cornwall with a fibreglass hull, forward wheelhouse, trawl winch and powerful engine, she was about the same length as a traditional coble but had the catching power of a 50ft boat and deck space unseen on a boat of her size. This class of inshore trawler became very popular in Hartlepool, as in other ports around the UK, replacing many traditional-style boats. The *Cygnus* was initially used for working crab pots, but was adapted for the winter prawn trawling season where the boat soon proved her worth. Various other boats of similar design appeared in the port, with the size of this class going up to 44ft (15m). With the large deck space available, hydraulic net drums and power blocks became standard equipment; this enabled the crew to be reduced down to two men. The weight of equipment on the deck was compensated for by the broad beam and deep draught of the design. A traditional coble of 32ft would draw about 2ft whereas the new design would draw 5–6ft (1.75–2m); this also gave space for a small fish room and a cabin up in the bows.

Rule Changes

During the latter part of the twentieth century, changes in fishing rules and regulations for various classes of boats had a profound effect on the design of vessels to suit these changing circumstances. In particular the design and catching capabilities of the under 10m (registered length) class changed radically. (The registered length is taken from where the bow leaves the water to the centre line of the rudder post.) This class has often been described as 'rule beaters' because of the way that the fishing regulations are interpreted.

The *Friarage*, at 10.03m registered length, is a traditional coble that was built to the individual skipper's requirement as to the length and beam and for the type of fishing to be carried out, and before tight restrictions.

The *Cygnus*, at 9.27m registered length, was developed in the South West and rapidly replaced the coble for the same registered length. The increased beam gives space for a trawl winch to be installed, and the catch can be stored below decks in a shallow fish room. A change in construction from wood to fibreglass with the hull built in a mould was another radical change from the traditional construction methods.

The *Endeavour*, at 9.95m registered length, shows a move to steel in the construction of the newer class of under 10m fishing vessels. Everything that a 15–20m fishing boat has is contained on this vessel: a powerful engine, hydraulic net drum, trawl winch, shelter deck, and a wheelhouse full of the latest electronics.

Friarage, registered length 10.06m.

Cygnus, registered length 9.25m.

Endeavour, registered length, 9.95m.

The build changes of these three examples has increased beam and draft to compensate for the increase in top-weight. The coble would typically draw 1–2ft, the *Cygnus* 5–6ft, and the *Endeavour* would have 7–8ft under the water.

The bigger classes of vessel have also shown a significant change in design, as can be seen from the photo overleaf. The traditionally built Danish design *Grenna Star*, in the centre, has a registered length of 17.9m, whereas the *Lindisfarne*, to the right, is 16.7m.

Grenna Star (centre), registered length 17.9m. Lindisfarne (right) registered length 16.7m.

The Demise

With the advances made over the years, not just to boat design, but in the technical side – fish finding, sonar, satellite navigation, and the wheelhouses of fishing boats looking more like the cockpit of an aircraft – the fish stocks could not keep pace with the catching power chasing them.

Add on the Common Fisheries Policy, designed by politicians who have never been to sea, and the effect on the fishing fleet of Hartlepool and the rest of the UK was disastrous. With the turning of the twenty-first century the Hartlepool fleet was down to its lowest numbers for many years and the quota system in place needed a lawyer to sort out what you could and could not catch. Rules and regulations have been piled onto the catching fleet, the local fishmonger has virtually disappeared, and the supermarket has taken over, mainly selling fish from the other side of the world. Even the fish and chip shop, once so numerous, has reduced in numbers and those remaining sell imported frozen fish from Iceland, Norway, Russia or the Faroes.

Preservation

It may be worth noting that two ex-Hartlepool fishing boats have been listed in the Historic Ships Register: the *Scanboy* (GY 579), which was owned in the port for a short while, and the *Sovereign* (HL 165).

Sovereign, now under restoration on the Tyne.

Strandby in dock at Ramsgate.

Sovereign is now owned by the North East Maritime Trust and is undergoing restoration. She is normally berthed in St Margaret's Marina in North Shields, along with two other small keel boats owned by the Trust.

Another ex-Hartlepool vessel which spent some time 'in limbo' awaiting preservation was the *Strandby* (HL 7). After moving to North Shields from Hartlepool, she went south to Ramsgate where she was taken over by the local maritime museum when her fishing days were over. *Strandby* was placed in dry dock adjacent to a steam tug, also awaiting preservation, but, after spending many years awaiting development and left to deteriorate without even any care and maintenance, she was scrapped in 2007. Other local vessels in preservation are the coble *Friarage*, which is now in the care of Hartlepool Council Museums and is moored alongside two local smaller cobles next to the *Wingfield Castle* in the town's marina. On the Tyne is the restored 1925-built coble *Peggy* (HL 2) which was owned in the town on two occasions. Perhaps more examples of fishing vessels should be preserved before an important part of social history disappears forever.

Friarage in the care of Hartlepool Museums.

Opposite: **PAINT-UP TIME**
A *Wayside Flower* on the ferry. **B** *David Helen* on the ferry. **C** *Tetsuko* on the ferry. **D** *David Helen*, *Press On* and *Endeavour II* on the Old Pier. **E** *Maruel* on the ferry. **F** *Alexandra* on the Old Pier.

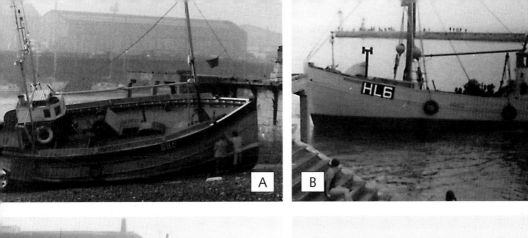

A

B

C

D

E

F

G *Prince Igor* coming alongside the Old Pier. H *Golden Hope* on the Old Pier. I *Cromlech* on the Old Pier. J *Maureen* on the ferry.

8

WARTIME

The First World War

On the morning of 16 December 1916, John Horsley of 21 Bedford Street was heading to sea in the motor fishing boat *Children's Friend* (HL 40) when, along with three other boats, he spotted three warships flying the Union Jack and Red Ensigns. Shortly after they hauled these flags down and German flags were hoisted aloft. When the warships opened fire on the town, the *Children's Friend* headed back to port and sheltered inside the breakwater, while the other boats ran ashore on the North Sands in an effort to keep out of the way. At one point the *Children's Friend* was no more than half a mile from the battle fleet and they could see the shells from the Heugh gun battery hitting or bouncing off the German ships. From an uncomfortably close position, John Horsley and his crew were witnessing the bombardment of Hartlepool. (Extracted from *The Hartlepools at War*.)

The outbreak of the First World War had a huge effect on the fishing industry, which was enjoying a boom time, with new steam trawlers rolling off the stocks as never before. This was, of course, a blessing in disguise for the country as these vessels were ideal for the war effort, to be used as minesweepers, armed patrols, boom defence vessels, and performing dozens of other vital roles in the conflict. At the start of the war 100,000 fishermen were employed around Britain and the Government had plans to commandeer 200 trawlers. Eventually over 3,000 fishing boats were taken up, and over half of the crews served with their boats. The Admiralty had already been experimenting with trawlers, having purchased a number of vessels for trials as minesweepers. In 1910 a division of the Royal Naval Reserve had been set up, the RNR(T), as a stand-by organisation in case of war.

In 1914, between Hartlepool and North Shields, there were eighty-eight steam trawlers working out of both ports; by the end of 1915 there was only two remaining fishing, but with food shortages some trawlers were returned to the trade. As the war progressed, the active fishing fleet was reduced to about one third of its pre-war level. With the corresponding reduction in landings and a general shortage of food in the country, the value of fish increased sharply. There were whispers of big pay days for the skippers and crews of the trawlers and cobles which continued fishing; this was confirmed as 'quite possible' according to the quarterly reports of the North Eastern Sea Fisheries Committee. Herring drifters were grossing up to £350 a night and up to £1,500 a

Irene Wray in wartime guise.

week. Inshore motor fishing boats landing whitefish catches also showed a large increase in earnings. Although fishing was highly profitable, it also carried additional hazards alongside those normally associated with the industry, with submarines prowling around in coastal waters sinking any vessel they came across.

On 25 September 1916, a group of trawlers were fishing close together 20 miles north-east of Scarborough. Of this group, eleven trawlers from Scarborough were sunk by a German submarine, together with Hartlepool-owned *Loch Ness* (HL 71) and the ex-Hartlepool, Whitby-owned *St Hilda* (HL 50). (The submarine responsible, *U57*, sank twenty-nine trawlers in three days.) Together with the loss of four trawlers earlier in the war, this action all but wiped out the Scarborough fishing fleet, leaving the port with only four trawlers and one drifter. Any fishing boat was fair game for the German Navy; even cobles of 5 or 6 tons were sent to the bottom.

An account written by Skipper George Ray in 1939, who as a boy did not attend school very much, tells of a submarine attack, and is reproduced here verbatim:

Another experience at the age of nearly 13 years 9 month, I was deckhand on a fishing vessel bound to the fishing grounds when a German submarine overtakes us, fires his gun to stop ship. Then comes close orders us to get boat out, shouts to come on board of submarine. When we get close to sub with small boat the Commander shouts no one get out of that boat till that boy gets out as it was dangerous to board, that boy was me. The conversation on board was very interesting for instance our captain or skipper as we usually term, say to the officer on sub, what about letting us go, to put us on board of another ship. After a conversation in German with another officer on his submarine 'sorry but my orders are sink every vessel we come across there is someone on my ship reports me if I don't.' He towed our small boat as near to the land as he dared for his own ships safety. When getting into the small boat one of the Germans handed me my small sea boots, which I was very proud of that were new that day. I have often wondered what became of them and the gentleman that gave us courage. That night the weather got worse we had quite a trying time, we had to take two of the crew out of the other ships small boat as it was too small. Next morning we managed to get to another fishing vessel. after getting on board, a British gunboat hailed us to make enquiry what had happened and we told him, hoping at the bottom of our hearts that they would get home.

This incident possibly took place in 1916. George says he got his sea boots back; this was because the Germans took the sea boots off the fishermen as they were leather and must have been better quality than the German issue. I am deeply indebted to 'Sonny Ray', George's son, for being able to include this eyewitness account.

The First World War effectively saw the end of the sailing trawler era; with numbers already diminished with the coming of steam, during the conflict over 240 were sent to the bottom by gunfire or by bombs placed on board. U-boats were estimated to have sunk 578 fishing vessels in UK waters with ninety-eight fishermen losing their lives and over 300 fishermen ending up as prisoners of war.

Minesweeping was one of the main tasks for which the trawler was ideally suited. The sea lane down the east coast of the UK was especially vulnerable to this enemy activity, being within easy reach of the German bases on the Continent. There was a buoyed channel all the way up the east coast of England and Scotland; this was an area which had to be swept on a daily basis, as far as the weather would allow. There were occasions, apparently, when the trawlers would be recalled because of bad weather, but some would chance putting down their nets on their way back on the prospect of catching some fish.

Flotillas of minesweepers were based at major ports on the east coast, with Hartlepool-based trawlers coming under Tyne command. Sweeping continued after the Armistice when there

Princess Royal and *Bracken Lynn* (foreground) explode one of the first German mines to be cleared by trawlers in the North Sea off Scarborough.

A wartime mine trawled up by the *Margit*.

were estimated to be over 11,000 mines still to be cleared between Flamborough Head and the Tyne. For every mine swept after the war, 2s 6d (12.5p) was paid by the Government. The money paid for each mine would probably equate to eight or ten pints of beer, so the twenty-first-century equivalent would be about £25–30. It may be worth noting that in 1920, three Scarborough trawlers were sunk by mines.

Sweeping was generally carried out by trawlers working in pairs. A serrated wire was passed between them with a 'kite' close to either end; the 'kite' acted rather like a trawl door; it kept the wire off the seabed so that it caught the mooring line of the mine which floated just below the surface. The mooring line was cut and the mine floated to the surface where it was exploded by gunfire from the trawlers. Not all mines exploded unfortunately, many went to the bottom full of bullet holes, these gradually sank into the seabed only to be trawled up generations later.

Margit's crew and bomb disposal squad pose next to the mine in the net.

Minesweepers in Hartlepool: First World War

During the First World War, a minesweeping flotilla was based in Hartlepool, which was part of the Tyne command. The author's grandfather was Chief Skipper in command of a flotilla based in the port after being transferred from Aberdeen. His war record shows the trawlers listed below which he served on, so presumably these could have been some which were based in Hartlepool at some point.

Island Prince, SN148, 205 tons, steam, 74hp, built 1911, Eltringham, S. Shields
     1911, Boyle & Rayner, N. Shields
     1914, Navy, No.62, m/s, 1x6pdr
     1919, returned to owners

Princess Royal, SN209, 213 tons, steam, 56hp, built 1913, Alex. Hall, Aberdeen
     1913, Dodds S.F. Co. Aberdeen
     1914, Navy, No.518, m/s, 1x6pdr
     1915, renamed, *Princess Royal II*
     1940, J.S. Boyle, Glasgow, r/n *John Watterson*
     1957, scrapped

Sanserit, GY996, 212 tons, steam, 78hp, built 1916, Alex. Hall, Aberdeen
    1916, W.H. Beeley, Grimsby
    1917, Navy, No.2997, m/s, 1x6pdr
    1919 returned to owners
    1920, C.H. George, Hull
    1923, A. Bruce, Aberdeen
    19??, A. Main & D. Wood
    1947, G. Robb, r/n *Viking Enterprise*
    1960, scrapped

Pekin, steam, built 1917, Smiths Dock as 'non-standard' Castle Class trawler
    1917, built as *Festing Grindall*
    1919 r/n *Pekin*
    1920 sold, r/n *Festing Grindall*

City of Perth, steam, built 1917, Duithie, Aberdeen, as Strath Class trawler
    1917, built as *William Ashton*
    1919, r/n *City of Perth* while on loan to US Navy
    1922, Crampin S.F. Co. Grimsby, r/n *William Ashton*
    1929, Walker Aberdeen, r/n *Star of Victory* (A 4)
    24-10-1939, wrecked at Keiss, Wick

The Second World War

As in the First World War, the Navy called up vast numbers of trawlers and drifters for the conflict. Over 800 trawlers and 200 drifters, many with their crews, were requisitioned, representing about 75 per cent of the fleet at the time, and consequently landings of fish dropped from 22,417,780 cwt in 1938 to 7,771,016 cwt in 1941 (1 cwt = approximately 55 kilos). As a consequence the price of fish rose until the Government stepped in with fixed price controls in 1941 (see table).

Fishing for crabs and lobsters has always been one of the main features of inshore fisheries operations off the north-east coast of England, and as the war progressed it became even more lucrative. As the price restrictions on whitefish came into effect in 1941, there was a switch by boats from whitefish to shellfish catching as there was no restriction on prices and they continued to rise in value. This threw the balance of landings out, reducing the supply of whitefish even further. The Ministry of Food intervened in 1943 and brought in restrictions to regulate shellfish catching off the Northumberland and Durham coasts. Licences were issued by the Ministry's Port Fisheries Captain, based in North Shields, to vessels which had previously been engaged in this side of the industry and not to 'newcomers' who had changed over from whitefish, however eventually controls had to be imposed on crab and lobster prices by the Ministry.

		Cod. s. d.	Haddock. s. d.	Hake. s. d.	Saithe s. d.	Halibut. s. d.	Plaice. s. d.	Sole. s. d.
1938 ..	..	1 8	2 4	4 8	0 8	9 11	6 5	16 6
1939								
August ..	..	1 11	2 4	4 8	0 10	9 8	5 7	16 9
September..	..	—	—	—	—	—	—	—
October ..	..	5 9	5 0	6 9	3 1	12 0	7 8	13 9
November..	..	5 6	5 11	7 10	3 7	13 8	8 3	14 8
December	..	4 6	5 6	7 11	2 9	13 9	11 1	20 9
1940								
January ..	..	5 5	7 1	7 4	3 10	15 0	11 6	20 9
February ..	..	4 3	5 5	7 8	2 1	12 7	10 1	13 11
March ..	..	4 10	5 9	8 5	2 7	15 9	11 4	13 9
April ..	..	4 1	5 5	7 11	2 5	16 6	10 8	17 3
May ..	..	3 1	3 11	5 7	1 11	13 5	8 7	20 4
June ..	..	4 1	6 0	6 0	3 3	14 6	10 9	22 1
July ..	..	7 0	6 3	7 3	4 4	13 8	11 4	22 11
August ..	..	8 8	7 5	9 6	5 2	16 8	11 4	26 4
September..	..	9 8	9 2	11 8	6 7	16 5	12 4	26 1
October ..	..	9 5	9 9	12 9	6 6	20 0	13 7	27 0
November..	..	9 4	10 2	14 1	5 11	19 1	14 7	32 1
December ..	..	12 3	13 0	16 2	10 11	24 2	16 9	35 5
1941								
January ..	..	13 4	14 5	20 1	11 4	25 10	21 5	37 1
February ..	..	13 1	15 9	22 4	9 7	27 2	19 11	41 6
March ..	..	10 3	13 0	22 0	7 2	29 3	18 6	38 7
April ..	..	14 2	16 11	25 3	14 7	34 5	20 11	42 1
May ..	..	13 6	14 6	20 8	12 8	27 9	17 2	32 7
June ..	..	12 2	13 7	15 7	11 2	25 0	15 11	28 7
July ..	..	8 0	7 10	15 5	7 8	21 10	13 11	20 10
August ..	..	8 0	7 10	15 2	7 7	21 11	14 3	20 10
September	..	8 0	7 11	15 4	7 3	21 11	13 9	21 1
October ..	..	7 1	7 0	9 6	7 0	20 11	13 5	20 9
November	..	7 1	7 0	9 6	7 0	20 11	13 1	20 10
December ..	..	7 0	7 0	9 6	7 0	21 0	13 11	20 11

Table showing the effect of wartime price control.

As there were only twenty years between the wars, many trawlers from around the country were called up by the Navy for a second time. Vessels which had been, or still were, owned in Hartlepool and served in both conflicts included *Ben Tarbet*, *Calypso*, *East Coast*, *George D. Irvine*, *Happy Days*, *Irene Wray*, *Loch Blair*, *Parkmore*, *Semnos* and *W.S. Burton*.

Most were on minesweeping duties but some served as boom defence or armed patrol vessels. More than 400 drifters and trawlers were lost in this second conflict. It will also be noted that trawlers were bought and sold while on charter to the Navy; this happened during both wars.

Following the Second World War, the Admiralty sold off its surplus stock of purpose-built trawlers: one local ex-Navy vessel was *Loch Blair*, launched as *James Began*, one of a class of over 140 'Strath' class trawlers built during the First World War. Another was the *Moreleigh* (HL 160), built of timber for the Admiralty as a general-purpose MFV at Rowhedge, Wivenhoe. Surplus vessels like these found a ready market in civilian life replacing trawlers lost in action. The reduced fishing effort during both wars gave the fish stocks time to recover with an increase in landings following both conflicts.

SOME TRAWLERS WHICH SERVED IN BOTH WARS
A *W.S. Burton*. B *George D. Irvine*. C *Loch Blair*. D *Calypso*.

Minesweepers in Hartlepool: Second World War

Below is a list of minesweepers based in Hartlepool during the Second World War. Changes to the list would have occurred during the war as ships were moved around various ports during the conflict. One notable name on the list is *Picton Castle*, still afloat in the twenty-first century, converted to a sailing ship and retaining her name.

Base Ship HMS *Paragon* (Destroyer)

Group 1 (purchased trawlers)
Hawthorn, T32 (ex-*Cape Guardafui*) 593 tons/1930
Sycamore, T37 (ex-*Lord Beaverbrook*) 573 tons/1930
Willow, T66 (ex-*Cape Spartivento*) 574 tons/1930

Group 22 (requisitioned trawlers)
Mount Keen, FY684, 254 tons/1936
Oku, FY660, 303 tons/1929
Stella Orion, FY?, 417 tons/1935

Group 23 (requisitioned trawlers)
Ben Dearg, FY690, 280 tons/1920 (ex-RN Thos. Alexander) retnd 6-1946
Picton Castle, FY628, 307 tons/1928, retnd 12-1945
Pointz Castle, FY630, 283 tons/1914, retnd 4-1945

Group 24 (Admiralty Tree Class, 530 tons, 164x27.5x10.5ft, 850 HP, 11.5 knots)
Birch, T93, built Cook, Weldon & Gammel, Beverley, engines by Holmes
Chestnut, T?, built Goole S.B. Co. engines by Amos & Smith
Rowan, T119, built Smiths Dock, South Bank
Walnut, T103, built Smiths Dock, Middlesbrough

Group 26 (Admiralty Tree Class)
Fir, T129, built Inglis, Glasgow, engines by Aitcheson Blair
Mangrove, T112, built Ferguson, Port Glasgow
Olive, T126, built Hall Russell, Aberdeen

Group 41 (requisitioned trawlers)
Milford Haven Earl
Phineas Beard, FY, lost 8-12-1941
Teroma, FY527 (ex-RN Isaac Heath) retnd 3-1945
William Cale, FY535 (ex-RN) retnd 3-1945

Group ? (purchased trawlers)
Ceder, T01 (ex-*Arab*) 649 tons/1933 sold 7-1946
Cypress, T09 (ex-*Cape Finisterre*) 548 tons/1930 sold 1946
Holly, T19 (ex-*Kingston Coral*) 590 tons/1930 sold 1946

Drifters (requisitioned)
Boy Alec, FY?, retnd 1945
Lizzie Birrel, FY1547, retnd 4-1946

9

THE *DUNELM*

Sailing from Hartlepool on 22 October 1959 for Dogger Bank, the *Dunelm* (HL 89) was seen by the Grimsby seine netter *Bay Wyke* five days later; that was the last sighting anyone would have of the *Dunelm*.

One of the saddest incidents in the history of Hartlepool's fishing industry was about to unfold.

Dunelm had been completed by the Scottish boatyard of George Thompson of Buckie in December 1958. She was a sister ship to the *Scema* (HL 79), built in 1957. Both vessels were 51ft long (17m), 24 tons, with Danish-type hulls and of very similar layout, apart from the *Dunelm*'s wheelhouse being slightly longer. *Dunelm* had been working the summer from Grimsby and had returned to her home port in October to work the winter. She had been under the command of Skipper Gunner Moller until then but he had to come ashore for an operation and the command was taken over by Skipper James Murray, of Buckie, who had on board his son Ian (sixteen years old) and two Hartlepool men, Harry Smith (twenty-six) and Thomas Andrews (twenty-seven).

She was expected to be away for up to eighteen days – her previous longest trip was nineteen days – and people ashore began to feel anxious after no contact was made after twenty days. Although the *Bay Wyke* had spotted the *Dunelm* early in her trip, she had been unable to make radio contact and at first the reason for the silence was thought to be a problem with the radio.

However, an air and sea search was instigated on 14 November, with radio calls being made from Cullercoats' radio every 2 hours, but nothing was seen or heard and all hope was abandoned on 27 November.

She could have been run down by a merchant ship or overwhelmed by the sea; as there were gale-force winds blowing through the area she was fishing at the time of her disappearance, that was a distinct possibility, but no one will ever know. No wreckage was found in the area she was supposed to be in, but the *Banffshire Advertiser* reported on 24 December that a lifebuoy had been found on the island of Unst, the most northerly of the Shetland Islands, a long way from the Dogger Bank.

The *Scema* continued to fish from Hartlepool and was sold out of the port for further fishing in 1984.

(Information and photographs from Ray Andrews.)

A Returning from sea trials. **B** Alongside at the builders. **C** At sea fishing.
D On the slip. (Photos courtesy of Ray Andrews)

10

TABLES AND ADVERTS

The following pages contain a miscellany of fishing–related documents, tables and adverts.

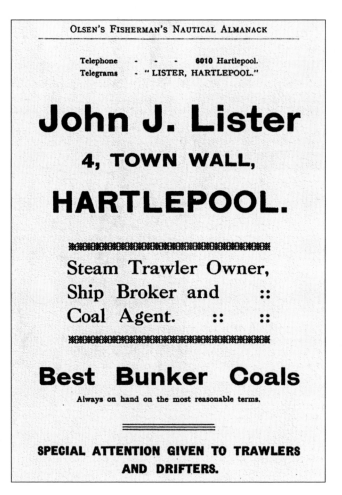

Advert for Lister.

FISH FROM HARTLEPOOL

reaches the under-mentioned towns at times shewn :—

Aberdeen	7 30 a.m.		Kettering	7 0 a.m.
Abergavenny Jct.	7 0 ,,		Leamington	4 0 ,,
Aldershot	7 30 ,,		Leeds	4 55 ,,
Arbroath	6 0 ,,		Leicester	5 30 ,,
Ascot	8 15 ,,		Liverpool	8 30 ,,
Aylesbury	9 0 ,,		Llandudno	8 30 ,,
Banbury	3 0 ,,		Llanelly	11 30 ,,
Barnstaple	10 30 ,,		London	2 0 ,,
Basingstoke	7 0 ,,		Loughborough	6 0 ,,
Bath	5 30 ,,		Macclesfield	6 30 ,,
Berwick	4 0 ,,		Maidstone	8 0 ,,
Birkenhead	7 30 ,,		Manchester	1 0 ,,
Birmingham	4 30 ,,		Margate	10 0 ,,
Bishop Auckland	3 10 p.m.		Market Harborough	7 30 ,,
Blackburn	9 30 a.m.		Matlock	4 30 ,,
Blackpool	9 30 ,,		Merthyr	10 0 ,,
Bournemouth	9 0 ,,		Milford Haven	3 45 p.m.
Bradford	6 0 ,,		Monmouth	12 noon.
Brighton	7 30 ,,		Newbury	8 45 a.m.
Bristol	6 0 ,,		Newcastle	5 45 p.m.
Burton-on-Trent	3 0 ,,		Newport	8 30 a.m.
Buxton	8 30 ,,		Northampton	8 30 ,,
Canterbury	9 0 ,,		Nottingham	12 30 ,,
Cardiff	9 0 ,,		Oxford	3 30 ,,
Carmarthen	12 30 p.m.		Perth	5 30 ,,
Chatham	8 0 a.m.		Plymouth	10 0 ,,
Cheltenham	9 36 ,,		Poole	9 15 ,,
Chester	5 30 ,,		Portsmouth	9 0 ,,
Chesterfield	6 0 ,,		Preston	8 30 ,,
Chichester	9 0 ,,		Ramsgate	10 30 ,,
Crewe	2 30 ,,		Reading	6 0 ,,
Darlington	12 24 ,,		Rhyl	6 30 ,,
Derby	2 30 ,,		Rugby	2 0 ,,
Devonport	10 15 ,,		Salisbury	8 0 ,,
Dewsbury	5 30 ,,		Sheffield	1 3 ,,
Dorchester	10 30 ,,		Shrewsbury	4 30 ,,
Dover	9 30 ,,		Southampton	8 0 ,,
Dundee	5 30 ,,		Southport	9 0 ,,
Durham	2 46 ,,		South Shields	10 50 p.m.
Eastbourne	8 30 ,,		Stockport	1 0 a.m.
Edinburgh	5 30 ,,		Stockton	8 36 ,,
Exeter	9 0 ,,		Sunderland	1 41 p.m.
Farnham	8 45 ,,		Swanage	10 15 a.m.
Fishguard	3 45 p.m.		Swansea	10 30 ,,
Folkestone	9 30 a.m.		Swindon	4 45 ,,
Glasgow	5 30 ,,		Taunton	8 0 ,,
Guildford	7 0 ,,		Torquay	10 15 ,,
Halifax	4 0 ,,		Tunbridge Wells	7 30 ,,
Harrogate	10 34 ,,		Tynemouth	7 48 p.m.
Hastings	8 45 ,,		Warrington	8 30 a.m.
Hereford	6 30 ,,		Weymouth	10 0 ,,
Hexham	8 0 p.m.		Whitchurch	8 0 ,,
Holyhead	11 30 a.m.		Winchester	7 30 ,,
Huddersfield	5 0 ,,		Woking	6 30 ,,
Ilfracombe	11 30 ,,		Wolverhampton	5 0 ,,
Ilkley	12 42 p.m.		Worcester	8 30 ,,
Inverness	10 0 a.m.		Yeovil	9 30 ,,
Keighley	7 30 ,,			

Information table taken from *Fishing Ports served by the LNER, 1923*, showing the arrival times in various towns of fish dispatched from Hartlepool.

APPENDICES TO ANNUAL REPORT OF PROCEEDINGS

APPENDIX II.—QUANTITY and VALUE of FISH landed at each STATION in ENGLAND and WALES in 1906.

Stations.	Quantity. Wet Fish.		Value. Wet Fish.		
	Other than Mackerel, Herring, Pilchards, and Sprats.	Mackerel, Herring, Pilchards, and Sprats.	Other than Mackerel, Herring, Pilchards, and Sprats.	Mackerel, Herring, Pilchards, and Sprats.	Total, including Shell Fish.
	Cwts.	Cwts.	£	£	£
EAST COAST.					
Berwick	5,384	62,922	18,257	15,957	34,455
Holy Island	1,417	628	649	121	2,732
North Sunderland	1,573	107,075	799	22,110	23,980
Beadnell	506	9,983	534	1,669	4,034
Newton	287	—	463	—	1,086
Craster	742	14,867	456	2,870	4,657
Boulmer	569	14	876	3	1,500
Alnmouth	184	—	628	—	628
Amble	147	—	477	—	582
Hauxley	324	—	1,234	—	1,922
Cresswell	105	—	446	—	687
Newbiggin	3,932	640	2,808	211	3,756
Blyth	225	—	385	—	508
Cullercoats	1,956	96	3,723	113	5,241
North Shields	395,651	297,036	279,589	78,360	363,393
Sunderland	25,115	870	16,870	270	17,632
Hartlepool	62,337	80,589	47,006	18,848	66,721
Redcar	1,812	—	1,447	—	1,721
Staithes	4,603	—	2,463	—	4,361
Whitby	2,488	4,585	2,201	1,922	4,939
Robin Hood's Bay	506	23	597	13	1,389
Scarborough	58,058	130,881	35,652	44,555	81,698
Filey	5,107	—	4,150	—	5,155
Flamborough	6,407	—	4,297	—	7,383
Bridlington	2,445	535	2,000	260	3,155
Hornsea	207	114	213	118	1,201
Hull	1,779,135	—	855,680	—	855,680
Grimsby	3,238,377	271,975	2,638,671	120,299	2,770,710
Boston	125,847	3,977	96,594	205	105,241
Lynn	505	—	474	—	10,916
Wells	20	—	13	—	2,773
Blakeney	82	—	58	—	680
Sheringham	1,553	192	893	181	4,464
Cromer	832	351	814	185	4,361

Landing statistics for 1906.

TABLE 2A.—QUANTITY AND VALUE OF EACH KIND OF FISH OF BRITISH TAKING LANDED AT EACH STATION IN 1938.

(i) MAJOR DEMERSAL STATIONS.

Kinds of Fish.	EAST COAST.							
	North Shields.		Hartlepool.		Whitby.		Scarborough.	
	Quantity.	Value.	Quantity.	Value.	Quantity.	Value.	Quantity.	Value.
	Cwts.	£	Cwts.	£	Cwts.	£	Cwts.	£
Bream..	—	—	—	—	—	—	—	—
Brill ..	75	171	31	150	40	112	197	818
Catfish..	2,850	3,173	1,013	1,195	—	—	223	375
Cod — Large	60,015	81,760	5,544	8179	1,494	2,632	9,110	15,402
Cod — Medium	33,897	37,244	7,541	10,653	1,880	2,150	4,456	6,402
Cod — Small	11,045	6,994	11,310	11,544	956	694	5,082	4,837
Cod — Unsorted	—	—	—	—	—	—	—	—
Cod — Total	104,957	125,998	24,395	30,376	4,330	5,526	18,648	26,641
Conger Eels ..	78	77	72	56	68	72	170	179
Dabs ..	393	419	598	622	2	7	232	366
Dogfish ..	333	118	262	99	57	48	34	14
Dory ..	—	—	—	—	—	—	—	—
Flounders ..	88	59	—	—	—	—	11	6
Gurnards and Latchets	2,870	921	1,215	613	—	—	561	459
Haddock — Large	1,035	1,655	305	484	—	—	697	1,383
Haddock — Medium	3,836	5,527	771	1,006	207	424	1,001	1,510
Haddock — Small	19,374	23,275	20,184	17,987	—	—	2,394	3,064
Haddock — Unsorted	74,944	81,228	—	—	—	—	—	—
Haddock — Total	99,189	111,685	21,260	19,477	207	424	4,092	5,957
Hake — Large	—	—	—	—	—	—	—	—
Hake — Medium	60	137	2	4	—	—	—	—
Hake — Small	89	105	5	10	—	—	—	—
Hake — Unsorted	—	—	—	—	—	—	—	—
Hake — Total	149	242	7	14	—	—	—	—
Halibut ..	1,961	9,164	168	829	—	—	9	53
Lemon Soles ..	9,461	36,066	1,275	5,435	—	—	719	3,362
Ling ..	8,360	8,117	1,211	1,245	275	284	921	1,141
Megrims ..	127	171	10	19	—	—	—	—
Monks (Anglers)	6,228	4,281	487	540	—	—	248	262
Mullet, Red ..	—	—	—	—	—	—	—	—
Plaice — Large	464	1,378	525	2,544	—	—	320	1,125
Plaice — Medium	2,466	8,490	511	1,636	63	282	654	2,920
Plaice — Small	1,950	3,556	998	2,095	26	59	1,312	3,723
Plaice — Unsorted	—	—	—	—	—	—	197	871
Plaice — Total	4,880	13,424	2,034	6,275	89	341	2,483	8,639
Pollack ..	1,531	955	—	—	—	—	38	33
Redfish ..	—	—	—	—	—	—	—	—
Saithe (Coalfish)	6,076	2,997	746	458	—	—	72	35
Skates and Rays	6,957	7,512	1,769	1,834	67	124	1,124	3,058
Soles — Large	—	—	6	42	—	—	—	—
Soles — Medium	—	—	56	339	—	—	—	—
Soles — Small	—	—	89	428	—	—	—	—
Soles — Unsorted	47	255	—	—	60	468	655	5,340
Soles — Total	47	255	151	809	60	468	655	5,340
Torsk (Tusk) ..	984	562	11	7	—	—	—	—
Turbot ..	3,959	10,685	1,200	3,974	53	133	1,338	4,535
Whiting ..	34,535	24,605	3,347	2,181	71	107	1,839	1,811
Witches ..	2,432	4,862	320	754	—	—	2	6
Livers ..	16,527	4,085	1,443	222	—	—	649	244
Roes ..	3,081	3,221	443	646	—	—	141	209
Other Kinds or Mixed	1,232	823	—	—	—	—	—	—
Total Demersal ..	319,360	374,648	63,468	77,830	5,319	7,646	34,406	63,543
Herrings ..	159,654	53,354	+26,591	9,008	72	30	6,137	2,392
Mackerel ..	6,650	2,686	2,455	1,216	6	1	604	288
Pilchards ..	—	—	—	—	—	—	—	—
Sprats ..	—	—	—	—	—	—	—	—
Mullet, Grey ..	—	—	—	—	—	—	—	—
Whitebait ..	—	—	—	—	—	—	—	—
Total Wet Fish	485,664	430,688	92,514	88,054	5,397	7,677	41,147	66,223
Shell Fish..	100's		100's		100's		100's	
Crabs ..	1,393	1,095	1,711	1,215	2,960	3,086	4,645	4,241
Crawfish ..	—	—	—	—	—	—	—	—
Lobsters ..	113	623	269	1,999	565	4,633	498	2,479
Oysters ..	—	—	—	—	—	—	—	—
	Cwts.		Cwts.		Cwts.		Cwts.	
Escallops and Queens	100	21	—	—	—	—	584	383
Norway Lobsters ..	2,050	2,816	12	7	—	—	—	—
Total Value of all Fish	—	435,243	—	91,275	—	15,396	—	73,326

Landing statistics for 1938.

HARTLEPOOL FISH CO. LIMITED

FISH QUAY · VICTORIA DOCK · HARTLEPOOL · TS24 0JH
Tel: 01429 891198   Fax: 01429 891175

PORT OF SALE: **HARTLEPOOL**   SKIPPER: S. Yoasley T.

DATE SOLD: 29.07.04   AREA OF ORIGIN 2

VESSEL: Noalood   PLN: LY347

SPECIES	WEIGHT	MERCHANT	UNIT PRICE	VALUE
Lemons	1¼	LD	24.50	30.63
Lemons	2	Trivv	14.00	28.00
Lemons	1	N/Picker		14.00
Lemons	4¾	Fillets	9.20	43.70
Lemons	26¾	LD	5.70	152.48
Hadd 3	2	Trivv	6.80	13.60
Hadd 4	5¼	Fillets	2.22	11.66
Whit	49	LD	1.20	58.80
Cod 1	4¾	Trivv	13.00	61.75
Cod 3	4	Fillets	9.00	36.00
Cod 4	3¾	W/h	6.50	24.38
Cod 4	2	N/Pickin	6.50	13.00
Cod 5	8½	W/t	5.60	47.60
Cod 5	4¼	W/t	5.40	22.95
Plaice 1	1	LD		15.00
"	2¼	Fillets	5.50	12.38
Mxd	1½	LD		6.60
124		**TOTAL**		592.53

Company Reg. No. 3230887   VAT Reg. No. 3453 02 686

Last auction in the Fish Co. Hall.

Sternus, the drifter which became *Swiftwing*.

AN ATTRACTIVE DIESEL DRIFTER/TRAWLER

"SWIFTWING"

BUILT	1925 by Cochrane & Sons Ltd., Selby, U.K.
TONNAGE	99.13 gross. 44.78 net.
DIMENSIONS	92 ft. × 18.6 ft. × 9 ft. Overall.
DRAFT	5 ft. forward — 10 ft. 6 ins. aft.
ENGINE	1954 by Ruston & Hornsby Ltd. 240 B.H.P. 4 cylinders 10¼ ins. × 14½ ins. stroke. Auxiliary — Ruston 2 cylinder.
SPEED	About 9 knots.
TRAWL WINCH	Belt driven from main engine. Approx. 220 fathoms capacity.
CAPSTAN	Elliott & Garrood. Electric/Hydraulic.
ACCOMMODATION	Skipper's Berth and Bunks for 10 men.
FISHROOM	37 tons fish. Served by 3 hatchways. Insulated on after bulkhead with sub-division and shelving.
ELECTRONIC EQUIPMENT	Kelvin & Hughes Echosounder. Boat's property only.
LIFE SAVING APPARATUS	Lifeboat, Elliot Liferaft, etc., conforming to the requirements of the Merchant Shipping Rules, 1958.
GENERAL	This vessel was converted to diesel machinery in 1954 and is presently engaged on drift net fishing.

OWNERS' IDEA OF PRICE :

"SWIFTWING"

Advert for *Swiftwing*.

Discharge papers for Park Cowling, who served aboard Hartlepool trawler *Ostrich*.

NORTH EASTERN SEA FISHERIES COMMITTEE

QUANTITIES AND VALUES OF FISH LANDED AT THE
SEVERAL PORTS AND STATIONS IN THE COMMITTEE'S DISTRICT

NOTE: These figures are supplied by the Ministry of Agriculture, Fisheries and Food and are subject to revision.

PORT OR STATION	QUARTER ENDED 31st DECEMBER, 1968								TOTAL VALUE £
	Wet Fish		Crabs		Lobsters		Other Shellfish		
	Cwts.	Value £	Cwts.	Value £	Cwts.	Value £	Cwts.	Value £	
Hartlepool	5253	25027	44	177	32	2127	476	6170	33501
Redcar	94	335	51	167	25	1769	-	-	2271
Staithes	46	204	135	562	21	1316	-	-	2082
Whitby	4458	21170	1848	7189	102	6719	-	-	35078
Scarborough	11197	57770	216	866	59	3448	-	-	62084
Filey	3078	14659	-	-	-	-	-	-	14659
Flamborough	704	2905	2	32	1	44	-	-	2981
Bridlington	13088	66361	-	-	-	-	-	-	66361
Hull	1041079	3526359	-	-	-	-	-	-	3526359
Grimsby	788978	3316757	-	-	3	132	654	706	3317595
TOTAL	1867975	£7031547	2296	£8993	243	£15555	1130	£6876	£7062971

Total quantity of Wet Fish landed during present quarter - 1,867,975 Cwts.

Total quantity of Wet Fish landed during corresponding quarter of last year - 1,687,238 Cwts.

Total value of all kinds of Fish landed during present quarter - £7,062,971

Total value of all kinds of Fish landed during corresponding quarter of last year - £6,440,181

County Hall,
BEVERLEY.

21st February, 1969.

Statistics for the fourth quarter of 1968.

11

FRIERS AND MONGERS

Fried Fish Shops

The following list has been drawn from Kelly's and Ward's Directories, and from other sources. The establishments were listed as 'fried fish dealers' or 'fried fish shops' in the Directories, not, as they were known in later years, as 'fish & chip shops'. Some shops have changed hands over the years, as different names occupy the same address, but I have no explanation as to why different names appear at the same address in the same year, apart from the fact that the shop could have been sold during that year. This list refers to Old Hartlepool and Middleton; it does not include any in West Hartlepool.

1896/7

J.E. Archbold	21 Brunswick St
Jane Burgon	3 Northgate
Wm Boaz	7 St Mary St
Mary Ann Brotchie	98 High St
Mrs Jane Brough	Commercial St
Chas. Collet	26 Frederick St
Wm McCarthy	Watson St
Mrs Sarah Nance	16 Prissick St

1900/01

Mrs A. Boaz	7 St Mary St
Mrs J. Burgon	3 Northgate
Miss Margaret Crombie	Commercial St
George Henry Heal	Arch St
David Martin	21 Bruswick St
George Maynard	98 High St
Mrs M.A. McCarthy	Watson St
J. McCourt	155 Durham St
Harry Turner	16 Prissick St
William Walker	168 Durham St
Mrs C. Cox	97 Durham St
Mrs M.E. Parnaby	46a Middlegate

1902/03

Mrs A. Aitkin	Watson St
Miss A. Boaz	7 St Mary St
Mrs C. Cox	97 Durham St
J. Grady	Commercial St
G.H. Heal	Arch St
D. Martin	Brunswick St
G. Maynard	98 High St
J. McCourt	155 Durham St
Mrs M.E. Parnaby	46a Middlegate
H. Turner	16 Prissick St
J. Wood	168 Durham St

1906/07

J.G. Allen	168 Durham St
Mrs J. Burgon	3 Northgate & 22 Stephenson St
Michael Craig	12 Brougham St
Walter Crawford	21 Brunswick St
Jeremiah Grady	Commercial St
Mrs Elizabeth Hall	Watson St
Mathew Hastings	98 High St
G.H. Heal	Arch St
Margaret Ann Horsley	16 Prissick St
Mrs Margaret Parnaby	46 Middlegate & 153 Durham St
Wm Scott	11 Alliance St
Mrs Mary Ann Shreebe	32 Corporation Rd
Robert Tabley	7 Commercial St

1920

Jane Burgon	3 Northgate
Pearl Curry	16 Prissick St
Robert Hudson	Commercial St
Oliver Jackson	25 Corporation Road
Mrs J. Lee	21 Brunswick St
Mrs Charlotte Nitch	48½ Alliance St
Mrs M. Parkinson	15 Prissick St
Thos Parrish	70 Commercial St
Wm Scott	11 Alliance St
Mrs Hannah White	49 Watson St
Harry Whitfield	98 High St
John Cawley	12 Brougham St
Wm Fullagar	170 Durham St
Mrs Elizabeth Hall	49 Watson St

Wm Horsley	98 High St
Wm Mean	49½ Alliance St
Alexander Muir	Arch St
Mrs Margaret Parnaby	16 Prissik St

1929/30

J. Andrews	15 Prissick St
Mrs J. Burgon	3 Northgate
E. Cappleman	16 Arch St
J.H. Dixon	32 Middlegate
E. Mason	49½ Alliance St
Mrs J. Mathewson	21 Bruswick St
Mrs I. Mitchell	78 Frederick St
J. Mitchell	98 Hart Road
J. Oliver	7 & 70 Commercial St
C.G. Parkinson	31 Mary St
J.W. Plaice	40 Corporation Road
Mrs E. Raine	120 Durham St
W. Simcox	51a Watson St
Mrs E. Straughton	33 Corporation Rd
T. Valentine	108 Durham St
F. Verrill	98 High St
J.E. Young	58 High St

1933/1934

Mrs J Burgon	3 Northgate
Mrs E.M. Foster	40 Corporation Rd
E. Gadsby	15 Prissick St
J.R. Jarvis	49½ Alliance St
H. Manuel	78 Frederick St
Mrs J. Mathewman	21 Brunswick St
W. Meadley	51a Watson St
O. Mitchell	31 Mary St
J. Oliver	68 Commercial St
J. W. Plaice	32 Middlegate
Mrs E.M. Raine	120 Durham St
W. Smith	16 Arch St
Mrs E. Straughton	33 Corporation Road
T. Valentine	108 Durham St
F. Verrill	98 High St
J.E. Young	58 High St

1938

Miss Hilda Andrews	Prissick St
J. Bretall	68 Commercial St
Mrs Caroline Fleetham	33 Corporation Rd
Wm Meadley	49 Watson St
Oliver Mitchell	31 Mary St
Frank Raine	120 Durham St
Stan. Rowbotham	3 Northgate
Thos Rowbotham	49½ Alliance St
Mrs Doris Simmonds	21 Brunswick St
J. Wheatley	16 Arch St

Fishmongers

The following list was compiled with the help of Kelly's and Ward's Directories, starting at 1880 and up to to 1938. The list concentrates on the Headland area or Old Hartlepool, and while it may not be complete it shows the number of fresh fish retailers in the area. The list also shows that shops changed hands over the years with different names at the same address:

R. Charlton	62 Northgate
Wm. Corner	49 Northgate
Cuthbert Coulson	11 Middlegate
Jacob Cox	Clifton St
Geo. Holder	12 Brougham St
Joseph Holmes & Bros	Town Wall
Thos. Swales	21 Town Wall
Williamson Thorp	36 Town Wall
Wm. Baxter	33 Northgate
Mrs Cicely Cox	97 Durham St
Richard Elliot	17 Northgate
Robert Nellis	2 St Mary St
James Collins	12 Brougham St
Robinson Hopper	13 Northgate
T. Browning	12 Brougham St
Wm. Cappleman	50 Northgate
Mrs Wardell	5 Middlegate
J. Melville	Abbey St & 59 Northgate
Joseph Beadnell	58 Northgate
Mrs Margaret Barker	50 Northgate
J.J. Wilkie	59 Northgate
Mrs Malling	19 Prissick St
Harlows	43 Northgate

12

REGULAR VISITORS

The following is a list of steam trawlers and drifters which used to land at or work out of Hartlepool on a regular basis in the 1920s and '30s. The names of the vessels come from a handwritten list which was passed on to me some years ago. Some further details have been added, but the list is by no means complete.

NAME	BUILT	BUILDER	HISTORY
Anderlucian	–	–	–
Andrameda	–	–	–
Auk	1901	Alex. Hall	1929, Ellis, Scarborough, scrapped 1936
Bell Isle	–	–	–
Ben Alder	1899	Hall Russell	1922, Holbeck, Scarborough
Ben Hope	1900	Hall Russell	Hope F. Co., North Shields
Bombay	–	–	–
Conqueror	–	–	Paddle
Conquest	1885	–	Paddle (SN 1089)
Constance	–	–	Paddle
Cooper	–	–	–
Crimenco	–	–	–
Dalhousie	–	–	–
Dandini	1917	Alex. Hall	Milburn, Whitby, sank 7-5-1938
Diana	–	–	(A 149)
Draco	–	–	–
Dreadnaught	1907	Hall Russell	ON 123386, 1919, Monkshaven, Whitby, scrapped 1956
Dunrobin	–	–	Paddle
Eccles Hill	–	–	–
Elsie	1896	Cochrane	ON 105100, 1920, Gamecock, S/boro (SH 280), 1926, Pattison, H/pool
Emulator	–	–	Scarborough (SH 83)
Endiminion	–	–	–
Euphony	–	–	Scarborough
Evening Star	1900	Duthie	H/pool & North Sea F. Co. Scarboro', sank 12-8-1908

116

Expert	1907	Hall Russell	Drifter
Express	–	–	–
Fort George	1902	Hall Russell	ON 115583, 1927, T. Round, S/boro, 1931 sold to France
Glen Gordon	–	–	–
Helen MacGregor	–	–	Paddle (SN 1097)
Isle of Wight	1905	Earls	ON 123211
Jack Johnson	1919	Hall Russell	–
Jeanie Stewart	1916	Hall Russell	ON 139287 (HL 82) 1919, Alliance, S/boro, 1920, Ball, N. Shields
John Elliot	–	–	Scarboro'
John Evans	–	–	–
Lynmouth	1892	Dixon	ON 98832, 1920, Robinson & Crosthwaite, M/boro (MH 118)
Magnolia	1898	Duthie	ON 108432, Stepney, S/boro', 1923 Co-op S/boro, sank, 1928 (SH 160)
Otter	–	–	–
Patrick Donovon	–	–	–
Persian Empire	–	–	Scarboro'
Ratapeco	1912	Duthie	ON 129379, 1920, Stepney, S/boro, (SH 221) 1922, Co-op (SH 39)
Renaisance	–	–	–
Rob Roy	–	–	–
Romanoff	–	–	Paddle (SH 373)
Savaria	–	–	ON 145053 (GY 1341)
Scorpio	–	–	–
Scorpion	–	–	–
Seal	–	–	–
Skerne	–	–	–
St Cloud	–	–	Paddle (GY 856)
St Elsie			Paddle (SH 280)
Star of England	–	–	–
Star of the East	1912	Hall Russell	ON 133605, 1920, Co-op S/boro (SH 321)
Star of the Empire	1912	Hall Russell	1920, Stepney, S/boro, 1923, Co-op, S/boro
Star of the Isles	1912	Hall Russell	On 129380, 1920, Stepney, S/boro, 1923, Co-op, S/boro.
Strathdee	1906	Hall Russell	1920, Derwent , S/boro, 1926, Sutton, S/boro (SH 136), scrapped 1938
Stratheric	1906	Hall Russell	ON 123373, 1921, Musgrove, S/boro
Strathlorne	–	–	–
Strathord	1906	Hall Russell	1919, McConkey, S/boro, mined, 23-2-1920

Strathspey	1906	Hall Russell	–
Thalarope	–	–	–
Torleif	–	–	–
Tyndrum	–	–	–
Victoria	1911	Smiths Dk.	ON 128759, 1920, Stepney, S/boro, 1922, Co-op, S/boro, scrapped 1950

ON	=	Official Number
S/boro	=	Scarborough
NS	=	North Shields
SH	=	Scarborough
GY	=	Grimsby
MH	=	Middlesbrough

On board *Emulater*, a regular visitor to Hartlepool from her home port of Scarborough.

13

THE HARTLEPOOL FISHING VESSEL REGISTER

From 1 March 1869

The information for compiling this list has come from the original handwritten registers which are held at the Teesside Archives in Middlesbrough and the European register which is available from the Internet. Other vessels which have been included are the Hartlepool-owned vessels which kept their original port of registration.

The Sea Fisheries Act came into force on 1 March 1869 and from that date all fishing vessels had to be registered and port letters and register numbers were issued which had to be painted onto the boats. On many old photographs of Hartlepool you can see boats with 'H' on their bows, not 'HL' – these were local pilot cobles, not fishing boats.

On the opening day of the register over 120 fishing vessels registered; the vast majority were for Hartlepool itself, but vessels based at West Hartlepool and Seaton Carew are included.

The first boat on the register was *Blue Eyed Maid* (HL 1) owned by Pounder Davidson. The average size of boats on the early register is between 18–30ft (6–10m), and these were mostly open boats. Crews were between three and five men; a typical 18ft coble would have three crew. This must have represented a considerable percentage of the town's population in the late 1800s. On the opening day a number of boats were registered with the same name, e.g. *Elizabeth*, and several registered to the same owner.

There are occasional question marks in the listings, mainly in the entries for the late 1800s and early 1900s, and this is because in the original ledgers all entries were handwritten and when a boat was sold or taken off the register, a line was drawn through that entry, making deciphering particularly difficult.

The early entries only show the owner's name but later into the 1890s they begin to show the owner's name and address. This then reveals the area of the town where the majority of the fishermen lived, which is, as expected, around the Croft, the Town Wall and Southgate; basically the area around the Fish Sands.

The handwritten registers stopped in 1988, the last fishing boat listed being *Callarias* (HL 100); the registration was then handed to the Cardiff office of the Shipping Register. When contacted about a list of vessels from 1989 they were unable to oblige. Fortunately, a list is available from the Internet via the European website. This gives basic vessel information only and no owners' names.

Although Hartlepool owned, no reference has been made to the trawlers of The West Hartlepool Steam Navigation Co. (Talisman Trawlers) which worked from Lowestoft and were Lowestoft registered; other publications are available covering their history.

Every endeavour has been made to ensure the accuracy of this list, but as information is coming forward all the time, the list can only be accurate up to a point. With the coming of metric measurements, a change can be seen in the listings reflecting this, with metres for length and kilowatts for power.

NAME & MATERIAL	NO.	YEAR	LENGTH	POWER	WEIGHT	DETAILS
ACACIA wood	BF 199	1960	60'	180hp Gardner	40t	built Nobles Fraserburgh, fished seine, trawl 1969, B. Nicol, & others, Gardenstown 1-5-1970, Hartlepool Seiners, Victoria Dock (W.K. Grigg-agents)
ACHIEVE wood	HL 257	1997	9.9m	126kw	13.3t	built Polruan 30-4-1997, Tony Greenwood, H/pool 2008, Scrabster
ACTIVE wood	HL 329		41'	sail	17t	decked boat, fished nets, crew 5 28-11-1882, Henry Hall, H/pool 4-3-1883, lost off Scarboro'
ADA wood	HL 201		15'	sail	0.5t	punt boat, crew 1, fished lines, nets, based Seaton Carew 17-1-1871, Ambrose Storer, reg. closed 21-8-1872
ADA wood	HL 260		15'	sail	2.5t	open boat, fished lines, crew 2 1-2-1876, Ambrose Storer, H/pool
ADAPTABLE wood ON 341771	HL 41	1972	43'x15'x6'	150hp Gardner	24t	built Middlesbrough, seine, trawl 21-12-72 Tommy Raw & Robert Robinson, H/pool 19-7-1974 Northgate F. Co. H/pool (Lola, agents) 2001, based N. Shields, r/n *Bethsaida*
ADMIRAL wood	HL 70		29'x6'x2'	sail	4.2t	coble, crew 3, fished pots, lines, built Whitby 17-8-1903, Thomas Hoyle, 3, Pier Stones?, Sandiside? H/pool
ADVANCE wood	HL 235	1881	19'	sail	3t	coble fished lines, crew 3, 12-11-1873, Robert Boagey, H/pool 11-3-1876, William Marshall, H/pool
ADVANCE wood	HL 292		18.5'	sail	3t	coble, fished nets, lines, crew 3 7-5-1878, James Moore, H/pool, lost at sea, 16-11-1881
ADVENTURE steel ON 109728	HL 19	1906	110'x21'x12'	steam	184t	built Hall Russell, Aberdeen, yard No.398, crew 9 4-4-1906, Henry A. Tweddle, Greatham Tce, West H/pool ?, Imperial Cold Storage & Supply Co. Aberdeen 7-9-1912, Mason & Wright, Fleetwood (FD 154) r/n *Lincolnia* 1914, Brooklyn Tr. Co. Fleetwood 1914-1918, Navy, minesweeper, 1x6pdr. AA. (A.2771) 1918, J. Mitchell, Fleetwood, Skipper, Sharman (H/pool)
AGNES wood	HL 80		21'	sail	4t	coble, crew 4, fished lines 1-3-1869, James Burgon, West H/pool 1875, re-reg. Berwick when family moved North
AGNES INNES wood	HL 95	1903	69'x20'x10'	sail & motor	76t	lugger, crew 7, fished lines, nets, built Port Seaton 22-8-1918, Francis Pounder, Ashvale, Park Road, West H/pool 1925, scrapped
AGNES MARIA wood	HL 163		30'	sail	12t	coble, fished nets, crew 4 19-5-1869, John Shaw, H/pool 17-6-1878 sold to Whitby (WY 534)
AILEEN wood	HL 12	1921	29'x10'x4'	sail & motor	5.9t	built Anstruther, lugger, crew 4, fished nets, lines 10-6-1925, Geo. Horsley, 18, Clayton St, H/pool 18-10-1934, took fire and sank, 3 mile NNE H/pool
A-L wood	HL 253		18'	sail	3t	coble fished lines, crew 3 8-5-1875, Robert Hood, H/pool
ALARM wood	HL 245		24'	sail	3t	coble, fished trawl, lines, crew 2 27-7-1874, Francis Ward, H/pool 9-1874, sold to Middlesbrough
ALARM wood	HL 361		20'	sail	3t	coble, fished lines, crew 3 21-3-1885, George Shephard, H/pool
ALBION wood	HL 198		40'	sail	15t	yawl, fished nets, trawl, crew 6 18-10-1870, John Shaw Jnr, H/pool 27-5-1875, re-reg. in Yarmouth

NAME & MATERIAL	NO.	YEAR	LENGTH	POWER	WEIGHT	DETAILS
ALBION wood	HL 243		19'	sail	2t	coble, fished nets, crew 2 27-5-1874, Mathew Lamb, H/pool
ALBURY wood	HL 11		20'x7'x2'		1.6t	crew 2, fished lines 27-7-1950, Stanley Alder, 40, Durham Rd, W. H/pool 10-7-1954, P.G. Jummet, 47, Percy St W. H/pool sold 1961
ALEXANDRA wood	HL 163 ex GY 423	1917	48'x13'x6'	sail & motor	18t	built Fano, Denmark, seine, trawl, single-cylinder engine 29-12-1965, Wm. Alex. Leonard, Pudsey House, H/pool & E.W. Haylock, Station Hotel, Seaton Carew 21-6-1966, R.E. Massey, Isle of Sheppey 2-1968, reg. trans. to Rochester 1982, E.W. Haylock, 32, Fraser St, Grimsby
ALICE wood	HL 120		18.5'	sail	3t	coble, crew 3, fished lines 1-3-1869, Robert Heron, H/pool 8-3-1875, Cuthbert Moor, H/pool
ALISON JANE grp	HL 229	1974	9.9m	57kw	2.63t	built Southampton 15-1-1991, H/pool
ALICE & ANN wood	HL 216		18.5'	sail	3t	coble, fished lines, nets, crew 3 18-4-1872, Joseph Rammsdon, H/pool 16-7-1877, Robinson Booth, H/pool
ALICE COUSON wood	HL 102	1905	21'x6'x2'	sail	2.5t	built Hartlepool, lugger, crew 3, fished lines 5-11-1918, Frank Coulson, Dial House, Town Wall, H/pool
ALICE ISABEL wood	HL 307		19'	sail	3t	coble, fished lines, crew 3 4-10-1879, George Shephard, H/pool 25-6-1886, Peter Burgon, 18, Commercial St, H/pool
ALLIANCE wood	HL 244		18.5'	sail	1.5t	coble, fished lines, crew 3 15-7-1874, William Staunch, H/pool
ALLIANCE wood	HL 263		19.5'	sail	2.5t	coble, fished lines crew 3 16-3-1876, Charles Cambridge, H/pool scrapped 1883
ALLIANCE wood	A 95	1955	66.4'	Kelvin	50t	built Wilson Noble, Fraserburgh fished trawl, seine 1955, Brebner F. Co. Aberdeen 1969, Croft Fishing Co. (Lola), H/pool
ALMADAD? wood	HL 40		44'x16'x5'	sail	16t	keel boat, decked, fished nets, lines, crew 6 18-1-1895, J.W. Holman, 7, Brougham St, H/pool
ALONZO wood	HL 174		30'	sail	6t	coble, fished lines, crew 4 3-6-1869, John Wray, H/pool 18-7-1873, John Turnbull & John Walker, H/pool 4-3-1876, James Pounder & John Walker, H/pool
ALPHA wood	HL 354	1884	66'	sail	91t	built Pounder, Hartlepool, cutter, fished trawl, crew 11 25-7-1884, Francis Pounder, H/pool 1887 sold to Grimsby
AMANDA steel	RO 23	1990	11.5m	280hp Volvo	24t	built Hull, inshore stern trawler ? W. Hodgson, H/pool
AMANDA D wood	WY 106	1973	10.55m	58kw	6.5t	built Whitby, coble ? H/pool
AMANDA D grp	WY 781	1984	8.53m	90kw	5.2t	built Falmouth, inshore trawler 1984, *Mystic Lady*, Weymouth 5-1998, *Amanda D*
AMBITIOUS	HL 127		26'x8'x3'		5.5t	crew 2, lines, pots 19-4-1961, Thos. H. Platts, 9, South Cres., H/pool, reg. closed 1971
AMY H	LH 223					inshore stern trawler ? David Horsley, H/pool
ANAIS steel	HL 50	1987	9.33m	120kw	5.01t	built H/pool 1989 *Osprey* H/pool 1-1-1992, *Anais* H/pool

NAME & MATERIAL	NO.	YEAR	LENGTH	POWER	WEIGHT	DETAILS
ANCIENT BOROUGH wood	HL 33	1914	50'x13'x7'	sail & motor	32t	built Hartlepool, lugger, crew 7, fished nets, lines 25-9-1914, owned by local group, H/pool 6-11-1930, scrapped
ANDREA JANE wood	HL 55	1982	9.9x4.2x1.7m	94kw	11.3t	built Fleetwood 18-4-1988, T.M. English, Seaham
ANGELA wood	HL 15		25'x7'x3'	sail & motor	2.6t	Ex-*Pioneer II*, lines, pots, crew 3 7-7-1948, A. Pritchard, Horden 11-10-1949, Robson, Wilson, Jones, Blackhall Rocks 4-6-1951, Jones, Jones, Jones, Blackhall Coll. reg. closed 1982
ANGLER wood	HL 284		38'	sail	8t	keel boat, fished nets, crew 5 18-9-1877, John French, H/pool
ANMARA steel	H 91					inshore stern trawler, built Knottingley 1982, Jack Robinson (Trawlers) Ltd Hull ? H/pool
ANN wood	HL 246		19'	sail	3t	coble, fished lines, crew 3, ex-*Swift* 31-7-1874, James Bond, H/pool 5-1875, sold to Thos. Burton, Whitby
ANN wood	HL 241		19'	sail	2t	coble, fished nets, crew 2 3-3-1874, Robert Davison, H/pool
ANN	HL 86		36'	sail	14t	keel boat, fished nets 1-3-1869, John & Peter Robinson, H/pool 1869, in severe gale blown round Flamborough Head crew, Peter Robinson, Henry Waite 1873, sold
ANN wood	HL 152		34.5'	sail	10t	keel boat, crew 4, fished nets 21-4-1869, Sammuel Mullins, West H/pool 18-2-1870, Christopher Bell, West H/pool 2-8-1873, sold out of fishing
ANN wood	HL 227		18.5'	sail	3t	coble, fished lines, crew 3 17-4-1873, Thomas Cooper, H/pool, sold 1907
ANN wood	HL 350		18'	sail	3t	coble, fished net, lines, crew 3 26-4-1884, Wm. Hodgson, H/pool
ANN wood	HL 79	1933	20'x6'x2'	sail	1.3t	built Hartlepool, crew 2, fished lines, pots 22-5-1942, John Humphrey, Brunswick St, West H/pool sold 1948
ANN wood	HL 203	1954	9.8x2.7x1.1m	26kw	4.6t	built Whitby, coble, lines, pots 18-3-1983, John Boylen, Elwick Rd, West H/pool, reg. closed 1989
ANN	HL 158		24x7x2'		1.7t	fished lines, trawl 21-9-1965, Henry Mason, Clavering Rd, H/pool, reg. closed 1989
ANN BULMER wood	HL 68		18.5'	sail		coble, crew 3, fished lines, nets 1-3-1869, Thornton Bulmer, H/pool 4-2-1873, Ann Bulmer, H/pool
ANN BULMER wood	HL 266		18.5'	sail	2t	coble, fished lines, crew 3 16-3-1876, Charles Cambridge, H/pool, scrapped 1883
ANN CORNER wood	HL 106		18.5'	sail	1.8t	coble, crew 3, fished lines 1-3-1869, Genge? Corner, H/pool, sold for pilot coble 1870 12-3-1875 Nathan Sotheran, H/pool
ANN JAYNE wood	HL 270		23'	sail	3.5t	coble, fished nets, crew 2 21-8-1876, Thomas Horsley, H/pool
ANN LYNN wood	HL 85	1973	30'x9'x2'		2.9t	built Whitby, coble fished lines, pots, crew 2 7-4-1975, Alan Fleetham, Bruce Cres., H/pool
ANN MARIA wood	HL 309		21'	sail	4t	coble, fished lines, crew 5 17-10-1879, William Pounder, H/pool

NAME & MATERIAL	NO.	YEAR	LENGTH	POWER	WEIGHT	DETAILS
ANN MARY wood	HL 2		28'	sail	2t	coble, fished lines, crew 3, sold to Sunderland 1899 22-8-1893, Peter Burgon, Commercial St, Middleton, H/pool
ANN POUNDER wood	HL 203		31'	sail	10.5t	coble, crew 4, fished nets 27-5-1871, Thomas Pounder H/pool 17-7-1876, William Pounder H/pool
ANN SCOTT ON 333967 wood	GY 150	1969	56'x17'x7'	171kw	48t	built Hunterstead, Denmark, fished seine, trawl 1980, Ingrams, Stringer, Dixon, Grimsby 1982, Ingrams (GY) Ltd 1987, Bekimael F. Co. & Stringer & Dixon, Grimsby 1993, Jubilee F. Co. Grimsby (GY 150) ?, Major Hartley, H/pool
ANNE LYNN wood	HL 85	1973	9.42m	74kw		built Whitby ? H/pool
ANNABEL grp	SN 349	1997	9.95m	134kw	9.36t	? H/pool
ANNE wood	HL 158	1989	24'x7'x2'	14kw	1.7t	crew 2, lines, trawl ? H/pool
ANNIE wood	HL 42	1888	21'x5'x1.5'	sail	2.2t	canoe (double ender), crew 3, fished lines 6-12-1923, Geo. Davison, 7, York Place H/pool sold 1927
ANNIE ON 106973	HL 53	1898	105'x21'x12'	steam 55hp	152t	built Edwards Bros. N. Shields, ketch rig trawler, crew 9 engine 3cyl. by H.G. Edwards, S. Shields 28-2-1898, H/pools Steam F. Co,. Victoria Tce, West H/pool 1899, sold to Denmark
ANNIE BAINBRIDGE grp	WY 50	2008	9.4m	74.6kw	4.5t	? Tommy Smith, H/pool
ANNIE JOSEPHINE wood	HL	1868		sail		? J. Shephard, H/pool
ANYA wood	HL 33	1935	8.8m	33kw	2.0t	built Amble 5-11-2004 H/pool
ARCTIC SOLITARE	HL 100	1981	10.2x3.6x1.3m		20.3	18-5-1982, S. Nutbrown, Brotton
ARGONAUT wood	HL 4	1978	9.2x2.9x1.9m	59kw	4.7t	built Sandsend, coble 16-9-1986, Geo. Baul, Peterlee
ARIEL wood	HL 211		24'	sail/oar	3.7t	smack, fished lines, crew 2 4-8-1871, Francis Ward, H/pool, re-reg. at Whitby 1871
ARIEL wood	HL 220		21'	sail	3t	coble, fished nets, crew 2 26-8-1872, Robert Horsley, H/pool
ARIES grp	HL 149	1990	10m	179kw	5.23t	built H/pool 15-8-1990, H/pool
ARTEMIS wood	HL 237	1979	9.5m	60kw	6.7t	built Fleetwood 31-7-1991, H/pool
ASGARD grp	WK 787	1989	9.81m	108kw	8.5t	inshore stern trawler, based H/pool Marina ?, Peter Rolf
AURORA grp	HL 10	2002	6.66m	61kw	1.22t	built Tiree 20-8-2002, H/pool
AUSPITIOUS wood	HL 30		29.5'	sail	10t	coble, crew 4, fished nets 1-3-1869, Mark Davidson, H/pool 30-12-1872, sold
AVONDALE wood ON 187227	HL 112	1958	46'x15'x6'	95hp Gardner	24t	builder, Nobles, Fraserburgh, seine & trawl, re-engined John Deere 3-3-1958, Mrs. D.L. Truman, H/pool 7-1-1969, Truman family members, H/pool 2002 sold

Acacia

Achieve

Adaptable

Alexandria

Alliance

Amanda

NAME & MATERIAL	NO.	YEAR	LENGTH	POWER	WEIGHT	DETAILS
BARRACUDA wood	HL 94	1989	8.1x2.8x0.5m	52kw	1.7t	
BARBARA ANN wood	SH 231					25-10-1988, E. Winn, Peterlee Whitby coble, fished creels ? Matty McLean
BARBARA & ALICE wood	HL 47		28'x6'x2'	sail	3.9t	built Hartlepool, coble, crew 3, fished lines 21-1-1896, Coulson Moore, Chapel St, H/pool 25-6-1906, Benjamin Hood, 5, Bedford St, H/pool 1932 sold to Seaham Harbour
BARBARELLA	HL 195		5.5x1.8x1m		1.2t	10-5-1982, W. Payer, Jameson Rd, H/pool
BARRIE - M wood	HL 97		7.9x2.4x0.9m	63kw	2.9t	built H/pool 16-11-1988, H. Gretton, Dundee Rd, H/pool
BARRY B wood						coble ? Barry Buglass, H/pool
BAY JOE wood	WY 810	2001	6.73m	26kw	1.43t	built Whitby by Steve Cook & Lennie Oliver, coble ? H/pool
BEATRICE wood	HL 209		19.5'	sail	3t	coble fished nets, crew 2 19-7-1871, Charles Cambridge, H/pool 1873, sold to Staithes
BEATRICE steel ON 127408	HL 16	1907	120'x21'x11'	87hp steam	239t	built Smiths, N. Shields, yard No.362, ketch rig, trawler, crew 7 launched 2-11-1907, engine by MacCall & Pollock, S/land 1914–1919 Navy minesweeper 8-4-1919, Harry Middleton, Eamont Gdns, West H/pool 5-5-1919, Middleton St Tr. Co. 36, Church St, West H/pool 26-5-1922, W.J. Wood, H/pool & J.E. Kennedy, N/cle 12-8-1922 sold to Holland
BEE wood	HL 302		23'	sail	2t	coble, fished lines, crew 3 18-10-1878, Thomas Crombie, H/pool
BELVOIR CASTLE wood ON 146880	GY 435	1918	53'x20'x7'	motor, fore main, jib sails	35t	built Viken, Denmark, fished seine, crew 6 ex-Thelma 26-4-1923, Crampin family, Grimsby 24-2-1930, Chapman & Craske, Grimsby 22-6-1935, G. Roberson, Sevenoaks 30-11-1936, W.E.W. Craske, Grimsby 17-9-1938, W.E.W. Craske, 41, Town Wall, H/pool 6-8-1948, stranded Seaton Carew, became total loss
BEN ADEN ON 112935 steel	HL 2	1900	106'x21'x12'	62hp steam	176t	built Hall Russell, Aberdeen, yard No.338, ketch rig crew 9, 3cyl. engine by builder 1900 North British S.F. Co. Aberdeen (A 303) 12-1-1914, R.H. Davison, 4, Beaconsfield Sq. H/pool 19-10-1915, A.H. Davison, Fish Quay, H/pool 14-7-1916, sunk by sub. 15miles East of H/pool
BEN-MY-CHREE wood	HL 71		23'x6'x2'	sail & motor	1.6t	lugger, crew 2, fished lines, pots 12-12-1938, Robert Hood, 11, York Place, H/pool, sold 1948
BEN-MY-CHREE wood	HL 12		26'x8'x3'		3t	18-3-1948, Robert Hood, 11, York Place, H/pool 21-11-1951, G.F. Whitfield, 156, Stockton Rd, West H/pool
BEN TARBET steel ON 133607	HL 21	1912	115'x22'x12'	78hp steam	197t	built Hall Russell A/deen, yard No.514, ketch rig trawler, 9 crew launched 14-8-1912, engine by builder, trawler 1912, Irvine, N. Shields (A 476) 1915–1919 Navy, boom defence vessel 9-7-1920 Alpha S. Co. 7-12-1923, Friarage S.T. Co. H/pool 19-4-1930, Skipper & crew awarded medals for rescue of 11

THE HARTLEPOOL FISHING VESSEL REGISTER

NAME & MATERIAL	NO.	YEAR	LENGTH	POWER	WEIGHT	DETAILS
						Norwegian seamen in hurricane force winds
						1940–1946, Navy, APV., BDV, M/S, stores carrier (Z 212)
						1955 sold to Belgium for scrap
BENJARMIN wood	HL 73		18'	sail	3t	coble, crew 3, fished lines
						1-3-1869, Joseph Hood, H/pool
						15-11-1870, Thomas Hood, H/pool
						31-1-1874, Nicholas Denton, H/pool
BERND	SN 104		60'			built Sweden ?
						? Sonny Ray
BERTHA ON 124306	HL 22	1906	115'x21'x13'	steam	207t	built Hepple S. Shields, yard No.559, ketch rig
						launched 6-6-1906, otter trawl
						1906, T.H. Peverill, 96, Northgate, H/pool
						1910 sold to Norway, scrapped Belgium 1955
BERTIE wood	HL 96	1908	21'x6'x2'	sail	2.3t	built Hartlepool, lugger, crew 3, fished lines
						30-9-1918, Robert Cambridge, 13, Wells Yard, H/pool
BETHEL wood	HL 74		18.5'	sail	3t	coble, crew 3, fished lines
						1-3-1869, Johnson Pounder, H/pool
						7-10-1875, William Winspear, H/pool
						23-5-1877, Richard Sharp, H/pool
BETSY & ANN wood	HL 228		24'	sail	2t	coble, fished nets, crew 3
						3-5-1873, John Henry Franklin, H/pool
BETTY wood	HL 25		20'x6'x2'	sail & motor	1.2t	built River Tees, lugger, crew 2, fished lines
						19-4-1940, John Humphry, 30, Archer St, West H/pool
						8-6-1942, David Hodgson, 106, Stockton St, West H/pool
BETTY H. grp	HL 255	1984	7.0m	54kw	4.37t	built Scarbrough
						11-3-1992, H/pool
BETTY W. grp	HL 233	1991	33'	112kw	12t	built H/pool
						1993, Cedric Williams, H/pool
BIRD wood	HL 33	1913	28'x9'x4'	sail & motor	6t	built St Monans, fished nets, lines, pots, lugger, crew 3
						6-12-1939, Thos. Horsley, 5, Milbank Cres, West H/pool
						26-6-1942, Wm. Craske, 41, Town Wall, H/pool
						1-9-1942, to Grimsby
						19-5-1944, to Brigg, Lincs.
						21-6-1946, to Kings Lynn, HL reg. closed 1946
BLESSING wood	HL 34	1907	42'	sail & motor	18.5t	coble, crew 5, fished nets, lines
						19-5-1909, John Humphrey, 3, Richmond St, M/boro
						15-1-1915, Sarah E. Humphrey, 15, George St, West H/pool
						28-4-1916, sunk by sub
BLOSSOM II wood	HL 1	1924	33'x10x3'		9.8T	built Eyemouth, crew 3, from Berwick
						13-10-1954, Owen Gilmore, Easington Coll.
						5-9-1956, Leonard Robinson, 10, Victoria Place, H/pool
						4-10-1958, Wm. A. Richards, Redcar, sold out of fishing 1968
BLUE EYED MAID wood	HL 1	1869	29'	sail	12t	coble, crew 5, fished lines
						1-3-1869, Pounder Davidson, H/pool
						10-7-1885, sold to M/boro
						the first H/pool boat registered under the Sea Fisheries Act
BLUE EYED SON wood	HL 5		32'	sail	14t	coble, crew 4, fished nets
						1-3-1869, William Davidson, H/pool
						26-4-1881, Pounder Davison, H/pool
BLUE JACKET wood	HL 180		29'	sail	8.25t	coble, crew 3, fished nets
						3-8-1869, Thomas Webber, ? H/pool
						5-2-1872, Alfred Smith, H/pool, scrapped 1875
BLUE MIST wood	HL 37	1966	8.2x2.7x1m		3.3t	built Whitby
						12-5-1986, G. Navin, Turnbull St, H/pool

NAME & MATERIAL	NO.	YEAR	LENGTH	POWER	WEIGHT	DETAILS
BON ACCORD steel ON 127151	HL 92	1908	115'x22'x13'	76hp steam	214t	built Hall Russell, A/deen, trawler, ketch rig engine 3cyl. by builder 1918, East Coast F. Co. A/deen (A 231) 1914–1918, Navy, m/s, 1 x 6pdr Admiralty No.510 1-5-1918, Grahams, H/pool 16-5-1919, Friarage S. Co. H/pool 5-7-1920, Leonard Brown, S. Shields 14-4-1921 R. Irvine, N. Shields 15-11-1940, James Mackie, A/deen, HL reg. closed ? J. Lewis A/deen (A 168) scrapped 1960
BONNY LASS grp	HL 125	1992	6.4m	21kw	2.7t	Cygnus fast inshore boat 3-8-1992, *Chatterbox* H/pool 30-12-2005, *Boy Scott* 4-11-2008, *Bonny Lass*, Plymouth
BUONO FORTUNA wood ON187222	HL 27	1955	37'x10'x4'	86kw	9t	built Hartlepool, coble, crew 3, fished lines, pots 11-10-1950, Frank Golightly, 5, Bell St, H/pool the last 'Whitby' coble built in the town. Built by Bob Young in Graham's shed on the Wood Quay (formerly the ice store)
BONITO wood	HL 236	1965	9.9m	12kw	3.33t	17-9-1991, H/pool
BORDER LASS	HL 38	1941	22'x6'x2'		1.7t	built Bergan, fished lines, pots 29-11-1968, A. Grungefield, Patterdale St, H/pool 6-10-1965, Robin Carter, Montague St, H/pool 3-7-1978, Martindale & Manchester, Station Town Co. Durham
BOY DAVID wood	HL 107	1921	29'x10'x4'	sail & motor	6t	built St Monance, fished lines, trawl, ex-*Volunteer* (ML 105) 21-10-1949, Frank Golightly, 5, Bell St, H/pool & Geo. Horsley, 7, Coverdale St, H/pool 26-7-1954, Geo Horsley, 25, Duke St, West H/pool 1955, sold to Whitby
BOY DAVID II wood ON 187223	HL 38	1956	32'x8'x2'			built H/pool, coble, fished pots, trawl 20-8-1956, George Horsley, 31, St Hilda St, H/pool 22-6-1960, James Rowley, Scarboro', re-reg. SH 57 27-8-1962, George Stewart, 98, Northgate, H /pool 14-4-1980, M.M. Stewart, Arkley Cres. H/pool
BOY KEN wood	HL 82	1916	29'x10'x5'	sail & motor	8.5t	crew 3, fished lines, pots, trawl, ex-*Maggie Deas* 9-6-1952, Graham, Pickford, Jopling, Easington Coll. 30-10-1953, Graham, Pickford, Jopling, & Mathwin, H/pool 9-9-1955, James Flounders Potts, 3 Croft Tce, H/pool 24-9-1956, Cuthbert Leighton, 19, Cleveland Rd, H/pool 21-3-1957, Wm. Grigg, 11, Gladstone St, H/pool 1959, sold to Sunderland
BOY SCOTT grp	HL 125	1992	6.4m	21kw	2.73t	built Falmouth 3-8-1992, H/pool as *Chatterbox* 30-12-2005, H/pool as *Boy Scott*
BRIER ROSE wood	HL 132		29'x8'x3'		4t	fished lines, pots 25-9-1961. G.S. Havelock, Blackhall Coll.
BRIER ROSE	HL 45		28'x9'x3'		3.4t	fished lines, pots 20-4-1972, Leslie McDonald, Easington Rd, H/pool
BRIGHTER HOPE wood	HL 44	1919	28'x7'x2'	sail & motor	2.3t	built Flambrough, fished, lines, salmon creels, crew 3 6-5-1931, Alfred Davison, 3, Sussex St, H/pool 1934, sold to Staithes
BRIGHTER HOPE wood	HL 44	1924	44'x12'x5'		19t	built East Cowes, trawler, crew 2 1924–1950, Teesmouth Lifeboat, RNLB *J.W. Archer*

NAME & MATERIAL	NO.	YEAR	LENGTH	POWER	WEIGHT	DETAILS
						1950–1954 Amble Lifeboat, sold out of service 1956
						1-10-1956, Wm. Melvin Carter, 20, Moor Tce, H/pool
						16-3-1971, Joseph Hughes, 50, Parkside Seaham
						2006, afloat River Crouch, Essex, bad condition
						9-2010, returned to Teesside for restoration
BRILLIANT	HL 296		96'	steam		Paddle trawler, fished trawl, crew 6
						10-7-1878, George Wright, H/pool
BRILLIANT STAR steel ON 106537	SH 46	1896	96'x19'x10'	45hp steam	125t	built Alex. Hall, A/deen, yard No.358, launched 3-4-1896
						1896 (new) T. Walker, A/deen (A 791)
						1908, T. Davison, A/deen
						1918–1919, Navy, Fishery Reserve
						1920, J.R. Ditchburn, A/deen
						1925, E. Jenkins A/deen
						1926, A.R. Sutton H/pool, scrapped 1937 (SH 46)
BRITISH ADMIRAL wood	HL 15		44' keel 49'x15'x5.5'oa	sail-2 lug & jib	32t	keel boat, fished nets, lines, crew 6
						8-6-1889, Hugh Lowrie, Clayton St, West H/pool
						4-6-1892, Burgon, Reay & Robertson, H/pool sold 1899
BROTHERLY LOVE wood	HL 63	1907	30'x6'x2'	sail lug rig	4.3t	built H/pool, coble, fished nets, lines, crew 3
						19-2-1901, Edward Davison, 10, Chapel St, H/pool
						29-9-1913, Frank Coulson, 1, Sandside, H/pool
						19-12-1917, sold out of fishing
BROTHERLY LOVE wood	HL 97	1914	21'x6'x2'	sail & oar	2.3t	built H/pool, lugger, fished lines
						24-9-1918, John Davison, 20, Chapel St, H/pool
						1938, sold & r/n *Two Pals*
BROTHERS wood	HL 2		18.5'	sail & oar	3t	coble, fished lines, crew 3
						1-3-1869, Benjamin Robson, H/pool, sold 1872
BROTHERS wood	HL 82		33'	sail & oar	12t	keel boat, crew 5
						1-3-1869, James Jnr. & John Burgon, West H/pool
						1875 re-reg. in Berwick when family moved North
BROTHERS wood	HL 204		18.5'	sail & oar	2.5t	coble, fished lines, crew 3
						1-3-1869, Robert Robson, H/pool
BROTHERS wood	HL 234		18.5'	sail	3.5t	coble, fished lines, crew 3
						20-10-1873, Thomas Pounder, H/pool
BROTHERS wood	HL 278		36'	sail	12t	keel boat -lugger, fished nets, crew 6
						31-1-1877, James & John Burgon, H/pool sold to Berwick 1881
BROTHERS wood	HL 321		50'	sail	10t	keel boat, fished nets, lines, crew 6
						6-3-1882, Walker, Thorp & Walker, sold to Berwick 1895
BUELA	HL 180		22'x7'x3'		3.7t	fished pots, lines
						1-6-1971, M. Moore & M. Owen, H/pool
BUENAMIGO wood	HL 15	1905	29'	motor	2.4t	coble, crew 3, fished pots, trawl, salmon
						17-2-1936, Thos. Oliver, M/boro, ex-*Four Sons*, Whitby
BURNSIDE	HL 46		9.4x2.9x0.5m		1.7t	
						20-3-1987, L.H. Pearce, H/pool, sold to Berwick (BK 40)
C. WILLIAM wood	HL 98		25' x 8' x 3'	sail & motor	4.6t	crew 2, fished lines & trawl
						3-9-1947, Herbert Bell, St Oswald St, West H/pool
CAIRNESS ON 110853	HL 44	1899	110'x21'x11'	steam	174t	built Hall Russell, A/deen, yard No.322, ketch rig trawler launched 19-9-1899, crew 9
						1899, Fraserburgh & North of Scotland S.T. Co. A/deen
						26-6-1909, J.T. Graham, H/pool
						8-11-1911, run down by Spanish ship, SS *Santiago*, 2 lost (Edwards & Taylor), Skipper Tommy Hall. *Santiago* lost after running aground at Redcar, some years later
CALABRIA iron	HL 56	1894	90'x20'x10'	steam 45 nhp	121t	built Edward Bros. N. Shields, ketch rig trawler launched 18-9-1894, yard No.495, 3cyl. engine & boiler

Amanda D

Amy H

Anmara

Ann Scott

Asgard

Aurora

NAME & MATERIAL	NO.	YEAR	LENGTH	POWER	WEIGHT	DETAILS
ON 104185						by N.E. Marine Engineering Co., Sunderland
						1894, Grimsby Alliance Screw F. Co, Grimsby
						1898, J. Edwards, Grimsby
						5-1-1899, Charles Henry Ford, H/pool
						1903, sold to Holland
CALEB & JOSHUA wood	HL 84		30'	sail & oar	9t	coble, crew 4, fished nets
						1-3-1869, Mathew Hunter, H/pool, sold 1884
CALLARIAS wood	HL 100	1971	11.3x3.2x1.0m	46kw	7.9t	built Whitby
						? B. Wiemer, Elwick
						16-11-1988, John Turner, Powlett Rd, H/pool
CALYPSO steel ON 112460	HL 53	1901	110'x20'x10'	53hp steam	187t	built Duthie, A/deen, yard No.230, launched 12-10-1901, trawler engine 3cyl., by Lidgerwood, Glasgow, 10 knots, ketch rigged
						1901, D. Pettit, Milford Haven (M 168)
						1915, B.S. Massey, Hull, transferred to Scarboro' 1916
						1917, W. Hill, Grimsby (GY 1083)
						1917-1919, Navy, Fishery Reserve
						1918, W. Hill & Victorian S.F. Co., Grimsby
						1920, J. Johnson, Fish Market, Newhaven, Granton
						1922, Walker, A/deen
						1929, Croft, A/deen (A 934)
						9-8-1932, J.T. Graham, H/pool
						1938–1949, Navy, scrapped 1951
CALYPSO wood	HL 108	1946	36'x10'x3'		6.7t	fished pots, lines, trawl
						29-9-1978, C.& D. Burns, Port Clarence, reg. trans to M/boro 1986
CARDEW ON 133320	HL 157	1913	115'	steam	208t	built Eltringham, Stone Quay, S. Shields, yard No.299 launched 30-10-1913, ex-*Northern Prince*
						1913, Prince F. Co. North Shields (*Northern Prince*)
						?, A. Sutton
CAROL MARY steel	HL 69	1987	9.9x3.3x0.5m	90kw	5.3t	built Hull
						9-11-1987, F. Zwart, M/boro
						1-9-1998, *Christy G.* (WY 788), Whitby
						16-8-2006, *Guiding Star* (N 932), Newry
CAROLE	HL 145		22'x6'x2'		1.7t	fished trawl, nets
						11-1-1980, Alfred Moor, Corporation Rd, H/pool
CAROLINE wood ON 182625	HL 85	1934	50'x15'x6'		26t	built Skagen, Denmark, fished seine, crew 4
						18-9-1958, Geo. Coull, 4, Wharton Tce, West H/pool
						30-1-1959, Linthorpe F. Co., Victoria Dock, H/pool
						5-3-1962, Kis F. Co. Victoria Dock, H/pool
						20-3-1962, W.H. Grigg & Co., Victoria Dock, H/pool
						2-1-1960, T.&G. Scales, Scarboro'
CAROLYN grp	INS 276			Daewoo 160hp		inshore stern trawler
						? John Wallace, H/pool
CARRIE wood	HL 80		22'x7'x2'	sail & motor	2t	fished lines, pots, crew 2
						12-5-1942, John Henry Chappel, 73, Commercial St, Middleton
						20-2-1945, boat wrecked
CASTLE BRAE wood	HL 117		37'x12'x5'		9.9t	fished lines, nets, crew 3
						4-4-1959, John Robinson, 7, Francis St, H/pool
CASTLE EDEN wood ON 189229	HL 115	1958	46'x15'x6'	95hp-5LW Gardner	24t	built Nobles, Fraserburgh, fished seine, trawl crew 4
						11-7-1958, H/pool Seiners, Victoria Dock, H/pool
						1968, caught fire sank off Redcar
CASTLE MOIL wood			56'			rigged for trawling
						8-11-1970, H/pool

NAME & MATERIAL	NO.	YEAR	LENGTH	POWER	WEIGHT	DETAILS
CATANIA iron ON 104193	HL 57	1895	90'x20'x10'	steam 29hp	121t	built Edwards Bros. N. Shields, ketch rig trawler, crew 8 engine 3cyl. by N.E. Marine S/land 5-1-1899, Charles Henry Ford, trans. from Grimsby 1903, sold to Holland
CATHERINE wood	HL 308		20'	sail	3t	coble, fished lines, crew 3 14-10-1879, Wm. Hastings, Wells Yard, H/pool
CHALLENGE C. steel	HL 7		9.67m	112kw	11t	inshore stern trawler ? *Manannan*, Douglas I.O.M. 15-8-2003, *Challenge C* (SH 294), Scarborough 9-2-2004, *Challenge C*, H/pool
CHAMPION iron ON 12933	HL 37	1894	101'x20'x11'	45hp steam	150t	built Cook, Weldon & Gammel, ketch rig trawler crew 9, engine 2cyl., by Bailey & Leetham, Hull 10 knots 1894 R.W. Crawford, Scarboro' 16-12-1922, J. Pattison, Greatham Tce, West H/pool 1915–1919, Navy, BDV 3-8-1929, Tyneside group scrapped 1931
CHARISMA grp	HL 115	1989	10.7m	100kw	13.3t	built Penryn, inshore stern trawler 20-7-1989, *Charisma* H/pool 27-1-1995, *Charisma* (OB 588), Oban 19-2-2008, *Two Brothers* (N 588), Newry
CHARITY	HL 110	1975	31'x9'x2'		3.2t	built Whitby, fished lines, nets, pots 1-7-1976, M. Watson, Seaton Carew 9-11-1979, John Robinson, Newbiggin, reg. trans to Blyth 1980
CHEERFUL wood	HL 141		33'	sail & oar	12t	keel boat, crew 5, fished nets 3-3-1869, Thomas Dickinson, H/pool 28-4-1871, William Bartlett, H/pool
CHILDRENS FRIEND wood	HL 40	1914	50'x13'x6'	sail & motor	29t	lugger, crew 5, fished nets, lines 27-10-1914, Local group, sold to Scarboro' 14-9-1918 skipper John Horsley, 21, Bedford St, H/pool
CHILDRENS FRIEND wood	LH 177	1983	14.6m	186kw	49t	built Seahouses, inshore stern trawler ? Major Hartley
CHRIS	HL 91		19'x6'x2'	sail & oar	1.4t	built H/pool, crew 2, fished lines, pots 23-7-1942, C.E. Steel, 17, Harbour Tce, West H/pool 12-5-1947, M.L. Headley, 11, Murray St, West Hp/ool 11-11-1947, G.F. Whitfield, 158, Stockton Rd, West H/pool
CHRISANDALE grp	HL 699	1992	8m	90kw	6.65t	built Falmouth & Hull 18-12-1992, H/pool
CHRISTINA wood	HL 356		44'	sail	14t	lugger, fished herring nets, crew 6, ex-Kirkcaldy 17-9-1884, John Wm. Holman, & Robert A. Rowe, H/pool
CHRISTIANIA	HL 76		27'x8'x3'		3t	fished lines, pots, crew 2 8-5-1958, Steven Mason Gowler, Seaton Carew 6-12-1958, Albert Goodchild, 68, Durham St, H/pool 16-1-1969, Alan Colvin, 38, Benson St, H/pool 21-9-1972, Joseph Lawson, 41, Rokeby St, H/pool 26-5-1981, Colin Williams, 28, Wynstay Gdns. H/pool 6-1-1983, Robert Ainsty, 41, Tredegar Walk, H/pool
CHRISTINE wood	HL 63	1949	20'x6'x2'		1.5t	built Thornaby, crew 2, fished lines, pots, ex- Mboro, MH 98 30-1-1953, Laurance Carter, 4, St Hilda St, H/pool
CHRISTINE wood	HL 140	1949	20'x6'x2'		1.3t	fished lines, pots 21-9-1962, Geo Townsend, 50, Southgate, H/pool 3-5-1973, W. Glaister, 5, Suffolk St, West H/pool
CHRISTINE	HL 83		10x2.5x0.2m		1.1t	11-1-1988, J.S. Clark, Billingham
CHRYSTAL SEA grp	HL 106	1988	9.15m	80kw	2.2t	built Liverpool 1989, *Shaun Dawn* 2007, *Chrystal Sea*

NAME & MATERIAL	NO.	YEAR	LENGTH	POWER	WEIGHT	DETAILS
CICERO wood	HL 28		28'x5'x2'	sail -lug & jib	2t	coble, fished lines, crew 3, ex-pilot boat (H 49) 14-3-1892, John Davison, 10, Chapel St, H/pool
CLARA wood	HL 267		18'	sail	1.5t	coble, fished lines, crew 2 1-5-1876, John Stevenson, H/pool 9-1876, sold to Middlesbrough
CLARA SUTTON wood ON 139832	HL 88	1917	89'x20'x10'	35hp steam	102t	built Colby Bros, Oulton Broad, Lowestoft, dandy rig, drifter yard No.44, crew 10, engine by Crabtree, Gt Yarmouth 20-9-1917, A.R. Sutton 7-4-1925, A.R. Sutton's new address, Clyde House, Baptist St, H/pool 1940, Navy, sold to Navy 1941
CLARE S steel	HL 75	1978	32'x12'x3'	89kw	5.2t	built Sunderland, inshore stern trawler, fished trawl pots, nets 16-5-1979, F.C. & C.F. Train, Tempest Rd, H/pool 16-8-1983, G. Morter, Station Lane, Seaton Carew 1989, (K 257), Kirkwall
CLARE LOUISE wood	MH 296	1980	7.5m	41kw	2.7t	
CLEVELAND steel	HL 93	1959	97'x22'x9'	432hp Blackstone	160t	built Richards, Lowestoft, yard No.450, launched 22-6-1959 1959, Star Drift F. Co. as *Boston Valliant* (LT 277) 3-8-1972 Albert F. Co. (Lola), H/pool, r/n *Cleveland* 23-2-1978, Putford Enterprises, Lowestoft, as oil rig stand-by r/n *Monkleigh*, 1989 sold
COMPANION ON 110210 steel	HL 60	1903	112'x21'x12'	65hp steam	163t	built Hall Russell A/deen, yard No.369, launched 26-2-1903 engine 3cyl., by builder, trawler 1903, J. Inglis, Peebles (GN 23) 24-11-1903, Towed S.T. *Columba* (GN 43) from 35m E of May Island 1910, T. Devlin, Granton 1917–1919, Navy, m/s, & training vessel, Portland 24-3-1924, towed S.T. *Glamis Castle* (GW12), 250m to Granton 1930, Dodd S.F. Co. A/deen 12-7-1933, Dalkins, 6, Baltic St, West H/pool (J.B. Graham) 1937, scrapped Stockton
CONFIDE grp	HL 23	1978	9.4x3.5x1.8m	101kw	7.2t	built Penrhyn, inshore stern trawler, ex-*May Archer* (SM 26) 3-7-1985, Peter Coull, Billingham 13-6-1986, David Horsley, Jesmond Gdns, H/pool 30-10-1986, C. Trewitt, Peterlee
CONFLICT wood	HL 364		22'	sail	3t	coble, fished lines, crew 4 19-10-1885, John Archbold, 47, Mary St, & Geo. Whammond 3-8-1889, Geo. Whammond, 4, Lily St, West H/pool
CONSTANCE wood	HL 77	1915	51'x13'x5'	sail & motor	29t	built Filey, lugger, crew 5, fished nets, lines 17-11-1915, local group, H/pool 15-10-1928, Mathew Hastings, 17, Wells Passage, H/pool 1932, sold to Arklow, Ireland
CONSTANT FRIEND wood	BH 212	1958	11.29m	81kw	8.2t	
CORMORAN grp	PZ 4	1999	6.19m	37kw	2.87t	inshore open boat ? 'Philly' Coul
COUNTESS of ? wood	HL 194		22'	sail	5t	smack, crew 2, fished nets 2-4-1870, Thomas Shaw 9-7-1873, sold to Portsmouth

NAME & MATERIAL	NO.	YEAR	LENGTH	POWER	WEIGHT	DETAILS
COURTIER wood	HL 39	1949	32'x9'x3'		4.5t	built Amble, fished lines, nets, pots, crew 2 11-11-1971, F.S. Pratt, Horden
COURTIER	HL 182		9.9x2.7x1m		4.5t	fished lines, nets, pots 16-3-1983, Dennis Davey, Easington Coll.
CRAIGMORE steel ON 139828	HL 83	1916	115'x22'x12'	78hp steam	210t	built Hall Russell A/deen, yard No.585, launched 13-6-1916 ketch rig trawler, crew 9 19-7-1916, local group, inc. R.H. Davison, H/pool 1916-1919, Navy, m/s (A.3294) 1926, K.R. Hoare, H/pool 20-12-1927, R.W. Sutherland, A/deen (A 309) as *Star of Peace* 1929, Walker S.T. Co., A/deen 1941 H.J. Horwood, Milford Haven (M 133) 15-10-1948, lost off the Smalls
CRIMOND steel ON 110851	HL 42	1899	110'x21'x12'	steam 50hp	173t	built Hall Russell A/deen, yard No.321, launched, 17-8-1899 ketch rig trawler, engine 3cyl. by builder 1899, Fraserburgh & North of Scotland S.T. Co. 26-6-1909, J.T. Graham, Fish Quay, H/pool 25-10-1910, Walker, A/deen 9-2-1912, ashore, near Sanday, Orkney, 4 crew lost when small boat wrecked, remaining crew rescued by Stronsay motor lifeboat, refloated 23-2-1912 19-5-1915, captured by sub, sunk by bomb, 50m E of Wick
CROMLECH wood	PH 125	1964	48'	150hp Boudouin	22t	built Port Louis France, rigged trawling ? Keith Kennedy, H/pool
CRYSTAL SEA grp	HL 106	1988	9.15m	80kw		built Liverpool. 4-4-1987, *Shaun Dawn* 24-7-2007, *Crystal Sea*
CUTHBERT wood	HL 21		18.5'	sail & oar		coble, fished lines, crew 3 1-3-1869, Robert Scott Pounder, H/pool sold 9-1869
CYCLONE grp	H 1059	1995	8.09m	175kw	3.9t	built Cornwall, fast inshore boat 17-4-1996, H/pool
CYGNUS grp ON 364706	HL 107		32'x12'x4'	105hp Ford	10t	built Falmouth, inshore stern trawler, fished pots, nets, trawl (Cygnus 32) first of its type on coast 20-5-1976, Alan Cook, Durham St, H/pool 23-5-1984, Alan & Anthony Greenwood, Winterbottom Ave, H/pool 6-3-1996, *Boy David* - Belfast 2003, re-engined, 118kw
DAGNY wood	HL 46	1939	46'x16'x6'		20.5t	built Risor, Norway, fished lines, nets, pots, crew 3 20-4-1972, Thos. Brian Smith, Stockton Rd, H/pool 3-4-1973, R.E. Foster, Park Road, H/pool, re-reg. Blyth 10-1973
DAISY wood	HL 90		29'	sail& oar	9t	coble, fished nets, crew 4 1-3-1869, Robinson Carter, sold to Sunderland, 1876
DALTON LASS wood	HL 46		28'	sail & oar	11t	coble, fished nets, crew 4 1-3-1869, Margaret Lister, H/pool, lost 16-6-1869
DANIEL wood	HL 57		18'	sail & oar		coble, fished lines, crew 3 1-3-1869, James Moor, H/pool, sold 1873
DANIEL wood	HL 87	1883	53'x15'x7'	sail & motor	36t	lugger, fished nets, lines, trawl, crew 7 23-5-1917, Thomas Hatton, 365, Linthorpe Rd, M/boro 1918, sold to Scarboro'
DASHER grp	HL 700	1984	6.6m	19kw	2.4t	built Gosport 13-6-1996, H/pool
DAVID wood	HL 268		14'	sail	2t	coble, fished lines, crew 2 31-5-1876, George Copeman, H/pool

Avondale

Barbara Ann

Bay Joe

Ben Tarbert

Bernd

Bonny Lass

NAME & MATERIAL	NO.	YEAR	LENGTH	POWER	WEIGHT	DETAILS
DAVID ANDREW grp	HL 1064	1998	7.45m	48kw	3.08t	built Dorset 28-7-1998, H/pool 17-7-2001, *David Andrew* (CE 59) Coleraine
DAVID HELEN wood ON 182648	HL 6	1949	47'x14'x8'	112hp Kelvin R6	22.4t	built Gilleleje Denmark, fished seine net, trawl 1949, K.W. Alder, London as *Aldersea*, 80hp engine 1968, Delga F. Co. Grimsby, 60hp engine 3-2-1969, Victor Deer, Broomhill Gdns, H/pool as *David Helen* 28-11-1988, R.J. Penfold, Brixham (BM 205) 1992, R.W. Hobbin, Cornwall, laid up Plymouth 1996 2005, sold for private use, refitted, re-engined Gardner 6LX
DAVID WILLIAM wood	BH 228	1958	16.1m	223kw	24.2t	
DAWN of HOPE wood	HL 38		18.5'	sail & oar	3t	coble, fished lines, crew 3 1-3-1869, John Hood, H/pool, sold 1873
DEER HOUND wood	HL 48		18.5'	sail /oar		coble, fished lines, crew 3 1-3-1869, Richard Pounder, H/pool
DELIGHT wood	HL 63		18.5'	sail /oar	3t	coble, fished lines, crew 3 1-3-1869, Robert Pounder, H/pool 3-6-1873, John Davison, H/pool
DEREEKA	HL 47		26'x9'x3'		3.9t	fished lines, pots, crew 2 4-10-1972, S Weegram, 11, Ashby Grove, H/pool
DEREEKA wood	HL 206	1963	7.5x2.9x1m	45kw	2.5t	built Whitby, coble 21-8-1984, Benson & Crosby, Peterlee, & Otterwell & Mitchell, H/pool
DEVOTION grp	HL 5	1978	9.6x3.5x1.1m	72kw	6t	built Cornwall, inshore stern trawler 8-10-1987, Alan & Anthony Greenwood, Winterbottom Ave, H/pool 2009, de-commissioned, Scarborough
DEWDROP wood	HL 39		18.5'	sail/oar	3t	coble, fished lines, crew 3 1-3-1869, Jacob Hood, H/pool, sold 1883
DEWDROP wood	HL 9		42'x16'x4'	sail - lug & mizzen	12t	decked boat, fished nets, crew 5 11-10-1887, Wm. Hastings, 3, Sussex St, H/pool, trans. from Berwick 19-8-1891, Mary Jane Hastings, 3, Sussex St, H/pool & J.A. Armstrong, 7 Brougham St, H/pool
DIANA POUNDER wood	HL 17		18.8'	sail/oar	3t	coble, fished lines, crew 3 1-3-1869, Thomas Coulson, H/pool 8-10-1878, Arthur Southern, H/pool
DIANE wood	HL 110		25'x8'x4'	sail & motor	4t	coble, fished lines, pots, crew 3 24-12-1947, Stanley Moore, & R.G. Davis, West H/pool
DICK WHITTINGTON wood, ON 65218	HL 332		71'	sail	63t	ketch, fished trawl, crew 5, transferred from Hull (H 679) 18-5-1883, H/pools Fishery Co. 1888, sold to Grimsby
DILIGENT wood	HL 86	1901	39'x14'x4'	sail & motor	12t	built Aberdeen, lugger, fished lines, nets, crew 4, ex-PD 298 27-9-1941, Thygeson, Ross & Leonard, H/pool 14-3-1942, Leonard, Ross & Webb, H/pool 25-6-1947, T.H. Harper, Blyth 22-4-1949, S. Wright, Seaham, reg. trans. to Sunderland, 1949
DOCTOR LIVINGSTONE wood	HL 95		29'	sail	8t	coble fished nets, lines, mussel dredging crew 4 12-1-1877, Ann Davison, H/pool 9-9-1878, James Ballantine
DOLLY GRAHAM wood	HL 135	1932	44'x13'x5'	sail & motor	19t	built Banff, fished trawl, nets, pots, crew 4 (ex-OB 68) 13-2-1962, Arthur Fenwick, Billingham 7-1965, reg. trans. to Shoreham

NAME & MATERIAL	NO.	YEAR	LENGTH	POWER	WEIGHT	DETAILS
DOLORES wood	HL 19		28'x7'x3'	sail & motor	4.3t	fished lines, pots, crew 3 16-8-1950, R.P. Manners, 8, Eltringham Rd, West H/pool
DOLPHIN wood	HL 127		14'	sail/oar	0.5t	small boat, crew 3, fished sweep net 3-3-1869 John H. Franklin, Seaton Carew, sold 1883
DOLPHIN wood	HL 119	1929	22'x7'x2'		3.6t	fished lines, pots, crew 2 14-8-1959, Spence & Gardner, West H/pool 31-12-1968 re-reg. HL 133, G. Metcalf, Easington Coll.
DOLPHIN steel	HL 231	1990	9.6m	216kw	14t	built H/pool 8-4-1991, H /pool 18-2-2002, *Dolphin* (DA 27), Drogheda, Ireland
DONNA M. wood	HL 1056	1992	7.32m	13kw	2.41t	24-4-1992, H/pool
DOREEN wood	HL 34		16'x6'x2'	sail & motor	1.0t	fished lines, pots, crew 2 15-12-1947, Phillip Peek, 3, Todd Sq. H/pool 2-8-1950, A.G. & E. Barber, West H/pool 2-9-1955, Edward Barber, West H/pool
DOREEN JOAN steel	HL 204	1982	9.4x3.8x1.5m	89kw	8.8t	built Hull 14-6-1984, Leslie Allison, Billingham 29-9-1999, *Sapphire* (WY 786) 10-5-2005, *Carona* (WY 786)
DORILEEN wood	HL 35	1912	22'x6'x2'	sail & motor	1.6t	built Hartlepool, coble, fished lines, pots, crew 3 28-10-1935, Harold Smalley, 14, Hart St, H/pool 1938, scrapped, ex-*Hilda* (HL 28) 1921
DORIS wood	HL 5		21'x6'x2'	sail & motor	1.5t	dandy, fished lines, pots 31-12-1929, Arthur Bell, 5, Raeburn St, West H/pool 8-10-1938, W.G. Collitt, 19, Arch St, H/pool 1955, destroyed by fire
DORIS BURTON ON 124315 steel	HL 11	1914	115'x22'x12'	steam,	197t	built Hall Russell, A/deen, yard No.549, launched 31-3-1914 ketch rig, trawler, crew 9 5-5-1915, Doris Burton S.T. Co. Fish Quay, H/pool 1915 left Aberdeen, went missing
DOROTHY wood	HL 75		28'x5'x2'	sail/oar	3.4t	built Hartlepool, coble, fished lines, nets, crew 3 24-2-1915. John Pounder, 1, Sussex St, H/pool 2-6-1917, sold to Seahouses
DOROTHY wood	HL 35		26'x8'x3'	sail & motor	5t	coble, fished lines, crew 3 18-10-1921, Robert Pounder, 1, Sussex St, H/pool 3-8-1927, Geo. Davison, 7, York Rd, West H/pool, scrapped 1927
DOROTHY wood	HL 166	1938	49'x15'x6'	66hp Kelvin K3	22t	built Alex. Aitken, Anstruther, lines, trawl, pots ? Sam Chapman, Grimsby (GY 545) 20-4-1967 F.C. Sutherland, 85, Marine Drive, H/pool 21-4-1967, Matty McClelland, Danny Cole, H/pool 8-9-72, Daniel Coull, Gibb Sq. H/pool 9-2-1976, David Wilson, 47, Milton Rd, H/pool
DOROTHY WALL wood	HL 76		31'	sail/oar	10t	coble, fished nets, crew 4 1-3-1869, John Wall, H/pool, sold 1876 6-6-1876, Robert Rowntree, H/pool
DOT	HL 51		14'x5'x2'		1.0t	fished pots, 20-4-1972, Alfred Moore, 11, Corporation Rd, H/pool
DOVE wood	HL 108		32'	sail/oar	12t	keel boat, fished nets, crew 4 1-3-1869, Alexander Johnson, scraped 1874
DOVE wood	HL 152	1921	25'x11'x4'		5.2t	built Hastings, trawler, 27-11-1967, John Brown, Easington Coll. 3-10-1969, J.R. Bryan, 6, Harlech Walk, H/pool

NAME & MATERIAL	NO.	YEAR	LENGTH	POWER	WEIGHT	DETAILS
DOVER steel ON 106681	HL 38	1896	104'x20'x10'	steam 45hp	163t	built Mackie & Thompson, Govan, yard No.124, launched 2-11-1896 engine 3cyl. by Muir & Houston, Glasgow. 1869, Hagerup & Doughty, Grimsby (GY 142) 1906, Consolidated S.F. & Ice Co. Grimsby 1914–1918, Navy, m/s, 1x3pdr, Admiralty No.630 30-12-1922, G. Wardell, 5, Middlegate, H/pool 1924, sold to Lowestoft
DULCIA LIVINGSTONE wood	HL 95		29'	sail/oar	8t	coble, fished nets, crew 4 1-3-1869, Robert Davidson, H/pool, sold 1877
DUNDARG wood	PD 97	1939	62'	150hp Gardner	48t	built Nobles Fraserburgh, cost £3,000 1939, Richie, Fraserburgh (FR 121) 1965, Richard Donnan, Co. Down 1969, Peterhead (PD 97) 1975, A.P. Blades, Cleveland, sold 1988 2006, working as a diving boat, West of Scotland
DUNELM wood ON 187230	HL 89	1958	47'x15'x6'		24.9t	built Thompsons, Buckie, seine netter, Danish style crew 4 16-12-1958, The Hartnes S.F. Co. Fish Quay, H/pool 11-1959, lost with all hands, skipper John Murray & son Iain from Buckie, Harry Smith & Tom Andrews, H/pool
EARLY MORN wood	HL 25	1927	29'x8'x3'	sail & motor	4t	built Hartlepool, lugger, fished lines, trawl, pots, crew 3 14-9-1928, Geo. Davison, 7, York Place, H/pool 15-5-1930, R.H. Pilcher, 146, Hart Rd, H/pool 8-7-1930, W.H. Whelpton, H/pool scrapped 1933
EARLY MORN wood	HL 88		26'x8'x3'		3.1t	fished lines, pots, 16-8-1950, Albert Parker, 41, Winterbottom Ave, H/pool 18-11-1952, Eric Green, 46, Vine St, Darlington
EARLY ON wood	E 238	1965	9.8m	95kw	4.2t	inshore trawler
EAST COAST steel ON 123378	HL 94	1907	115'x22'x12'	68hp steam	207t	built Alex. Hall, A/deen, engine 3cyl. by builder, yard No.427, trawler 1907, built as *Horace Stroud* (A 122) 1913, r/n *East Coast*, sold to Portugal 1914, purchased by Navy, m/s 1-5-1918, J.T. Graham, H/pool 1919 sold to Belgium 1923 Don Trawling, Aberdeen (A 935) 1944–1945 Navy 7-11-1947 sinking 30m off Ballycotton, crew rescued, towed by Milford Haven trawler *Slebech* and beached 1958, scrapped, Wards Castle Pill
EASTER MORN wood	WY 820	1947	6.4m	14kw	1.5t	
EBENEZER wood	HL 205		31'	sail/oar	9t	coble, fished nets, crew 4 29-5-1871, Wm. Horsley
EBENEZER wood	HL 275		39'	sail	8t	lugger, fished nets, crew 5 7-10-1876, Barnet, Davis, Shaw & Mowby, H/pool 15-4-1878, Barnet, Shaw, Mowbray, & Davis, H/pool
EBENEZER wood	HL 318		19'	sail	3t	coble, fished lines, crew 3 11-8-1881, Robert Pounder, H/pool 14-1-1890, Francis Sotheran, 11, Sussex St, H/pool
EBENEZER wood	HL 62	1895	41'x12'x5'	sail & motor	14t	built Montrose, lugger, fished lines, nets, crew 4 20-11-1936, local group 7-7-1948, sold to Ayr

NAME & MATERIAL	NO.	YEAR	LENGTH	POWER	WEIGHT	DETAILS
ECHO	HL 31		29'	sail/oar	10t	coble, fished nets, crew 4
						1-3-1869, Mark Davidson, H/pool sold 1874
						27-7-1874, Arthur Twaite, H/pool
ECLIPSE wood	HL 289		42'	sail	12t	keel boat, fished nets, lines, crew 6
						11-12-1877, John Shaw & Albert Coulson, H/pool
EDITH wood	HL 297		18'	sail	1.0t	jolly boat, fished trawl, crew 2
						12-8-1878, Edward Jobson, H/pool
EDNA T. wood	HL 101		22'x7'x2'		2.2t	fished lines, pots
						9-6-1954, W.T.B. Train, 7, McDonald Place, H/pool, sold 7-1955
EDWARD wood	HL 252		18.5'	sail	3t	coble, fished lines, crew 3
						9-3-1875, Pounder Davison, H/pool
EILEEN wood	HL 115		17'x6'x2'		1.3t	fished lines
						24-11-1947, John Grant, Billingham, reg. trans. to M/boro 7-1948
EILEEN wood	HL 95	1959	27'x8'x3'	motor	2.9t	coble, fished lines, creels
						17-3-1959. W.K. Grigg, Wansbeck Gdns, H/pool
						17-3-1960, Victor Deer, Cobden St, H/pool
						28-9-1962, Matty McClelland & Danny Cole, H/pool
						9-1964, reg. trans. to Sunderland, r/n *Patricia*
EILEEN wood	HL 146	1931	33'x12'x5'		9.2t	built St Monance, keel boat, fished lines, pots, trawl (ex-WY 34)
						13-8-1963, Victor Deer, 30, Cobden St, West H/pool
						28-1-1966, John White, Seaham, re-reg. Colchester 10-1967
EILEEN WRAY ON 123368 steel	HL 61	1906	120'x23'x13'	58hp steam	227t	built Duthie, A/deen, yard No.291, crew 9, trawler
						1906, Walker A/deen, as *Star of Liberty* (A88)
						sold to France, r/n *Graziella*
						1929, sold to A/deen as *Jane Stephen* (A 368)
						9-10-1933, W. Wray, 10, Jesmond Rd, H/pool, as *Eileen Wray*
						14-11-1940, St Andrews S.F. Co. Hull 1942 re- reg. (H 7)
						1948 Humber Trawlers, Grimsby (GY 108)
						5-1952 scrapped
ELEAZAR steel ON 104515	HL 51	1895	90'x19'x11'	steam 45hp	111t	built Hall Russell, A/deen, as long-liner, later trawler, yard No.294
						launched 18-9-1895, crew 8, engine 2cyl. by builder
						1895, Wood, A/deen
						27-10-1897, J.J. Lister, 4, Town Wall, H/pool
						23-5-1916, Barton, Whitby (WY 105)
						1917, Navy
						12-8-1917, captured by sub, sunk by gunfire
						25m SW by W St Ann's Head
ELEAZAR steel ON 139280	HL 31	1906	118'x21'x11'	steam	211t	built Mackie & Thompson, Govan, 9 crew, ketch rig trawler yard No.330, launched 4-4-1906
						1906, built as *J. Beals*
						1915, Steam Trawling Co. Hull
						1917, Fishery Reserve
						1919, Melville S.T. Co. Fleetwood (FD 362)
						1923, Transvaal S.T. Co, Fleetwood
						9-10-1928, J.H. Lister, 4, Town Wall, H/pool
						1937, scrapped Stockton
ELENOR wood	HL 233		25'	sail	5t	coble, fished lines, crew 4
						22-9-1873, Johnstone & James Borthwick, H/pool
						18-11-1875, James Borthwick, H/pool
ELENOR wood	HL 25		29'x6'x2'	lug sail & 4 oars	4.2t	built Hartlepool, coble fished lines, crew 3
						10-1-1891, John Horsley, Cambridge Tce, H/pool
						25-6-1906, John Horsley, 6, John St, H/pool
						5-10-1910, George Horsley, 12, Wells Yard, H/pool, sold 1915

Boy David

Brighter Hope

Calypso

Carolyn

Castle Eden

Challenge-C

Charity

Children's Friend

Clare-S

Cleveland

Confide

Constant Friend

NAME & MATERIAL	NO.	YEAR	LENGTH	POWER	WEIGHT	DETAILS
ELENOR MAY wood	HL 1082	1983	5.63m	33kw	1.05t	built Whitby, based Redcar 1-10-1998, Whitby (WY 8) 16-5-2007, H/pool
ELIZA wood	HL 240		18.5'	sail	3t	coble, fished lines, crew 3 27-2-1874, Robert Pounder, H/pool
ELIZABETH wood	?			sail		? 2-9-1863, run down off Seaham Harbour by *Jeune Adeline* of St Malo. Matt Williamson lost, survivors, Ben Robson, Rob Robson, Andrew Boagey
ELIZABETH wood	HL 26		30'	sail/oar	10t	coble, fished nets, crew 4, 1-3-1869, Robert Yeal, H/pool, wrecked 18-4-1877
ELIZABETH wood	HL 15		25'	sail/oar	6t	herring boat, crew 3 1-3-1869, Thomas Coulson, H/pool 8-4-1871, Robert Pounder, H/pool, scrapped 1875
ELIZABETH wood	HL 18		31'	sail/oar	8t	coble, fished nets, crew 4 1-3-1869, Elizabeth Corner, H/pool, skipper Thos. Corner 23-8-1880, Cuthbert Pounder, H/pool ?, sunk in collision with Sunderland herring boat off Huntcliffe, crew saved
ELIZABETH wood	HL 158		18.5'	sail / oar	3t	coble, fished lines, crew 3 29-4-1869, Nathan Sotheran, H/pool, wrecked 1875
ELIZABETH wood	HL 191		19'	sail / oar	2.5t	coble, fished lines, nets, crew 3 9-2-1870, Francis Bulmer, H/pool 11-2-1882, Thomas Pounder, H/pool
ELIZABETH wood	HL 230		36'	sail	8t	herring boat, fished nets, crew 5 27-6-1873, James Burgon, H/pool 8-11-1876, Ann Pounder, sold to London 1880
ELIZABETH wood	HL 272		19'	sail	1.5t	open boat, fished nets, lines, crew 2 18-9-1876, Harvey Peak, H/pool
ELIZABETH wood	HL 27		40'x15'x4'	sail – lug & mizzen	10.5t	keel boat, fished nets, crew 5, ex-SD 94 9-9-1891, John William Holman, 7, Brougham St, H/pool
ELIZABETH	HL 30		27'x7'x2'		2t	fished lines, pots, 22-9-1947, Richard Pounder, 7, Regent St, H/pool, sold 1957
ELIZABETH M. wood	HL 66	1945	27'x8'x3'		2.9t	built Aberystwyth, fished lines, pots 20-6-1957, Samuel Ainsley, 55, West View Rd, H/pool 18-9-1958, Robert Nolan Maiden, 15, Baptist St, H/pool
ELIZABETH & MARY wood	HL 319		39'	sail	10t	keel boat, fished nets, lines, crew 5, ex-Eyemouth 12-10-1881, Holman, Grievson & Frampton, H/pool 10-7-1888, J.W. Holman, 7, Brougham St, H/pool & Geo. Grievson, 157, Durham St, H/pool 22-5-1890, John William Holman, 7, Brougham St, H/pool
ELIZABETH ANN wood	HL 44		18.5'	sail / oar	3t	coble, fished lines, crew 3 1-3-1869, Cuthbert Moore, H/pool 13-4-1874, John Hood, H/pool
ELIZABETH ANN wood	HL 33		18.5'	sail / oar	3t	coble, fished lines, crew 3 1-3-1869, George Coulson, H/pool, sold 1882
ELIZABETH ANN wood	HL 105		18.5'	sail/oar	3t	coble, fished lines, crew 3 1-3-1869, Heron Pounder, H/pool 6-1-1871, George Corner, sold out of fishing 1886
ELIZABETH ANN wood	HL 164		30'	sail/oar	10t	coble, fished nets, crew 4 19-5-1869, Wm. Calling & Robert Sheldon, H/pool 14-10-1869, Wm. Calling, sold to Whitby, 1880
ELIZABETH ISOBEL wood	SD 129					Whitby coble, based in Marina ? H/pool

NAME & MATERIAL	NO.	YEAR	LENGTH	POWER	WEIGHT	DETAILS
ELIZABETH JANE wood	HL 7		18'	sail/oar	3t	coble, fished pots, crew 3
						1-3-1869, Pounder Davison, H/pool, sold to Redcar 1870
ELIZABETH MARY wood	HL 40		18.5'	sail/oar	3t	coble, fished lines, crew 3
						1-3-1869, Thomas Horsley, H/pool
						27-7-1876, Edward Appleton, H/pool
ELLEN wood	HL 218		18'	sail/oar	2.5t	coble, fished lines, crew 2
						15-7-1872, Joshua Southeran, H/pool
ELMO wood	HL 35		24'x8'x2'		2t	fished lines,
						3-9-1947, Robert Martin, 20, Duke St, West H/pool, sold 1949
ELSA wood	HL 104	1953	23'x7'x3'		2.3t	built Stockholm, fished lines, pots
						11-8-1959, Cyril Edmundson, Stockton
ELSIE iron ON 105100	SH 280	1896	110'x21'x11'	60hp steam	184t	built Cochrane & Copper, Beverly (ex-H 320) trawler
						engine 3cyl. by C.D. Holmes, Hull
						1896, Gamecock S.T. Co., Scarboro'
						1916–1919, Navy, 1x6pdr (A 944)
						1926, J. Pattison, H/pool
EMBRACE wood	KY 43	1933	44'	66hp	19t	ex- Pittenweem, fished creels, built as ring netter
						1933, Halley, Fisherrow (LH 158)
						1950, Alex. Wood, Pittenweem (KY 43)
						1960, Bill Horsley, H/pool
						1982, P.M. Townsend, Sheffield
EMMAUS wood	HL 213		18.5'	sail	3t	coble, fished lines, crew 3
						17-7-1876, William Pounder, H/pool
						21-6-1880, Wm. Corner, Wells Yard, H/pool
EMMA LOUISE wood	HL 147	1972	6.24m	37kw	1.8t	built H/pool
						31-7-1992, H/pool
EMMY LOU grp	HL 133	1991	6.2m	42kw	1.31t	built Falmouth
						24-3-1992, H/pool
EMPRESS iron ON 98541	HL 3	1890	93'x18'x11'	steam 40hp	104t	built Eltringham, Stone Quay, S. Shields, crew 8, ketch rig trawler
						engine 2cyl. by Clyne Mitchell, A/deen
						1890, Robert Laing Jnr, 82, Union Grove, Aberdeen
						12-4-1899, J.C. Graham
						30-3-1915, Walker S.T. Co. Aberdeen
						23-12-1915, overwhelmed in severe SE gale waiting to enter
						Aberdeen, skipper John Barber, Torry A/deen,
						lost with all hands
EMULATE	HL 101	1978	16'x5'x2'		1.0t	fished pots, trawl, built Barmston, Humberside
						14-12-1978, Colin Ellis, Stockton
ENDEAVOUR wood	HL 149		30'	sail/oar	8t	coble, fished nets, crew 4
						1-4-1869, Thos. Needham & John Fowler, H/pool
						31-7-1871, John Pattison, H/pool
ENDEAVOUR wood	HL 250		18.5' keel 25'x5'x3' oa	sail	3t	coble, fished lines, crew 3
						31-12-1874, Cuthbert Moor, H/pool
						16-10-1885, Johnson Pounder, 7, Dovecote Yard, H/pool
						17-5-1895, Johnson Pounder, 20, Bedford St, H/pool,
						1898, sold to Whitby,
ENDEAVOUR wood	HL 42	1974	16m	195kw Caterpiller	34.5t	built Portavogie, fished seine, trawl
						1989, Progress (B 22), Belfast
						21-1-1998, Endeavour (HL 42), H/pool,
						16-11-1999, Endeavour (LH 169), Leith
ENDEAVOUR steel	HL 42	2000	9.95m	200kw	11.67t	built Cleveland
						17-10-2000, Kenny Johnson, H/pool
ENDEAVOUR 2 wood	KY 356	1958		150hp Gardner	24t	built Scotland, fished trawl, seine, based H/pool
						1958, Phillip Picknet, Redcar & J.E. Picknet, H/pool

NAME & MATERIAL	NO.	YEAR	LENGTH	POWER	WEIGHT	DETAILS
ENDURANCE wood	HL 52	1944	24'x6'x2'			1989, Kenny Johnson, H/pool as *Supreme* (HL 42) 15-11-1989, J. Munro, Ayr, r/n *Numora III* (BA 42) fished lines, pots, crew 2 22-5-1954, J.W. MacConachie, 66, Bruntoft Ave, H/pool 9-6-1955, G.S. Tavistock, Blackhall Coll. 27-7-1958, M.H. Porritt, 17, Town Wall, H/pool 12-5-1967, S. Bradshaw, 84, Howard St, H/pool 21-6-1968, J. Brown, & Eric Ray, H/pool 23-10-1969, J. Brown, 6, Langley Flats, H/pool 3-8-1972, W.G. Turner, 86, Howard St, H/pool
ENDURANCE	HL 184	1977		27'x 8'x 4'	4.4t	built Bridgend, fished lines, nets 11-7-1980, John Roberts, Cameron Rd, West H/pool
ENDURANCE wood	HL 3	1978	9.07m	38.8kw	3.9t	built Whitby 15-7-2005, *Endurance* (SD 100), Sunderland 7-7-2008, *Endurance* (HL 3), Hartlepool
ENERGY wood	HL 89	1901	32'x11'x4'	motor	6.8t	built Anstruther, fished seine net, crew 4, ex-Berwick (BK 51) 5-5-1942, John Geo. Thos. Ray, Westbrook Grove, West H/pool 21-1-1948, sold to Seahouses, reg. trans to Berwick
ENTERPRISE wood	INS 11	1973	54.6'	Kelvin TA3C6	28.7t	built Thompson, Buckie, fished seine, trawl 1973, *Heather Anne* (BA 30) 20-11-1974, J.G. Henderson, Mallaig, r/n *Solam* (OB 239) 1982, A.M. Farquhar, Lossiemouth 2000, r/n *Enterprise* (INS 11) 2007, Major Hartley, H/pool
ENTERPRISE wood	HL 10		25'	sail	5t	coble, fished drift nets, crew 3 28-8-1888, John Beaton, 21, Laburnam St, & Joseph Perry, 35, Bengal St, West H/pool
ENTERPRISE wood	HL 108		24'x7'x3'		2.3t	fished lines, pots, trawl, crew 2 28-5-1949, Frank Golightly, 5, Bell St, H/pool
EQUITY grp	TH 377	1983	6.5m	55kw	1.5t	inshore open boat ? H/pool
ERIMOUSE? wood	HL 213		18.5'	sail	3t	coble, fished lines, crew 3 5-2-1872, Thomas Pounder, H/pool
ESCAPE wood	HL 327		35' keel 38x14x5' oa	lug, fore & trisail & 4 oars	12t	keel boat, fished nets, crew 5, ex- Berwick 2-10-1882, Thomas Hogarth Jnr. H/pool 15-8-1890, Alexander Bruce, 15, Back High St, H/pool
ESPERANCE? wood	HL 96		18.5'	sail	3t	coble, fished lines, crew 3 2-10-1874, Thos. Hood, H/pool, sold to Whitby 1878
ESPERANZA wood	HL 51		29.5'	sail/oar	7t	coble, fished nets, crew 4 1-3-1869, Thomas Pounder, H/pool
ESSIE ORR wood ON 168509	HL 179	1942	46'x16'x5'	85hp	25t	built Portavogie 1942, John Orr (B 312) Portavogie 19-2-1968, H. & A. Noble, Peterlee 19-1-1973 Balgowan, Shearer & Cormack, Stonehaven r/n *Gellachad Milis* (A 206) ?, last known fishing lines from Holyhead
ETHAL - MAC wood	HL 50		24'x7'x2'		3t	fished lines, pots, crew 2 8-5-1954, W.C. Pearson,& J.B. Robinson, H /pool
ETHEL wood	HL 39		30'x6'x2'	sail/oar	3.6t	coble, fished nets, lines, crew 3 14-12-1894, Cambridge & Coulson, H/pool 25-1-1911, Richard Hunter Coulson, 10, Duke St, West H/pool 1918, scrapped
EUPHENMIA & HELEN wood	HL 34,		36.5'x14'x5'	sail	12t	keel boat, yawl rigged, fished nets, crew 5 (ex-238 BK) 8-10-1892, Robertson, Mumsen & Pickard, H/pool 1917, sold for use as sleeping place for salmon fishermen

NAME & MATERIAL	NO.	YEAR	LENGTH	POWER	WEIGHT	DETAILS
EUPHRATES wood	HL 212		21'	sail/oar	3t	coble, fished lines, nets, crew 3 31-8-1871, Robert Hodgson, H/pool
EVA wood	HL 64		18'x5'x2'		1.0t	fished lines, nets, pots 4-7-1952, James Hastings, 9, Raby St South, West H/pool 29-7-1954, Albert Pugh, 3, Moor Parade, H/pool 24-10-1956, Matty McClelland, 11, Baptist St, H/pool, scrapped 1957
EVE II steel	HL 185	1980	36'x13'x3'	89kw	7.6t	built H/pool, fished lines, nets, trawl 11-9-1980, R.E. Leck, Stockton Rd, H/pool
EXCALIBUR grp	HL 131	1988	10.3m	239kw	7.98t	built Cornwall 13-2-1990, H/pool
EXCELSIOR wood	HL 22		32'	sail/oar	12t	coble, fished nets, crew 4 1-3-1869, George Horsley, H/pool, scrapped 1884
EXPERIANCE wood	HL 96		18'	sail/oar	3t	coble, fished lines, crew 3 1-3-1869, William Coulson, H/pool, sold 1874
EZMERELDA wood	HL 136	1978	34'x11'x2'	54kw	4.3t	built Stockton, fished nets, lines. 4-9-1979, Richards & Allison, Billingham
EZRA wood	HL 249		18.5'	sail	3.5t	coble, fished nets, lines, crew 3 30-12-1874, Thornton Bulmer, H/pool 11-2-1882, Francis Bulmer, H/pool 14-3-1888, James Pounder, 11, Sussex St, H/pool
FAIR LADIES wood ON 359271	HL 74	1973	35'x9'x3'	54kw	6.1t	built Amble, coble, fished lines, nets, pots, crew 2 17-10-1974, Barnes, Stewart, & Newton, Peterlee 16-9-1981, D. Robinson, 2, South View, Hart Village, believed to be the last coble built on sailing coble lines
FAIRY COVE steel ON 162470	HL 10	1955	102'x22'x12'	2SA-6cyl Crossley	182t	built Henry Scarr, Hessle, crew 10, trawler 1-4-1955, Grahams, H/pool 28-6-1963, Udastream Ltd, H/pool 9-7-1966, James Wilson, Fleetwood, r/n *Georgina Wilson* 9-11-1970, Hubert Jones (Trawlers) Ltd, Milford Haven 6-1978, Peter Wright – paid £11,225 together with 2 other trawlers when Hubert Jones goes bust
FAITH wood	HL 123		18.5'	sail/oar	3t	coble, fished lines, crew 3 1-3-1869, Anthony Davidson, H/pool 19-7-1971, Joseph Rawson, H/pool
FAITH wood	HL 214		18.5'	sail/oar	3t	coble, fished lines, crew 3 7-3-1872, Charles Cambridge, H/pool
FAITH wood	HL 15		25'x6'x2'	sail/oar	3t	built Whitby, coble, fished pots, crew 2 15-5-1906, Amos Major, Duke St,. West H/pool 2-9-1909, sold to Sunderland
FAITHFULL wood	HL 26	1916	30'x11'x3'	sail & motor	5.6t	built Anstruther, lugger, fished nets, lines, crew 3 12-10-1928, Wm. C. Snowden, 4, Lumley Sq. H/pool 20-11-1935, took fire and sank, H/pool Bay
FAMOUS grp	HL 118	1981	9.2x3.5x1.4m	97kw	8.6t	built Penrhyn, inshore stern trawler 20-10-1986, Cedric Williams, Hart Village 12-6-2006, *Optik* (AH 716) Arbroath
FAMOUS wood	HL 5	1933	46'x14'x5'		14.5t	built Lossiemouth (ex- AH 93) fished creels ? J. Young & others, Lossiemouth (INS 302) 1953, Arbroath (AH 93) 27-3-1969, Thos. & Elizabeth Williams,12, Gladstone St, H/pool 1-1977, reg. closed
FANNY & ETHAL wood	HL 69	1889	22'x7'x2'	sail/oar	3.4t	built Hartlepool, coble, crew 2 17-7-1902, Frederick Mumsea,12, Cundall Rd, West H/pool, sold 1903

Cormoran

Cromlech

Cygnus

David Helen

Devotion

Dorothy

NAME & MATERIAL	NO.	YEAR	LENGTH	POWER	WEIGHT	DETAILS
FATHER & SONS wood	HL 190		20'	sail/oar	3t	coble, fished lines, crew 3 2-12-1869, David Borthwick, H/pool 9-9-1872, Mary Borthwick, H/pool
FATHER & TWO SONS wood	HL 189		19'	sail/oar	3t	coble, fished lines, crew 4 5-10-1869, John & Alexander Johnston, West H/pool
FAVOURITE wood ON 56245	HL 337		70'	sail	61t	ketch, fished trawl, crew 5 29-5-1883, H/pools Fishery Co. 2-1884, lost at sea,
FELICITY wood	HL 91		24'	sail/oar	6t	coble, fished nets, crew 4 1-3-1869, Thomas Davidson, H/pool, sold 1872
FIDELITY wood	HL 8	1925	15'x5'x2'	sail/oar	1.3t	built Hartlepool, lugger, fished pots, nets, crew 3 16-2-1925, John Richardson, Seaham, sold to Sunderland
FIONA FAY wood ON 187228	HL 113	1958	46'x15'x6'	95hp - 5LW Gardner	24t	built Nobles, Fraserburgh, fished seine net, trawl, crew 4 24-4-1958, Janet Fishing Co., Victoria Dock, H/pool 27-11-1966, driven ashore on North Sands and wrecked, crew safe
FIREFLY grp	HL 20	1986	5.08m	26kw	0.69t	built Poole 2-7-1992, H/pool
FISHER LASS wood	HL 45		18.5'	sail/oar	3t	coble, fished lines, crew 3 1-3-1869, John Shepherd, H/pool
FISHER LASS wood	HL121		27'	sail/oar	6t	coble, fished nets, crew 3 1-3-1869, Cuthbert Pounder, H/pool, sold to Seaham, 1869
FISHER LASS wood	HL 320		18.5'	sail	3t	coble, fished lines, crew 3 17-11-1881, John Davison, H/pool
FISHER LASSES wood	HL 4		30'x 8'x 3.5'	sail		coble, fished nets, crew 4 15-8-1893, Frank Burgon, West H/pool, sold to M/boro, 1905
FIVE BROTHERS wood	HL 41		29'x 5'x 2'	sail	2t	coble, fished nets, lines, crew 3 6-2-1895, Frank & Geo. Southern, H/pool, sold 1910
FIVE BROTHERS wood	HL 62	1900	30'x 6'x 2'	sail/oar	4t	built Hartlepool, coble, fished lines, crew 3, ex-*Lord Roberts* 8-9-1906, Robert Heron Corner,9, Dovecote Yard, H/pool 25-10-1910, Frank Sothern, Sandwell Chare, H/pool
FLO wood	HL 72		20'x 5'x 2'	sail & motor	1.1t	lugger, fished lines, nets, pots, crew 2 28-9-1938, Arthur Bell, 5, Raeburn St, West H/pool, scrapped 1940
FLORANCE N. wood	HL 9		21'x 5'x 2'	sail & motor	1.5t	lugger, fished lines, pots, crew 3 27-1-1930, C. Armatage, 8, Olive St, H/pool
FLY wood	HL 130		14'	sail/oar	0.5t	small boat, fished draw net, crew 2 3-3-1869, Mathew Lamb, Seaton Carew, sold 1880
FLY wood	HL 32		22'x 6'x 2'	sail/oar	1.6t	lugger, fished lines, pots, crew 3 14-11-1928, Richard Turner, The Beach, Blackhall Rocks, scrap 1931
FLYING SPRAY wood	HL 53		30'	sail/oar	10t	coble, fished nets, crew 4 1-3-1869, James Pounder, H/pool, sold to Whitby as pilot coble 1874
FLYING SPRAY wood	HL 54		18'	sail/oar	2.5t	coble, fished lines, crew 3 1-3-1869, James Pounder, H/pool sold to Whitby 1875
FOAM wood	HL 24		22'x7'x2'	sail & motor	2.5t	lugger, fished lines, trawl, crew 3 27-5-1940, Charles Ingram, 8, Rowell St, H/pool, wrecked Nov. 1942
FOLLOW ME wood	HL 349	1884	20'	sail/oar	3t	built Hartlepool, coble, fished lines, crew 3 2-4-1884, Joseph Snowdon, H/pool 22-9-1906, Joseph Snowdon, 28, Chapel St, H/pool
FOLLOW ME wood	HL 349	1884	27'x7'x3'	sail/oar	4.25t	coble, fished pots, crew 3 8-1-1914, George Horsley Leighton, 38, Lily St, H/pool

NAME & MATERIAL	NO.	YEAR	LENGTH	POWER	WEIGHT	DETAILS
FORESTER wood	HL 175		27'	sail/oar	4t	27-12-1916, sunk by trawler, raised, scrapped coble, fished nets, crew 4 3-6-1869, John Wray, H/pool 8-6-1872, James Webber & Thos. Sanson, H/pool 1875, sold to Whitby
FORT RYAN steel ON 162283	A 190	1932	121'x22'x12'	68hp steam	255t	built John Lewis, A/deen, yard No.126, launched 5-5-1932 fitted with Hughes echo sounder 1932, J. Lewis & Son, A/deen 1939–1944, Navy, Boom Defence Vessel (Z 156) 1944, North Eastern F. Co. A/deen 26-11-1957, Binns Trawlers, H/pool
FORTH wood	HL 342		24'	sail	4t	decked boat, fished trawl, crew 2 20-8-1883, Joseph Smith, H/pool, wrecked Nov. 1885
FORTUNATUS wood	HL 164	1930	38'x12'x4'		10.8t	built McDuff, fished lines, nets, ex-BK 157 29-12-1965, Frederick Peason, 154, King Oswy Drive, H/pool 22-5-1969, John Johnson, Filey, reg. trans. to Colchester10-1974
FOUR BROTHERS wood	HL 258		19'		3t	coble, fished nets, crew 3 24-1-1876, Ralph Coulson, H/pool, sold to Stockton 1876
FOUR WINDS wood	H 207	1966	9.1m	40kw	3.8t	built Whitby 22-4-1992, H/pool
FOX wood	HL 239		20'	sail	4t	cutter, fished trawl, crew 2 27-1874, Gilbert Allen, H/pool, wrecked Oct. 1875
FRANCES wood	GY 465	1911	11.43m	63kw	6.87t	built Bridlington 1981, R.D. Wraith Grimsby 1984, A.H. & D.M. Aitchison, Whitley Bay 4-1984, W. Hutchinson, Sunderland 1993, James Henry Staunch, H/pool
FREDRICK wood	HL 11	1900	18'x5'x2'	sail, lug, jib 2 oars	1.0t	open boat, fished lines, crew 3, new boat 29-1-1900, Fredrick Beard, 21, Town Wall, H/pool, wrecked 1906
FREDERICK wood	HL 16	1892	18'x5'x2'	sail/oar	1.6t	coble, fished lines, crew 2 26-9-1906, Frederick Beard, 21, Town Wall, H/pool, lost at sea 17-2-1911
FREEDOM wood ON 53275	HL 334		69'	sail	63t	ketch, fished trawl, crew 4, transferred from Hull 22-5-1883, H/pools Fishery Co. 28-7-1884, T.W. Spencer, & 3 others, sold to Scarboro' 1886
FRIARAGE steel ON 139836	HL 18	1930	115'x22'x13'	69hp steam	215t	built J. Lewis, A/deen, yard No.119, crew 10, speed 10k 7-7-1930, Friarage S.T. Co. H/pool, Skipper Matty Waugh 1939–1945, Navy, APV, Examination vessel, 1x6pdr (FY 904) 6-11-1957 scrapped Belgium
FRIARAGE wood ON 359275	HL 80	1973	33'x9'x3'	59kw	5.9t	built Whitby, coble fished nets, pots, crew 2 11-6-1974, Derek Harrison, 121, Northgate, H/pool 24-6-1986, Stephen & George Horsley, H/pool 1990, donated to H/pool Museum
FRIENDS wood	HL 78		23'	sail/oar	4t	coble, fished lines, crew 4 1-3-1869, Henry Burgon, H/pool
FRIENDS wood	HL 176		28'	sail/oar	8t	keel boat, fished nets, crew 3 5-6-1869, Thos. Markwell & Wm. Haywood, West H/pool 13-6-1870, Thos. Markwell & Thos. Coverdale, sold to Berwick 1871
FRIENDS wood	HL 222		18.5'	sail	1.5t	coble, fished trawl, lines, crew 2 9-9-1872, Simeon Reay, H/pool
FRIENDS wood	HL 223		36'	sail	10t	Herring boat, fished nets, crew 5, ex-Berwick 4-2-1873, James & Johnson Borthwick, H/pool 21-6-1875, Johnson Borthwick, re-reg. Berwick 1880
FRIENDS	HL 236		18'	sail	3t	coble, fished lines, crew 3

NAME & MATERIAL	NO.	YEAR	LENGTH	POWER	WEIGHT	DETAILS
wood						20-11-1873, John Snowden, H/pool
FRIENDSHIP	HL 35		18.5'	sail/oar	3t	coble, fished lines, nets, crew 3
wood						1-3-1869, Robert Yeal, H/pool sold 1871
FRIENDSHIP	HL 215		18.5'	sail/oar	3t	coble, fished lines, crew 3
wood						18-3-1872, Thomas Pounder, H/pool, sold 1873
FROSTY	HL 104	1974	7.4x2.5x1.3m		3.8t	built Rye
grp						16-11-1988, G.J. Laverick, Stockton
						21-12-1992, *Frosty* (PT 55), Port Talbot
FRUITION	HL 91	1933	46'x15'x5'		18.3t	built Banff, fished drift, seine net, crew 3, keel boat
wood						9-7-1975, Brian & Micheal Graves, & Ray Eastwood, H/pool
						22-6-1976, Colin Robinson & Albert Cope, H/pool, sold 1977
GAFFER	HL 34	1986	33'x11'x3'	89kw	9t	built H/pool, inshore stern trawler
ON 706158						10-12-1986 Ken Davis, St Andrews Grove, H/pool
wood						
GALILEE	HL 20	1880	30'x6'x2'	sail/oar	3.7t	built Hartlepool, coble, fished pots, crew 3
wood						22-2-1890, James Pounder, 1, Hunter St, H/pool
						8-11-1912, George Horsley Leighton, H/pool, scrapped 1913
GARIBALDI	HL 111		22'	sail/oar		coble, fished lines, crew 4
wood						1-3-1869, David Borthwick, West H/pool
						9-9-1872, Mary Borthwick, West H/pool
GARLAND	INS 228	1949	56'	Gardner	30t	built Wilson Noble, Fraserburgh, fished seine, trawl
wood						31-5-1956, J.R. Moore
						23-1-1967, G.S. Stewart
						7-12-1970, W.H. Grigg, H/pool (skipper Jocky Gresham)
GEM	HL 181		20'	sail/oar	3t	coble, fished nets, crew 2
wood						13-8-1869, Robert Pounder, H/pool, sold 1871
GENERAL HAVELOCK	HL 153		30'	sail/oar	8t	coble. fished nets, crew 4
wood						21-4-1869, George Grievson, H/pool
GENERAL HAVELOCK	HL 351		30'	sail	8t	coble, fished nets, crew 4
wood						9-6-1884, George Grievson, H/pool
GENESIS	HL 1065	1977	9.75m	65kw	6.4t	built Falmouth, inshore stern trawler
grp						1-1-1992, *Paulanda* (LI 271), Littlehampton
						26-2-1992, *Paulanda* (M 6), Milford Haven
						27-10-1992, *Paulanda* (FH 177) Falmouth
						28-7-1998, *Genisis* (HL 1065) H/pool
GEORGE D. IRVINE	HL 20	1911	115'x22'x12'	78hp steam	194t	built Hall Russell, A/deen, ketch rig, yard No.494
steel						engine 3cyl. by builder
ON 129360						1911 Richard Irvine & Son
						1914–1919 Navy, minesweeper, 1x6pdr AA (A.116)
						20-5-1920, Alpha S.T. Co., NER Building, High St, H/pool
						7-12-1923, Friarage S.T. Co. H/pool
						1940–1945, Navy, bdv, m/s, stores carrier, 1x6pdr AA gun (Z.249)
						Post-war mine clearance based at Cromarty
						(under Lt T.T. Laurenson)
						1956 scrapped Belgium
GEORGE DUNCAN	HL 68	1988	9.9x4.3x1.2m	64kw	10.8t	built Toms, Polruan, inshore stern trawler
wood						15-11-1988, Clive Marrison, Hetton-le-Hole
						3-12-2003, decommissioned
GERTRUDE CAPPLEMAN	HL 74	1914	115'x22'x12'	steam	195t	built Hall Russell, A/deen, ketch rig, trawler, launched 12-1914
steel				78hp		yard No.562, engine, 3cyl. by builder, crew 9
ON 137106						27-1-1915, J.B. Graham, H/pool
						1915–1920, Navy, BDV

NAME & MATERIAL	NO.	YEAR	LENGTH	POWER	WEIGHT	DETAILS
						9-10-1930, Fairy Cove S.T. Co., N.E. Rly Bldg, High St, H/pool
						29-9-1936, R. Irvine, N. Shields, r/n *Ben Screel* (SN 78)
						25-12-1942, lost off St Abbs Head
GIDEON wood	HL 13		22'	sail	4t	coble, fished lines, crew 3
						6-12-1888, E.F. Davison, 20, Chapel St, H/pool
GIDEON	HL 90	1888	29'	sail/oar	4t	built Hartlepool, lugger, fished pots, lines, crew 3
						30-4-1918, Samuel Thomas King, 100, Brougham St, H/pool & James Pearson, Prissick St, H/pool
						6-6-1923, James Pattison, Fish Quay, H/pool
						14-9-1937 M. B. Nyquist, Lansdown Rd, West H/pool, scrap 1938
GIRL ANNIE wood?	YH 700	1910				built Lowestoft? drifter
						?, A.R. Sutton?
GIRL EMMA grp	HL 1061	1991	6.43m	22kw	2.85t	built The Wirral
						4-3-1993 (CH 116), *Girl Emma*, Chester
						27-1-1997, H/pool
GIRL PAT wood	HL 13		19'x6'x2'	sail/oar	1.4t	lugger, fished lines, pots, crew 2
						7-3-1940, Thos. Forsyth, 46, Southgate St, H/pool
						20-8-1941, Geo. W. Routledge, 27, Northgate, H/pool
						19-5-1944, Charles William Simpson, H/pool, scrapped 1948
GLADSTONE wood	HL 50		18.5'	sail/oar	3t	coble, fished lines, crew 3
						1-3-1869, Shephard Pounder, H/pool
						14-6-1880, Johnathan Pounder, H/pool
GLADSTONE wood	HL 122		30'	sail/oar	10t	coble, fished nets, crew 4
						1-3-1869, College Pounder, H/pool
						3-6-1871, Thomas Pounder, H/pool
GLADYS wood	HL 52	1932	25'x7'x2'	sail & motor	2t	built Hartlepool, lugger, fished pots, lines, crew 3
						23-6-1932, Robert Ridley, 58, High St, H/pool
						1-7-1933, John Moore, 31, Alexandra St, West H/pool
						scrap 1939
GLEANER wood	HL 104		31'	sail/oar	10t	coble, fished nets, crew 4
						1-3-1869, Thomas Rowntree, H/pool, sold 1891
GLEANER wood ON 73171	HL 336		74'	sail	79t	ketch, fished trawl, crew 5, ex-*Glance* (H971)
						29-5-1883, H/pools Fishery Co.
						1883, to Hull, 1884, to Leith
GLORIA	HL 44		30'x6'x4'		4t	fished lines
						11-6-1946, S.M. Gowler, 8, Garston Grove, West H/pool
GOLDEN BELLS steel	BK 28	1973	33'	98kw	14.6t	built Whitby, inshore stern trawler
						Keith Williams, Hart Village
GOLDEN BOY wood	FR 54	1963	54'x17'x6'	240hp Volvo	23t	built Eyemouth Boatbuilding Co., fished trawl seine, keel boat
						1963, J. Aitchison, Eyemouth, as *Fortunatus* (LH 432)
						1990, R. Fraser Wood, Aberdeen, as *Arcwood* (FR 54)
						2000, W. Hodgson, H/pool as *Golden Boy*, scrapped 2003
GOLDEN HOPE wood	AH 85	1964				built Macduff Eng. Co. keel boat, fished trawl, seine
						1964, G. Watt & others Macduff (BF 325)
						1983, Halcyon F. Co. H/pool
GOLDEN RAY wood						keel boat, fished trawl
						? Frank Bergan, H/pool
GOOD HEALTH wood	HL 365		21'	sail	1.5t	coble, fished lines, crew 3
						28-6-1886, Frank Burgon, 2, Back Commercial St, Middleton
GOOD INTENT wood	HL 195		18.5'	sail/oar	3t	coble, fished lines, crew 3
						25-4-1870, Cuthbert Coulson, H/pool, sold 1890
GRACE wood	HL 7		29'x8'x3'	sail & motor	6.3t	lugger, fished lines, pots trawl, crew 3
						13-3-1925, Frank Coulson, 34, Dial House, Town Wall, H/pool
						1934, sold to M/boro

Dove

Dundarg

Dunelm

Early On

Eileen

Eileen

Eileen Wray

Eleazar

Elizabeth Isobel

Emblem

Embrace

Endeavour

NAME & MATERIAL	NO.	YEAR	LENGTH	POWER	WEIGHT	DETAILS
GRANIA wood	HL 2	1948	12x4.2x1.8m		14.7t	
						24-2-1984, R.A. Burliston, Sunderland
GRATITUDE wood	HL 183		20'	sail/oar	3t	coble, fished nets, trawl crew 2
						13-8-1869, Robinson Carter, H/pool
						5-9-1874, Arthur G. Millingate (?), H/pool
						5-8-1875, Robinson Pounder, H/pool
GREEN BOAT wood	HL 132		14'	sail/oar	0.5t	small boat, fished sweep net, crew 2
						3-3-1869, Thomas Burton, H/pool, sold 1873
GRENNA STAR wood	HL 112	1968	17.9m	191kw	46t	built Grenna Haven, Denmark fished seine, trawl
						1982, Grenna F. Co. Grimsby (GY 145)
						1-1-1989, *Grenna Star*, Fraserburgh (FR 60)
						4-1-1990, r/n *Rebecca Anne*
						2-11-2000, Bob Truman, r/n *Grenna Star* H/pool (HL 1069)
						28-2-2005, re-reg. (HL 112)
GUIDE wood ON 47811	HL 328		45'	sail	25t	smack, fished trawl, crew 4, ex- Grimsby
						31-10-1882, W. Wise & A. Fernie, H/pool
						9-6-1886, Wm. King, Lincoln Lane, Boston
GUIDE ME wood	HL 6	1914	17'x5'x2'	sail & motor	1.0t	lugger, fished lines, pots, crew 3
						6-3-1939, Ralf Cole, 'Holmside', The Front, Seaton Carew, scrap 1948
GUIDE ME III wood?	BK 247	1907		steam?		built Banff
						? J.T. Graham
GUIDE ON wood	HL 122	1926	28'x6'x2'		3.3t	built Amble, fished lines, nets, ex-*White Heather* (BH 80), Blyth
						6-11-1959, Stephen M, Gowler, Gaston Grove West H/pool
GUIDING STAR wood	HL 118		37'	sail/oar	12t	keel boat, fished nets, crew 5
						1-3-1869, David Burgon, H/pool,
						3-6-1874, Margaret & Peter Burgon, H/pool,
GUIDING STAR wood	HL 80		31'x9'x4'		5.4t	fished lines, pots, trawl, crew 2
						19-9-1951, Wm. G. Charlton, Sea View Tce, H/pool, sold 1952
GUIDING STAR wood	HL 130	1942	22'x7'x2'		1.9t	fished lines, pots, crew 2
						25-8-1961, Larry Turner, 12, Clifton St, H/pool
GYPSY	HL 175		27'x8'x3'		3.6t	fished lines, pots
						16-7-1970, Stan Weegram, 11, Ashby Grove, H/pool
						8-10-1971, Wm. Durkin, Horden
GYPSY B.	HL 175		27'x8'x3'		3.6t	fished lines, pots
						3-8-1972, Geo. W. Bolton, 3, Radcliffe Tce, H/pool
GYPSY GIRL grp	HL 1085	1980	5.97m	14.9kw	2.71t	inshore open boat
						8-4-2008, H/pool
GYPSY QUEEN steel	HL 117	1989	24'x8'x2'	59kw	9.1t	fished lines, pots
						20-9-1977, Alan Hann, Gray St, H/pool
						8-12-1980, T. Hann, Sandsend Cres., H/pool
						15-11-1988, Alan Hann, Gray St, H /pool
HA'BURN wood	BF 269	1951	37'		14.2t	built T. Summers, Fraserburgh, keel boat, fished trawl
						1954, J. Runcie, Cullen
						1980, Paul Watson, H/pool
						1982, sold to Aberdeen (A 269)
						1982, sank, raised, fished as (INS 310) then (BA 79)
						1990, sank when mine she had caught was detonated too close to vessel by disposal squad
HAHNEN KAMM wood	NN 48	1985	8.46m	56kw	7.1t	fished pots, nets
						? Staunch H/pool
HALCYON wood	KY 177				23t	fished trawl, seine net
						? Kenny Johnson, H/pool
						1969, D.G. Allen, St Monance

NAME & MATERIAL	NO.	YEAR	LENGTH	POWER	WEIGHT	DETAILS
HALCYON wood	HL 138	1944	26'x8'x3'		3t	fished lines, pots, crew 2 5-6-1962, Frederick Evens, 4, Eden St, West H/pool 30-7-1966, T. Whelpton, 39, Stokesly Rd, Seaton, Re-reg. HL 169 27-4-1970, Margaret Whelpton, 39, Stokesly Rd, Seaton Carew 6-4-1972, Leslie Dobson, 4, Barra Grove, H/pool 3-8-1972, Geo. W. Bolton, 3, Radcliffe Tce, H/pool 30-8-1972, Leo Judge, 8, Avondale Gdns, H/pool 13-6-1975, E. Tweddle & W.S. Nimmo, H/pool
HANNAH wood	HL 24	1892	29'x6'x2'oa 24.5' keel	sail & oar	4t	built Middleton, coble, fished nets, lines, crew 3 8-12-1890, Thos. Wm. & Mary Coulson, Wells Yard, H/pool 31-1-1911, Mary Ann Coulson, 4, Wells Yard, H/pool 19-4-1911, Frank Coulson, Sandiside, H/pool, sold 1915
HANNAH wood	HL 43		21'x6'x2'	sail & motor	1.5t	built Middlesbrough, lugger, fished pots, lines, crew 3 7-3-1933, F. Southeran, 5, Croft Tce, H/pool, destroyed 1938
HANS TAUSON wood	SN 84	1918		132hp	22t	built Frederickhaven, Denmark 1969, Lawrence Olsen, N. Shields ?, H/pool
HAPPY DAYS wood ON 136575	LT 185	1914	88'x19'x10'	20hp steam	101t	built Colby, Lowestoft, yard No.4, drifter engine 2cyl. by Elliot & Garrard, Beccles 1914, L.R. Tripp, Lowestoft 1914–1919, Navy 1919, Stranton Drifters (R.H. Davison), H/pool 1926, J.C. Haywood, & H.E. Smith 1936 Vigilant F. Co. Lowestoft, r/n *Dorenta* 1939–1945, Navy m/s, scrapped 1948
HARRIET wood	HL 19		31'	sail/oar	8t	coble, fished nets, crew 4, skipper George Corner 1-3-1869, Elizabeth Corner, H/pool, sold to M/boro, 1876
HART wood	HL 317		20'	sail	3t	coble, fished nets, crew 3 8-6-1881, William Davison, H/pool
HARVEST HOME wood	HL 248		18.5'	sail	3t	coble, fished nets, crew 3 6-9-1876 Robert Davison H/pool (owner)?, drowned off Whitby? 30-5-1884, Thomas Pounder, H/pool 12-1-1877, Ann Davison, H/pool 13-2-1882, Robert Cambridge, H/pool
HARVEST HOME wood	HL 345		44'	sail	10t	keel boat, fished nets, crew 5, ex-North Shields 4-10-1883, George Horsley, H/pool
HARVEST MOON grp	HL 704	1971	9.98m	76kw	7.25t	built Eyemouth Boatyard 1-1-1989, *Georgina K.*, Leith (LH 49) 27-6-1990, *Brighter Dawn*, Kirkcaldy (KY 117) 20-1-1999, *Harvest Moon*, H/pool
HARVEST REAPER steel	HL 93	1988	9.9x4.2x1.5m		10.5t	built Sunderland, inshore stern trawler 4-11-1988, Peter Coull, Billingham skipper/owner
HARVESTER wood	HL 55	1918	25'x6'x2'	sail & motor	1.6t	built Amble, coble, fished, lines, pots, crew 2 25-9-1953, J.G. Stewart & S. Ainsley, H/pool 23-7-1954, J.G. Stewart, 11, Vincent St, H/pool 27-7-1955, Albert Goodchild, 18, Clifton St, H/pool 3-7-1956, F.B. Cuthbertson, 16, Francis St, H/pool 31-7-1956, C.A. Clayton, 10, Jersey St West H/pool
HAZEL wood	HL 37	1941	22'x6'x2'		1.7t	fished lines, pots 25-5-1949, John Monahan, 8, Skelton St, H/pool
HEADWIND grp	HL 1071	2001	6.71m	22kw	1.83t	built Scotland 11-12-2001, H/pool

NAME & MATERIAL	NO.	YEAR	LENGTH	POWER	WEIGHT	DETAILS
HEARTS CONTENT wood	HL 38		40'x13'x4'		11t	fished seine net, crew 3 6-11-1945, Ray Bros. Fishing Co.,33, Church St, West H/pool 1947, wrecked
HEATHER BELLE wood	LK 263	1948	46.5'		23t	built Noble Fraserbrugh, keel boat, fished trawl, seine 1948, D. McPherson, Gairloch, as *Mhaighdean Mhara* (UL 276) ? *Maggie McLean* (OB 30) (BK 213) 1968, L.A. Simpson, Whalsay, as *Heather Belle* (LK 263) 1977, Lola F. Co. & Colin Robinson, H/pool
HEATHER 1	HL 24	1966	17'x5'x2'		1.0t	built Whitby, fished lines, crew 2 30-9-1970, J.A. Pearce, Stockton
HELLEN wood	HL 353		23'	sail	4t	cutter, fished trawl, crew 2 25-7-1884, Francis Ward, H/pool 23-7-1889, John H. Impey, Doctors Passage, H/pool 7-1889, sold to Sunderland
HENDERSONS wood	HL 277		38'	sail	10t	coble-mule, fished nets, crew 6 27-12-1876, Robert Shieldon & Joseph Foster, H/pool 29-1-1879, Robert Shieldon, H/pool
HEORTNESS steel ON 124312,	HL 57	1911	112'x22'x12'	75hp steam	198t	built Hall Russell, A /deen, ketch rig, yard No.490 launched 27-4-1911, engine 3cyl., by builder, 15-5-1911, Hartness S.F. Co. Dock St, H/pool 1914–1919, m/s, 1x6pdr, AA (A 63) 23-8-1937, scrapped Stockton
HERO wood	HL 116		20'	sail/oar	4t	coble, fished nets, crew 2 1-3-1869, Robert Boagey, H/pool
HERO wood	HL 173		19.25'	sail/oar	5t	coble, fished trawl, crew 2 31-5-1869, Joseph Waller, H/pool, sold 1870
HERRING GIRL wood	HL 197		18.25'	sail/oar	3t	coble, fished lines, crew 3 2-7-1870, Pounder Davison, H/pool
HEUGH steel ON 137104	HL 64	1914	115'x22'x14'	steam 78hp	200t	built Alex. Hall, A/deen, ketch rig, yard No.507, crew 9 23-12-1914, Heugh S.T. Co. H/pool 1915–1919. Navy, m/s, 1x6pdr, 1x6pdr AA (A 1480) 27-1-1940, Walker S.T. Co. A/deen 1943, A. Bruce, A/deen (A180) 1944, G. Robb & Son, A/deen, r/n *Viking Honour*, scrap 1960 Received salvage award of £650 for the towing of steamer *Mons* for 53 hours
HIGHLAND LASSIE wood	HL 89		18'	sail/oar	3t	coble, fished lines, crew 3 1-3-1869, William Davidson, H/pool
HILDA wood	HL 28		22'x6'x2'	sail/oar	2.7t	built Hartlepool, coble, fished lines, nets, crew 3 25-11-1921, Richard Pounder, 14, Sussex St, H/pool sold 1934
HILDA wood	HL 27	1924	14'x5'x2'	sail/oar	1.0t	built Hartlepool, lugger, fished pots, lines, crew 2 5-6-1928, Eden Pounder, 88, Henry St, H/pool 28-10-1931, Phillip Peek, 3, Todds Sq., H/pool 1931, r/n *Dorileen*, scrapped, 1947
HILDA	HL 1		20'x6'x2'		1.0t	fished lines, pots, crew 2 27-9-1947, Albert Eden Parker, Winterbottom Ave, H/pool
HILDA ANN wood	HL 60		17'x6'x2'		1.0t	fished lines, pots, crew 2 22-9-1947, R.S. Leighton, 15, Lilly St, H/pool 14-7-1948, Kemp & McKnight, H/pool
HIRAM wood	HL 47		18.5'	sail/oar	3t	coble, fished lines, nets, crew 3 1-3-1869, Thomas Pounder, H/pool
HOPE wood	HL 188		20'	sail/oar	3t	coble, fished lines, crew 3 25-9-1869, Robert Snowden, H/pool sold 1874
HOPE wood	HL 247		19'	sail	3t	coble, fished lines, crew 2 20-8-1874, Wm. Spence, H/pool, sold to Middlesborough 1875

NAME & MATERIAL	NO.	YEAR	LENGTH	POWER	WEIGHT	DETAILS
HOW ABOUT IT grp	HL 1081	2007	5.9m	11kw	1.7t	2-3-2007, H/pool
HUSTLER grp	HL 3	1950	8.4m	67kw	1.03t	built Sweden 10-10-1990, H/pool
HYPATIA iron ON 101960	HL 10	1893	100'x20'x10'	40hp steam	143t	built Craggs, Stockton, ketch rig, yard No.96, launched 5-12-1892 engine 3cyl. by Westgarth, English & Co., M/boro 1893, Newbon & Brocklebank, Milford Haven 1896, Rushworth S.F. Co., Grimsby (GY 20) 1899, Rushworth S.F. Co., H/pool 26-7-1899, Richard Thompson 134, Frederick St, H/pool 5-1-1905, sank 6m E of Lambay Islands, Co. Dublin
IANTHE ? wood	HL 17		27'x6'x2'	sail/oar	3.6t	built Hartlepool, coble fished pots, lines, nets, crew 3 24-3-1914, George Horsley, 19, Clayton St, H/pool 26-6-1916, Nelson, Seahouses,
IMELDA wood	HL 76		22'x6'x2'	sail & motor	2.5t	coble, fished lines, pots, crew 4 8-8-1939, Wm. Blair, Wynyard Rd, Wolviston, boat lost Dec. 1947
IMMANUEL wood	HL 28		31'	sail/oar	12t	coble, fished nets, crew 4 1-3-1869, Robert Hodgson, H/pool 26-5-1873, Jane Hodgson, H/pool
IMPETUOUS wood	HL 87		30'	sail/oar	10.5t	coble, fished nets, crew 4 1-3-1869, James Pounder, H/pool, Lost 16-6-1869
INCENTIVE grp	WY 373	1998	9.84m	75kw	12t	inshore stern trawler, works from marina ? H/pool
INDIA DELTA	HL 122	1972	28'x7'x3'		2.9t	built Whitby, fished pots, lines, crew 2 29-3-1978, John Roberts, Havelock St, West H/pool
INDUSTRY wood	HL 155		30'	sail/oar	9t	coble, fished nets, crew 4 24-4-1869, Richard Hunter, H/pool 13-10-1881, Davidson, H/pool 5-4-1882, Wm. Davison, H/pool
INDUSTRY wood	HL17	1909	24'x9'x4'	sail & motor	6t	built Arbroath, lugger, fished nets, lines, crew 2 23-6-1927, Richard Pounder,14, Sussex St, H/pool 24-12-1940, sold to Stockton for Fire Service use
INO ? wood	HL 178		26'	sail/oar	9t	coble, fished nets, crew 4 30-6-1869, Nicholas Holman, H/pool, scrapped 1871
INTREPID grp	HL 1079	2006	9.9m	118kw	10.5t	inshore stern trawler (Cygnus GM 33) 2-10-2006, H/pool
IONA wood	HL 344		41'	sail	11t	decked boat, fished nets, crew 5 17-9-1883, Henry Hall, H/pool
IONA wood	HL 362		42' keel 44'x15'x5'oa	sail	10t	lugger, fished nets, crew 5 28-4-1885, Wm. Clithero, H/pool, 2-8-1892, Walker Cook, 8 Wood St, H/pool 1895, sold to Lowestoft
IONA wood	HL 41		24'x7'x3'		3.5t	built USA, fished lines, pots 28-4-1949, R. Greenhow, Oxford Rd, West H/pool 11-9-1951, J.W. Pearson, Shakespeare Ave, West H/pool 10-11-1952, A.E. Moore, 1, Regent St, H/pool, wrecked 1953
IRENE wood	HL 1		26'x5'x2'	sail & motor	2t	lugger, fished lines, pots, crew 3 8-12-1932, S. Lewis, 2, Henry St, H/pool, sank 1937
IRENE wood	HL 9	1970	6.6m	7kw	1.7t	built Whitby 17-8-1990, H/pool
IRENE WRAY steel	HL 73	1914	117'x22'x14'	78hp steam	216t	built Smiths Dock, S. Bank, ketch rig, yard No.615 engine 3cyl., by builder, launched 17-11-1914

Endeavour

Endeavour II

Endurance

Enterprise

Equity

Essie Orr

NAME & MATERIAL	NO.	YEAR	LENGTH	POWER	WEIGHT	DETAILS
ON 137103						1914, W. Wray 6, McDonald Place, H/pool
						1915–1919, Navy, m/s, 1x6pdr AA (A1456)
						1917–1918, based Lowestoft (Lt J.W. Powell)
						29-10-1919, Harris, Chapman & Colbrook, Grimsby
						1922, Regent S.F. Co, Grimsby
						1926, Harris & Rosenberg, Grimsby
						1926, sold to Holland r/n *Maria R. Ommering*
						1940–1945, Navy, m/s (FY 1785) chartered from Holland
						1951, J.C. Llewellin, Milford Haven r/n *Nolton*, scrapped 1956
IRIS wood	HL 42		18'x5'x2'	sail/oar	1.0t	built Hartlepool, coble, fished lines, nets, crew 3
						2-12-1935, Geo. Westhorpe, Harbour of Refuge Hotel, H/pool
						9-1-1937, sold
IRIS wood	HL 47		18'x5'x2'	sail/oar	1.0t	built Hartlepool, fished lines, pots, crew 2
						11-6-1942, R.J. Smith, Southburn Tce, West H/pool, sold 1948
ISABELL wood	HL 146		18.5'	sail/oar	3t	coble, fished lines, crew 3
						22-3-1869, George Horsley, H/pool, sold 1873
ISABELLA wood	HL 103		18.5	sail/oar	3t	coble, fished lines, crew 3
						1-3-1869, Thomas Rowntree, H/pool, sold 1878
ISABELLA wood	HL 326		19'	sail	3t	coble, fished nets, lines, crew 3
						31-8-1882, Henry Denton, H/pool
ISABELLA wood	HL 22	1913	38'x13'x5'	sail & motor	16.5t	fished lines, crew 5
						2-1-1945, Grigg, Sutton & Spink, H/pool
						14-4-1947, Alexander Devine, H/pool, sold to Fraserburgh
ISABELLA & ANN wood	HL 140		32'	sail/oar	11t	coble, fished nets, crew 4
						3-3-1869, John Trentholm, H/pool
ISABELLA CAMBRIDGE wood	HL 171		31'	sail/oar	10.5t	coble, fished nets, crew 4
						31-5-1869, James Cambridge, H/pool
						20-5-1870, sold to foreigners
ISABELLA CAMBRIDGE wood	HL 196		31'	sail/oar	10.5t	coble, fished nets, crew 4
						20-5-1870, James Cambridge, H/pool
						29-5-1876, Maurice Harper, H/pool
						6-9-1876, Robert Boagey, H/pool, sold to Staithes 3-6-1879
ISABELLA FOWLIE steel ON 129371	HL 19	1911	115'x22'x12'	78hp steam	196t	built Hall Russell, A/deen, ketch rig, yard No.501, launched 8-11-1911
						engine by builder, crew 9
						1911, William F. Dawson, 130½, Union St, A/deen (A 418)
						1915–1919, Navy, m/s, 1x12pdr, 1x6pdr (A 473)
						16-2-1920, Hartness S.T. Co.
						10-7-1941, lost by aircraft fire, 7m ENE Longstone
						3 crew lost
ISABELLA wood	HL 103		18.5'	sail	3t	coble, fished lines, crew 3
						1-7-1878, Thomas Pounder, H/pool
ISABELLE wood	HL 41		18.5'	sail/oar	3t	coble, fished lines, crew 3
						1-3-1869, Robert Moor, H/pool, sold to Whitby 1876
ISABELLE grp	FH 398					small inshore boat
						? H/pool
ISIS steel	HL 8	1984	9.6m	89kw	5.11t	built H/pool
						1989, Ruth Leslie
						27-2-1992, Isis
IT'LL DIUS steel	HL 78		9.1x3.4x1.4m		7t	built Co. Durham
						5-8-1988, J.W. Hays, & W. Huntington, Horden
IVY wood	HL 59		26'x7'x3'	sail/oar	3t	lugger, fished trawl, lines, crew 3
						8-7-1933, John Green 19, Back St Hilda St, H/pool
						4-5-1934, E.N. Wilkinson 9, Powlett Rd, West H/pool
						1934 r/n *Nancy*

NAME & MATERIAL	NO.	YEAR	LENGTH	POWER	WEIGHT	DETAILS
J. J. grp	HL 11	1990	32'	86.5kw	15.5t	built Cygnus, Falmouth, fished nets, trawl, salmon 8-11-1990, Keith Fletcher, H/pool 15-9-1997, *Provider* (SH 276), Scarboro'
J. J. grp	HL 11	1998	32'	180-8LXB Gardner	15.5t	built Falmouth, inshore stern trawler (Cygnus 32) 13-7-1998, Keith Fletcher, H/pool
JACKIE D. wood	HL 1058	1973	13.6m	159kw	25.9t	27-10-1994, *Midnight Moon* (HL 1058) 3-9-1996, *Jackie D.* (HL 1058) 23-9-1996, *Jackie D.* (LH 519) Leith
JAMES HARAH wood	HL 148		19'	sail/oar	3t	coble, fished lines, crew 3 30-3-1869, George Moor, H/pool, lost 1870
JAMES & ROBERT wood	HL 53	1882	46'x15'x5'	sail/oar	32t	built Eyemouth, coble, fished nets, lines, crew 6 7-9-1910, Frank Coulson, 1, Sandside, H/pool, sold 1912
JAMES B. GRAHAM steel ON124314	HL 9	1914	115'x22'x12'	78hp steam	198t	built Hall Russell, A/deen, ketch rig, launched 24-2-1914 engine by builder, trawler, yard No.547 1914, Hartness S.F. Co. H/pool 1914–1919, Navy, m/s, 1x3pdr (A 64) 15-1-1922, wrecked Holy Island
JAMES PETER DENNIS grp	HL 1052	1988	6.1m	26kw	2.72t	built Torpoint 13-11-1991, H/pool
JANE wood	HL 10		18.5'	sail/oar	3t	coble, fished lines, crew 3 1-3-1869, Mark Davidson, H/pool, wrecked 1874
JANE wood	HL 11		19'	sail/oar	3.t	coble, fished lines, crew 3 1-3-1869, Cuthbert Pounder, H/pool, sold 1872
JANE wood	HL 135		18.5'	sail/oar	3t	coble, fished lines, crew 3 3-3-1869, Joseph Hodgson, H/pool, sold 1872
JANE wood	HL 261		37'	sail	12t	keel boat, fished nets, crew 6 2-2-1876, Thomas Davison, H/pool
JANE wood ON 51235	HL 341		69'	sail	60t	ketch, fished trawl, crew 5 19-6-1883, H/pools Fishing Co. 1884, sold to Grimsby (GY 943)
JANE wood	HL 84		26'x6'x2'		2.2t	fished lines, pots, crew 2 (ex-MH 98) 21-4-1942, Richard Pounder, 7, Rowell St, H/pool, 1942 scrapped
JANE wood	HL 104		24'x8'x2'		3.3t	fished lines, crew 2 11-8-1951, Herbert Martin, Pine Grove, West H/pool
JANE & HARRIET wood	HL 207		20'		3.5t	coble, fished nets, crew 2 27-6-1871, George Davison, H/pool,
JANE & CHRISTINA wood	HL 17		44'	sail	12t	lugger, fished nets, crew 6 4-11-1889, J.C. Graham, 9, Union St, H/pool & James Holtman
JANE ANN wood	HL 12		18.5'	sail/oar	3t	coble, fished lines, crew 3 1-3-1869, Cuthbert Pounder, H/pool, wrecked 1878
JANE ANN wood	HL 29		30'x6'x2.5'	sail – lug & jib	3t	coble, fished lines, nets, crew 3 22-4-1892, Thos. Coulson, 19, Sussex St, H/pool, sold to Whitby 1910
JANE ANN wood	HL 2	1904	22'x5'x2'	sail/oar	2.2t	canoe, fished lines, crew 3 10-3-1924, John Horsley, 21, Bedford St, H/pool, sold Sept. 1924
JANE LOUISA wood	HL 134		30'	sail/oar	10t	coble, fished nets, crew 4 3-3-1869, George Loughborough, H/pool, sold to Whitby 1887
JANE ANN WORTHY wood	HL 99		18'	sail/oar	3t	coble, fished lines, crew 3 1-3-1869, Thomas Pounder, H/pool, broken up 1873
JANET	HL 26		16'x5'x2'	sail/motor	1t	fished lines, pots

NAME & MATERIAL	NO.	YEAR	LENGTH	POWER	WEIGHT	DETAILS
wood						18-9-1947, Francis Osbourne,1, Dock Gate Cottage, West H/pool
						21-11-1949, G.S. Havelock, Blackhall Coll.
						30-9-1952, W. Conners, Trimdon Station
JANET wood	HL 6	1918	51'x14'x5'		17.3t	built Denmark, motor ketch, fished seine, trawl, crew 4
						15-3-1955, E.W. Laycock, Sir Colin Campbell Inn, Durham St H/pool
						22-8-1955, Janet F. Co, H/pool
						29-6-1959, W.J. Baxter, S/land, reg. trans. to S/land 1959
JANET JENSON wood ON 379530	GY 421	1942	18.68m	195hp Cummins		built W.R. Byberg, Denmark, fished trawl, seine (ex-*Tony Neilson*)
						1979, Joy F. Co. & Togo F. Co., Grimsby
						1982, Togo & Delga F. Co.s, Grimsby
						1983, Togo & Sleight's F. Co.s, Grimsby
						1985, Hartlepool F. Co. Scarboro' St, H/pool
JANICE wood	HL 173	1966	29'x8'x3'		3.7t	built Whitby, fished lines, pots, trawl, crew 2
						28-7-1967, Noel Picknett, 66, Marine Dr., H/pool, to Scar'boro, 1970
JEANIE STEWART steel ON 139287	HL 82	1916	115'x22'x12'	steam	210t	built Hall Russell, A/deen, ketch rig, yard No.584, launched 18-5-1916
						5-6-1916, Robert & Mary Stewart, 6, York Place, H/pool
						1916–1919, Navy, fitted with Listening Hydrophones
						6-9-1919, Alliance S.T. Co., Scarboro
						6-3-1920, R.J. Ball Jnr, N. Shields (SN 18)
						1923, R. Irvine, N. Shields
						24-12-1938, presumed lost, mate, William Hopkins, from H/pool
JANORAS steel ON 397715	HL 1	1984	38'x16'x6'	185hp Volvo	31t	built Birkenhead/Fleetwood, inshore stern trawler, based H/pool
						5-7-1984, Joe. Gilmore, Seaham
						3-2-1986, M.A. Brook, Scar'boro
						2008, crabbing from Bridlington
JEAN wood	HL 305		40'	sail	12t	keel boat, fished nets. lines, crew 5
						16-9-1879 Colling, French & Hall, H/pool
JEAN wood	HL 28		24'x6'x2'		2.3t	fished lines, crew 2, ex-*Ethal*
						12-9-1947, Joseph William Davison, 7, South St, H/pool
						22-2-1950, Davison & Potts, H/pool
						13-1-1955, Frank Golightly, 5, Belk St, H/pool,1957, sold to M/boro
JEAN wood	HL 157		20'x7'x2'		1.2t	fished lines, pots, crew 2
						26-2-1970, Wm. Mathwin,28, Bruce Cres., H/pool
JEAN HORSLEY wood ON 131887	HL 51	1918	41'x13'x4'	sail & motor	13.7t	built Cockenzie, fished lines, nets, trawl, crew 4, ex-Kirkcaldy
						2-5-1946, Geo. Horsley Snr, 18, Penrith St, H/pool & Geo Horsley Jnr, 7, Coverdale St, H/pool
						10-11-1952, Edward Adams, 38, Wordsworth St, West H/pool
						17-2-1953, Adams & Robson, West H/pool
						1958, sold to Whitburn,
JEANETTE wood	HL 103		27'x8'x3'		3t	fished lines, pots, crew 2
						27-7-1954, Samuel Ainsley, 55, West View Rd, H/pool
JEM wood	HL 38		17'x5'x2'	sail & motor	1.0t	coble, fished lines, pots, crew 3
						28-10-1935, Jack Harrison, 17, Wells Yard, H/pool
						15-9-1937, R. Stevenson,46, Commercial St, Middleton, sold 1938
JENNY wood	HL 112		16'x6'x2'		1.3t	fished lines, pots, crew 2
						12-4-1948, Geo. Campion, 37, Priest St, West H /pool
						29-10-1949, Herbert Martin, 20, Duke St, West H/pool
JENNY 111 wood	HL 33		25'x7'x3'		2.8t	fished lines, pots, crew 3
						31-7-1956, F.B. Cuthbertson,16, Francis St, H/pool

NAME & MATERIAL	NO.	YEAR	LENGTH	POWER	WEIGHT	DETAILS
JESSIE wood	HL 259		16'	sail	1.0t	open boat, fished lines, crew 2 27-1-1876, John Lithgo, H/pool
JESSIE wood	HL 70		21'x6'x2'	sail & motor	1.5t	lugger, fished lines, pots, crew 2 31-5-1937 Stephen Measor, 36, Grace St, West H/pool 28-2-1938, Richard Gowler, 24, Crossley St, West H/pool, sold 1942
JESSIE ALICE	HL 81	1989	9.9m	111kw	8t	built H/pool 1-1-1989, *Morning Star* 12-7-1994, *Jessie Alice*, sold to Harwich?
JESSIE EVANS	HL 96		18'x5'x2'	sail & motor	1.0t	fished lines, pots, crew 2 24-12-1947, Edward Francis Sutheran, 4, Town Wall, H/pool 9-5-1958, A.E. Errington, M/boro. 1959, boat wrecked
JOANNE wood	HL 17	1970	31'x9'x4'	67kw	5.6t	built Whitby, fished trawl, lines, pots 1-6-1971, Alan Vale, 16, Tempest Rd, H/pool
JOHN wood	HL 3		18.5'	sail/oar	3t	coble, fished lines, crew 3 1-3-1869, Richard Booth, H/pool sold 1882
JOHNEEN wood	PZ 4	1968	7.62m	37kw	4.07t	built Looe 1-1-1989, based Penzance 26-1-1999, H/pool
JOHNS wood	HL 340		35'	sail	14t	decked boat, fished nets, crew 6 18-6-1883, James Burgon, H/pool 6-1883, transferred to Berwick
JOHN & SARAH wood	HL 154		30'	sail/oar	7t	coble, fished nets, crew 4 21-4-1869, George Grievson, H/pool
JOHN & SARAH wood	HL 26	1891	29'x6'x2'	sail/oar	4.2t	built Hartlepool, coble, fished lines, crew 3 19-8-1891, Thos. Snowden, 2, Bedford St, H/pool 8-9-1906, John Snowdon, 2, York Place, H/pool
JOHN BULL wood	HL 78	1915	46'x13'x5'	sail & motor	20t	built Flamborough, lugger, fished lines, drift, crew 4 17-11-1915, Robert Hunter Davidson, H/pool 14-8-1917, sold to Scarboro
JOHN H. VINCENT	HL 201	1938	12.8x3x1.4m		8.9t	built Goole 28-5-1982, B. Mills, Leeds
JOHN & EILEEN WEBSTER	HL 12		24'	sail	3t	boat, fished lines, crew 3 10-9-1888, James Webster, 10, Bedford St, H/pool
JOHN & SARAH wood	HL 144		30'	sail/oar	7t	coble, fished nets, crew 4 19-3-1869, Robinson Pounder, H/pool 13-6-1872, Johnathan Cambridge, H/pool 26-7-1872, Robinson Pounder, sold to Seaham 1873
JOHN O'HEUGH steel ON187224	HL 48	1957	102'x22'x9'	Crossley Diesel	182t	built Henry Scarr, Hessle, trawler 3-6-1957, Friarage S.T. Co. H/pool 11-7-1963, Pegasus T. Co. Lowestoft, as *Boston Trident* (LT reg) 1972, Carbiside Safety Ships, A/deen, 1979, Scrap Blyth
JOHN PAUL wood	HL 4	1953	24'x8'x2'		2t	built Seahouses, fished pots, crew 2 23-6-1970, John Watson, Blackhall Rocks, 26-8-1971, Bertie Cox, 5, Howlbeck Lane, H/pool
JOHN ROBERT wood	HL 1	1884	28'x6'x2'	sail/oar	3.4t	built Hartlepool, lugger, fished lines, crew 2 31-1-1919, J.R. Nicholson, 4, Northgate, H/pool, scrapped 1921
JOHN THE BAPTIST wood	HL 56		46'x12'x6'	sail & motor	24t	built Filey, fished nets, lines, pots, crew 4 30-12-1910, Wm. Frederick Croft, 39, Brougham St, H/pool 5-8-1911, sold to Whitby
JOHN WILLIAM	HL 107		23'	sail &	3t	coble, fished lines, nets, crew 4

Fairy Cove

Fiona Fay

Fort Ryan

Friarage

Friarage

Garland

Genesis

George D. Irvine

Gertrude Cappleman

Golden Bells

Golden Boy

Golden Hope

NAME & MATERIAL	NO.	YEAR	LENGTH	POWER	WEIGHT	DETAILS
wood				4-oars		1-3-1869, Alexander Johnson, West H/pool
						22-12-1883, John Johnson, H/pool
JOHN WILLIAM wood	HL 125		34'	sail/oar	10t	coble, fished nets, crew 4
						1-3-1869, Wm. Harper & John Trentholm, H/pool
						8-4-1871, Wm. Harper, H/pool, sold to Whitby 20-12-1884
JOHN T. GRAHAM steel ON 124313	HL 69	1912	122'x22'x12'	steam 76hp	198t	built Hall Russell, A/deen, ketch rig, trawler, yard No.511, launched 13-4-1912, engine 3cyl. by builder, crew 9
						29-4-1912, J. Graham, H/pool
						1914–1919, Navy, m/s, 1x6pdr AA (with time attatched to American m/s detatchment under Rear Admiral Strauss USN)
						9-10-1930, Fairy Cove S. Co., NER Bldg, High St, H/pool
						1937, scrapped
JOLADA ? wood	HL 72		18.5'	sail/oar	3t	coble, fished lines, crew 3
						1-3-1869, George Horsley, H/pool, sold 1873
JOLLY ROGER wood	HL 35		18'x5'x2'		1.6t	fished lines, pots, crew 2
						21-9-1955, Rodgerson, West H/pool
						22-7-1960, Links & Grangefield, West H/pool
						18-9-1964, J. Kavanagh, 78, Raby Gdns, West H/pool
						20-10-1966, D.W. Wreford, Seaton Carew
						28-7-1967, C.W. Maddison, Small Crafts Club, Middleton
						14-8-1972, G.W. Balderson, H/pool
JOSEPH & FANNY wood ON 68719	HL 339	1874	71'	sail	69t	ketch, fished trawl, crew 5
						11-6-1883, H/pools Fishery Co.
						1884, sold
JUBILEE wood	HL 3		24'	sail	3.5t	cutter, fished drift net, crew 2
						24-8-1887, J.S. Ballantyre, Back Tweddle St, H/pool, scrap 1889
JUDEANN steel	GY 26	1988	11.3m	134kw	21.7t	inshore stern trawler
						1988, P. & M. Trawlers, Cleethorpes
						? A. Hodgson, Whitby St H/pool
JUELAN grp	HL 238	1991	9.95m	112kw	16.3t	inshore stern trawler, works from Marina
						30-10-1991, H/pool
JULANTE wood ON 378886	HL 157	1978	34'x15'x6'	150hp.6LX Gardner	16t	built J.J. Harrison, Amble, fished trawl, nets, crew 2
						30-5-1978, G.E. & J.W. Price, Redcar (based H/pool)
						3-9-1981, D.P. Chapman, Padstow, reg. trans. to Padstow
						12-11-1982, Waterloo Marine, High Wycombe
						8-2-1988, P. & L.D. Letchin, Mevagissey
						23-2-1996, (BH 201) Blyth
						12-1-2007, (WD 242) Wexford
JULIE M.	HL 121		19'x6'x2'		1.4t	fished lines, pots, crew 2
						27-7-1977, Wilkinson & Harrison, Hutton Henry
						25-10-1978, J. Humphery, Dawdon
						18-12-1980, David Smith, York Place, H/pool
JUNE wood	HL 75	1937	20'x6'x3'	sail & motor	1.7t	built Hartlepool, coble, fished lines, crew 3
						8-10-1938, Herbert Thomas Carrick, Yew Tree, Snape, Bedale
						12-9-1947, Geo. Alfred Gilbraith, 39, The Front, Seaton Carew
JUNO wood	HL 29		28'	sail	9t	coble, fished nets, crew 4
						1-3-1869, Robert Hodgson, H/pool
JUST ABOUT grp	HL 1055	1989	9.8m	95kw	7.16t	built H/pool
						19-3-1992, H/pool
						28-2-2006, (G 567), Galway
JUST WILLIAM steel	HL 51	1985	8.7x2.8x1m		5t	built H/pool
						16-10-1987, W.T. Hunter, Challoner Rd, H/pool
						6-3-1990, Kingfisher, H/pool
						18-9-2006, Kingfisher (FD 516), Fleetwood

THE HARTLEPOOL FISHING VESSEL REGISTER

NAME & MATERIAL	NO.	YEAR	LENGTH	POWER	WEIGHT	DETAILS
K-FREE grp	PE 538	1976	8.3m	34kw	4.3t	
KAREN	HL 56		27'x8'x3'		3.1t	fished lines, pots 11-12-1956, Ian Smith, West View, H/pool 8-2-1960, John Wilson, West H/pool
KARRIE ANNE wood	WY 171	1968	9.1m	63kw	4.4t	
KATHLEEN wood	SD 107	1949	8.2m	12kw	2t	Whitby coble based in Marina ? H/pool
KATHLEEN	HL 57		24'x7'x2'		3t	fished lines, pots, trawl, crew 2, 11-2-1957, Geo. Stewart, Smith St, H/pool 26-1-1962, W.O. White, Eaglescliffe 10-9-1964, W.S. Fryer, 5, Dawlish Drive, West H/pool
KATHLEEN & DAVID	HL 30	1959	21'x7'x2'		1.9t	built Whitby, fished pots, crew 2, r/n Silver Spray 1971 16-3-1971, Robert Robinson, 40, Marine Drive, H/pool 29-10-1976, D. Hartley & T. Lamb, Peterlee 20-3-1980, D. Hartley, Murton
KATHLEEN BURTON steel ON 137102	HL 30	1914	115'x22'x12'	steam 57hp	197t	built Hall Russell, A/deen, ketch rig, trawler, crew 9 yard No.558, launched 10-9-1914, engine 3cyl., by Abernethie, A/deen 1914, Doris Burton S.T. Co. Fish Quay H/pool 1916–1919, Navy, m/s (A1469) 3-1919, towed to port, German ship Germot, which had been abandoned in a gale (ex-hospital ship) 1935, Wood A/deen, as Espera (A 246) 26-1-1937, sank 30m SE of Dennis Head, Orkney during storm, pumps manned for 36 hours, crew taken off by German trawler Este, of Hamburg, after tow broke twice, crew landed in Buckie, skipper Alex. Smith
KATREEN wood ON 139830	HL 85	1916		steam 33hp	104t	built Colby Bros, Oulton Broad, dandy rig, drifter, yard No.33, crew 9, engine 3cyl., by Crabtree, Gt, Yarmouth 29-11-1916, A.R, Sutton, 5, Clyde Place, H/pool 23-10-1931, H.R. Franklyn, Grimsby 1942, John Debner Ltd (as salvage vessel) 1944, Navy salvage vessel
KIA - ORA wood	HL 69	1934	48'x16'x6'		23.8t	built Lossiemouth, fished trawl seine net, crew 3 16-4-1973, Kenneth Johnson, 13, Lumley Sq, H/pool
KINDLY LIGHT	HL 149		33'x10'x3'		6t	fished lines, nets, trawl, crew 3, 31-8-1965, John Watson, Blackhall Rocks, sold to Gt. Yarmouth
KING FISHER wood	HL 115		30'	sail	10t	coble, fished nets, crew 4 1-3-1869, Robert Boagey, H/pool, sold to Seaham harbour, 1877
KINGFISHER wood	HL 113		27'x8'x3'		3.9t	built Glasgow, fished lines, pots, crew 2 12-4-1948, J. Hall, 121, Chester Rd, West H/pool
KINSMAN	HL 176		38'x7'x4'		8.3t	fished lines, crew 2 6-9-1977, E. & R. Gibbon, H/pool
KIS wood ON 162469	HL 77	1917	44'x13'x6'		22.6t	built Hobro, Denmark, fished seine, trawl, crew 4 18-1-1955, W.H. Grigg 11, Gladstone St, H/pool 23-8-1955, Kis F. Co. Victoria Dock, H/pool 6-6-1959, boat sank, 40m E of H/pool, all saved, crew, Hans Thygeson, Alan & Rodney Bell, & John Hanley
KISMET	HL 98		18'x6'x2'		1.1t	fished lines, crew 3 13-10-1958, Thomas Boagey, 24, Beaconsfield St, H/pool
KIZZY	HL 57		24'x7'x2'		2.9t	fished lines, pots, crew 2

NAME & MATERIAL	NO.	YEAR	LENGTH	POWER	WEIGHT	DETAILS
KLONDIKE wood	HL 67	1901	28'x6'x3'	sail	2.4t	30-10-1972, Stan Grylls, & Geo. Brown, H/pool 22-5-1975, J.R. Hope, Lister St, West H/pool 25-7-1977, A. Cannel, Sherwood Place, H/pool built Hartlepool, lugger, fished lines, pots, nets, crew 3 29-4-1902, John Horsley 15, Clayton St, H/pool 11-1-1926, Richard Pounder, 14, Sussex St, H/pool 1928, sold to Seaham
KNIGHT COMMANDER wood	HL 60		29'x6'x2'	sail	4t	built Hartlepool, lugger, clinker-built coble, fished lines, crew 3 22-10-1900, Robert Hood, 37, Town Wall, H/pool, ex-Whitby?
KRALDUM	HL 128		16'x5'x2'		1.0t	18-11-1915, Thos. Carver, Sutton, Thirsk fished lines, pots
KRISTINA	HL 52		8.7x3x0.6m		2.6t	19-4-1961, T. Currel, 47, Sandsend Cres., H/pool
KRISTIONA wood ON 187226	HL 111	1957	46'x15'x9'	95hp 5LW Gardner	24t	20-7-1981, Peter Craggs, Shotton Coll. built Fraserburgh, Danish style seiner/trawler 23-11-1957, Kis Fishing Co. (W.K. Grigg), H/pool 1994, decommissioned (spent all working life in H/pool)
KUDOS steel ON 129358	HL 93	1911	115'x22'x12'	steam 75hp	207t	built Hall Russell A/deen, ketch rig, trawler, launched 10-5-1911, yard No.491, engine 3cyl. by builder, crew 10 1911, East Coast S.F. Co. A/deen (A 374) 1915–1919, Navy, m/s, 1x6pdr (FY 1343) 1-5-1918, Grahams H/pool 16-5-1919, Friarage S.T. Co. H/pool, scrapped 1954
LA BELLE wood	HL 94	1912	29'x7x3'	sail & motor	4.5t	built Middlesbrough, fished lines, pots, trawl, crew 3 12-11-1942, Thomas Forsyth, 46, Southgate, H/pool
LADY BARBARA wood	HL 128	1974	28'x8'x3'		4.1t	fished lines nets, pots, crew 2 27-2-1979, Ossy Rennie, Turnbull St, H/pool
LADY BIRD wood	HL 97	1926	37'x9'x2'		3.7t	built Fraserburgh, fished lines, nets, pots, crew 4 4-11-1975, John Meakins, 20, Arabella St, H/pool
LADY EDITH wood	HL 114	1914	44'x12'x6'	sail & motor		built Ardsiahaig, fished pots, nets, crew 4 4-10-1947, Geo. Townsend, 50 Southgate & G.F. Graham, Thornaby 11-12-1951, Geo. Townsend, 50, Southgate, H/pool 11-1953, reg. closed
LADY EDITH wood	HL 54	1914	44'x12'x 6'	sail & motor	17t	built Ardrishaig, crew 4 25-5-1954, Geo. Townsend, 50, Southgate, H/pool 1963, sold to London
LADY HELEN	HL 98		27'x8'x3'		3.5t	fished pots, lines. nets, crew 2 25-2-1980, R. Martindale, Wingate 15-5-1981, A. Robinson, Alfred St, H/pool
LADY PATRICIA steel	HL 16	1984	33'	89kw	8.9t	built Hartlepool, inshore stern trawler, fished trawl, pots 1984, Peter Davis, H/pool 1993, Steven Veart, H/pool
LADY OF THE LAKE wood	HL 217	1872	42'	sail	12t	decked boat, fished nets, crew 5 29-4-1872, Joseph Hatton, H/pool
LADY Y.	HL 702	1986	9.93m	78kw	2.94t	built Guernsey 7-10-1998, H/pool
LAIRDS ISLE wood	HL17		24'x7'x3'	motor	2.7t	fished lines, crew 3 30-6-1949, Wilfred Colling,6, Wilson St, West H/pool 10-6-1954, Wm. Mason,1, Warren Rd, H/pool
LASS O'GOWRIE wood	HL 142		27'	sail	8t	coble, fished nets, crew 4 11-3-1869, David Burns, sold to Thomas Purvis, Whitburn
LAURA JUNE grp	FR 63	1978	6.6m	30kw	2.3t	? H/pool
LAVINIA	HL 3		19'x5'x1.5'	sail	1.0t	lugger, fished, nets, pots, crew 2 (ex-*Robin*)

NAME & MATERIAL	NO.	YEAR	LENGTH	POWER	WEIGHT	DETAILS
wood						5-3-1929, George Horsley, 6, King St, H/pool
						20-8-1929, R. & M.C. Cole, Holmside, Seaton Carew
						1948, scrapped
LAVINIA	HL 53	1927	8.8x2.7x0.5m	53kw	1.0t	
wood						25-1-1988, S. Rennie, Town Wall, H/pool
LAZARUS	HL 35		30'x6'x2'	sail	2t	coble, fished lines, nets, crew 3, built H/pool
wood				lug rig		14-11-1892, Mathew Hastings, 4, Sandside, H/pool &
						Thomas Sayer, 3, Dovecote Yard, H/pool
						28-9-1905, Mathew Hastings, 17, Wells Yard, H/pool
						29-5-1913, sold to Seaham,
LAZARUS	HL 281		19' keel	sail	3t	coble, fished lines, crew 3
wood			26'x5'x2' oa			10-2-1877, Francis Hastings, H/pool
						5-1-1891, Mathew Hastings, 3, Sussex St, H/pool
LET ME ALONE	HL 131		15'	sail	1.5t	small boat, fished lines, crew 3
wood						3-3-1869, Andrew Robson, Seaton Carew
LIBERTY	HL 280		19.5'	sail	3t	coble, fished lines, crew 3
wood						9-2-1877, James Moon, H/pool
LIBERTY	HL 295		20'	sail	2t	coble, fished lines, crew 3
wood						5-6-1878, Robert Pounder, H/pool
LIBERTY	HL 130	1989	10.67m	94kw-6LXB	9.9t	built Toms Cornwall, inshore stern trawler
wood				Gardner		20-6-1989, Ronnie Buglass, H/pool
						24-10-2000, (SH 287) Bridlington
						14-12-2005, *Aaron* (S 229), Skibbereen, Ireland
LIDIA	HL 73		15'x5'x3'	motor	1.4t	fished lines, pots, crew 2
wood						27-12-1951, Frank Southeran, 74, Blandford St, H/pool
LIL & PAT	HL 90		26'x6'x3'		2t	fished lines, trawl, crew 2, ex- Blyth
wood						23-10-1946, R.J. Smith, 45, Stockton St, West H/pool
						16-1-1948, James Hastings, 9, Raby St South, West H/pool
						15-2-1949, E.F. Southeran, 31, Prissick St, sold to Montrose 1955
LILLY	HL 325		16'	sail	1.0t	boat, fished nets, crew 2
wood						13-5-1882, Wm. Blenkinsop, H/pool
LINDAN	HL 134	1962	21'x6'x2'		1.4t	built Hull, fished lines, pots, crew 2
						22-8-1979, T.A. Forth, Dickens Grove, H/pool
LINDISFARNE	INS 51	1987	16.76m	298kw		built Garrard Arbroath, fished seine, trawl
wood						1-1-1989, *Ardgour IV*, Kirkcaldy (KY107)
						7-7-2000, G. Reid, Lossiemouth, as *Clarness* (INS 51)
						28-2-2008, H/pool as *Lindisfarne* (INS 51) sold 2009
LISANDRA	HL 151	1953	20'x7'x2'	motor		fished lines, pots, crew 2, ex-*Manatee*
						3-8-1965, J.P. Tuck, & A.R. Johnson, H/pool
						9-7-1968, A.R. Johnson, 4, Radcliffe Tce, H/pool
						7-10-1970, W.E. Bootland, 85, Elwick Rd, H /pool
						19-5-1978, John Maddison, Drayton Rd, H/pool
LISANDRA	HL 1074	2003	6.36m	10kw	1.49t	
wood						1-4-2003, H/pool
LITTLE BOB	HL 225		18'	sail	4.5t	coble, fished lines, crew 3
wood						5-4-1873, Thomas Pounder. H/pool
LITTLE DICK	HL 49		19'	sail	3t	coble, fished lines, crew 3
wood						1-3-1869, Hartley Pounder, H/pool
						25-3-1881, Joseph Leighton, H/pool
LITTLE FREDA	HL 12	1910	35'x9'x4'		6.6t	built Flamborough, fished lines, pots, crew 2
wood						28-11-1969, W.E. Bastle, 11, Baptist St, H/pool
						23-6-1970, R.W. Bell, Billingham,
LITTLE JENNY	HL 61		18'	sail	2.5t	coble, fished lines, crew 3
wood						1-3-1869, David Moor, H/pool

Golden Ray

Grenna Star

Gypsy Girl

Ha' Burn

Halcyon

Hans Touson

Harvest Reaper

Incentive

Intrepid

Irene Wray

Isabella Fowlie

Isabelle

NAME & MATERIAL	NO.	YEAR	LENGTH	POWER	WEIGHT	DETAILS
						4-11-1885, Joseph Roberts, Baptist St, H/pool, sold to Whitby, 1886
LITTLE MARGARET wood	HL 167		30'	sail	10t	coble, fished nets, crew 3
LIZ	HL 96		24'x8'x2'		1.9t	19-5-1869, Cuthbert Moore, H/pool fished pots, nets, crew 2
LIZZIE wood	HL 359		21'	sail	4t	10-3-1975, A. Moore, 11, Corporation Rd, H/pool, sank 1977 lugger, fished nets, lines, crew 3
LIZZIE wood	HL 2		18'x5'x2'	sail		20-11-1884, Cuthbert Moore, H/pool 1909, sold to be used as Pilot coble built Stockton, coble, fished nets, lines, crew 2
LIZZIE HOOD wood	HL 43		28'x5.5'x2.5'	sail	3.6t	14-1-1904, Thomas Armstrong, 6, Wood St sold to M/boro1904 built Hartlepool, open boat, fished lines, crew 3
LIZZIE JANE wood	HL 66		27'x6'x2'	sail	2.1t	24-4-1895, Thos, Hood, 4, John St, H/pool 1-4-1913, Thos. Hood Jnr, 76, Hart Rd, H/pool lugger, fished nets, lines, crew 3
LIZZIE POUNDER wood	HL 6		20' keel 26'x5.5'x2.5' oa	sail -lug & jib	3t	15-4-1902, Cuthbert Coulson, 9, John St, H/pool, sold 1916 coble, fished lines, crew 3 5-9-1887, Thos. Pounder, 15, Wells Yard, H/pool 13-5-1892, John Pounder,16, Bedford St, H/pool, scrap 1918
LOCH BLAIR steel ON 143845	HL 42	1917	115'x22'x13'	steam 57hp	215t	built Hall Russell, A/deen, yard No.620, speed 10 knots, 10 crew 9-10-1917, Admirality 'Strath' class *James Beagan* 1923, Bon Accord F. Co. A/deen, r/n *Loch Blair* 1939–1946, Navy (A 203) APV 1940, Malcolm Smith, H/pool 18-9-1948, Hartness S.T. Co, H/pool 1953, J.T. Graham, H/pool 11-1957 scrap Belgium
LOCH GARRY steel ON 115594	HL 32	1903	106'x21'x12'	steam 60 hp	179t	built Alex. Hall A/deen, yard No.400, launched 3-2-1903 engine, 3cyl. by builder, trawler 1903, Empire S.F. Co. A/deen 6-5-1908, J.B. Graham, 6, South Cres. H/pool ?, Samuel Francis, Whitby St, West H/pool 18-10-1912, Landed 17 survivors after collision between SS *Camargo* and SS *Etona* 1914–1916, Navy, APV 13-9-1916, foundered off Kirkwall while on Navy service
LOCH KATRINE steel ON 112933	HL 23	1900	103'x20'x12'	steam		built Alex. Hall A/deen, ketch rig, yard No.383, crew 9 engine, 3cyl. by builder, trawler 1900 Loch Line S.F. Co. A/deen 19-12-1906, J.T. Graham, H/pool 3-3-1914, Albert Sutton, 5, Clyde Place, H/pool 11-8-1917, Reliable S.F. Co. Scarboro' 4-7-1917, captured by sub and sunk by gunfire 85 miles ESE Sando, Faroe Islands
LOCH NESS steel ON 114199	HL 71	1901	106'x21'x12'	steam	176t	built Alex. Hall A/deen, yard No.390, launched 2-10-1901 engine 3cyl. by builder, crew 9. trawler 1901, Bon Accord S.F. Co. A/deen (A467) 1-3-1912, J.J. Lister, 4, Town Wall, H/pool 9-4-1912, helped 2 lifeboats tow SS *Fanny Crossfield* out of danger near Longscar Rocks 25-9-1916, sunk by sub, 20m NE Scarborough
LOCH RYAN steel	HL 7	1901	108'x21'x12'	steam	186t	built Hall Russell, A/deen, ketch rig, yard No.352, launched 5-7-1901 engine, 3cyl. by builder, crew 9, trawler

NAME & MATERIAL	NO.	YEAR	LENGTH	POWER	WEIGHT	DETAILS
ON 114198						1901 W.R. Wetherly, A/deen
						15-11-1915, J.T. Graham, H/pool
						26-9-1916, captured by sub taken to Germany, skipper, Whitleton
LONG ?? wood	HL 40		27'x10'x4'	sail & motor	5.7t	fished lines, trawl, crew 3, ex-*Boy Trev*, Sunderland
						13-6-1946, James Stewart, 94, Durham St, H/pool
						1947–1952, various groups, reg. closed 1958
LONGLANDS LADY grp	HL 132	1986	9.4m	239kw	6.41t	built Cornwall
						13-2-1990, Longlands Lady (HL 132)
						1-2-1996, Seahawk (HL 132)
LONGSCAR steel ON 162461	HL 16	1930	115'x22'x12'	steam 69hp	215t	built J. Lewis, A/deen, trawler crew 10, engine, 3cyl. by builder
						7-7-1930, Heugh S.T. Co. H/pool
						1935–1945, Navy, Examination vessel
						1945, returned to owners
						1961 scrapped Holland
LORD KITCHENER ON 109722 steel	HL 55	1899	104'x21'x11'	steam	158t	built J.T. Eltringham, Stone Quay, S. Shields, yard No.203
						ketch rig, crew 9, trawler
						13-1-1899, J.J. Lister, 4, Town Wall, H/pool, F.W. Mason,
						High St, T.H. Peverill, Northgate, &
						St Hilda S.F. Co., 4, Town Wall, H/pool
						22-3-1912, T.H. Peverill, 13, Albion Tce, H/pool
						22-7-1912, Brown, Mason & Peverill, H/pool
						1914, sold to Aberdeen
						6-4-1917, captured by sub, sunk by bomb, 45m, N by
						E, Kinnaird Head
LORD LORNE wood	HL 4		22'	sail	3t	coble, fished lines, crew 3
						26-8-1887, Frank Burgon, 21, Albion St, Middleton, H/pool
LORD ROBERTS wood	HL 62		30'x5'x2'	sail	1.8t	coble, fished nets, lines, crew 3
						17-11-1900, Robert Heron Corner, 9, Dovecote Yard, H/pool
LORNA wood	HL 105		20'x6'x2'	motor	1.5t	fished lines, nets, crew 3
						20-10-1947, George Hunter Grainger, 15, Sea Tce, Middleton, H/pool
						4-7-1951, Stanley Gray, Ferryhill
LORNE wood	HL 208		20'	sail	3.5t	coble, fished nets, crew 2
						27-6-1871, John Pounder, H/pool
LOUCIE CHARLIE wood ON 68249	HL 338		74'	sail	72t	ketch, fished trawl, crew 5
						11-6-1883, H/pools Fishery Co.
						1884, registration transferred to Grimsby (GY 933)
LOUISA BIRKETT wood	HL 68	1889	28'x6'x2'	sail	4.3t	built Hartlepool, coble fished nets, lines, pots, crew 3
						17-7-1902 Helen Lowrie, 44, Lily St, H/pool
LOWESTOFT LASS wood	HL 109		31'	sail lug-rigged	10t	coble, fished nets crew 5
						1-3-1869, Thomas Pounder Metcalf, H/pool
						20-9-1875, James Mowbray, H/pool
						20-7-1883, John French, H/pool
LOYAL FRIEND wood ON 135753	LT 64	1913	84'x19'x9'	steam 20hp		built John Chambers, Lowestoft, yard No.432, drifter
						engine, 3cyl by Elliot & Garrod
						1913, E. Catchpole, Lowestoft
						1917, R.H. Davison, H/pool
						1914–1918, Navy
						1929, F.E. Geane, & I. Kemp,
						1926, J.J. Coulby (Lowestoft?)
						2-6-1931, overwhelmed by heavy seas entering Aberdeen,
						crew rescued by breeches buoy
LUCIA grp	HL 1067	2000	9.96m	116kw Daewoo	12t	built Penryn, inshore stern trawler
						9-2-2000, Phill Walsh, H/pool

NAME & MATERIAL	NO.	YEAR	LENGTH	POWER	WEIGHT	DETAILS
LYNDA	HL 123		27'x8'x3'		3t	fished lines, pots
						27-5-1960, Kenneth Borthwick, 45, Walton St, H/pool
						14-4-1961, Ian Smith, 52, Annandale Cres., H/pool
M. K. NOER wood ON 167536	HL 84	1935	45'x14'x5'	65hp	24t	built Frederiksund, Denmark, engine, single cyl.
						16-12-1957, Jens Erikson Noer, 5, Amberton Rd, H/pool
						26-11-1968, Annie Langton Noer, 5, Amberton Rd, H/pool
						21-4-1971, F.W. Thompson, Wirral, Cheshire (HL reg. closed 11-1979)
						1972, seining from Fleetwood
						1979, scallopping from Rye (RY 42) scrapped Ramsey 1988
MACK wood	HL 66		26'x6'x2'	sail & motor	2t	lugger, fished lines, pots, trawl, crew 2
						10-12-1936, T. McNulty, 80, Whitby St, West H/pool. to Stockton 1938
MADAME SANDS wood ON 168572	SA 28	1946	60'	120hp	49t	built Cracknore Hard, Southampton
						1969, Lillian Rose, Bridlington
						also worked from Bridlington
MAGGIE wood	HL 363		21'	sail	3t	coble, fished lines, crew 3
						15-6-1885, Robert Davison & Geo. Shepherd, 10, Croft St, H/pool
						1915, scrapped
MANX HERO steel ON 138964	HL 103	1916	117'x22'x13'	steam 74hp	236t	built Smiths Dock, South Bank, ketch rig, trawler, crew 9 yard No.617, launched 20-3-1916
						1916–1919, Navy, m/s, 1x6pdr. AA (A.3291)
						23-11-1918, R.H. Davison, 7, Albion Tce, H/pool
						28-6-1919, Phillip Belman, A/deen, r/n Evelyn Belman
						1922, Manx Hero; 1929, Rotterdam; 1951, Steynton; 1956 scrap
MARGARET wood	HL 16		18.5'	sail, lug jib, mizzen	3t	coble, fished lines, crew 2
						1-3-1869, Thomas Coulson, H/pool
						6-1-1871, James Sanderson, H/pool
						15-8-1883, John French, H/pool
MARGARET wood	HL 24		18'	sail	3t	coble, fished lines, crew 3
						1-3-1869, William Rowntree, H/pool
MARGARET wood	HL 100		18.5'	sail	3t	coble, fished lines, crew 3
						1-3-1869, James Rowntree, H/pool, sold to Whitby 1876
MARGARET wood	HL 147		18.5'	sail	3t	coble, fished lines, crew 3
						30-3-1869, William Rowntree, H/pool
MARGARET wood	HL 172		31'	sail	10.5t	coble, fished nets, crew 4
						31-5-1869, James Cambridge, H/pool, sold to Whitby 3-9-1878
MARGARET wood	HL 18		31'	sail	8t	coble, fished lines, crew 4
						10-12-1870, Elizabeth Corner, & Cuthbert Pounder H/pool
MARGARET wood	HL 283		22'		3t	coble, fished nets, crew 2
						15-8-1877, Charles? Cambridge, H/pool
MARGARET wood	HL 312		20.5'		4t	coble, fished lines, crew 3
						14-6-1880, Shepherd Pounder, H/pool
MARGARET wood ON 67006	HL 360		42'	sail	23t	lugger, fished lines, nets, crew 6, ex- Shoreham
						15-12-1884, Isaac Barnard, H/pool
						12-7-1887, James Fordson, North St, Kings Lynn
MARGARET wood ON 114301	HL 92	1903	64'x17'x9'	sail & motor	50.8t	built Fleetwood ?, fished trawl, crew 4, ex-FD 208
						other records show, built West H/pool, as a smack
						1903, W. Leadbitter, Fleetwood
						17-12-1949, James Robert Sheader, 20, Sea View Tce, H/pool
						1954, scrapped

NAME & MATERIAL	NO.	YEAR	LENGTH	POWER	WEIGHT	DETAILS
MARGARET wood	HL 29	1916	21'x6'x2'	sail & motor	1.4t	built Hartlepool, coble, fished lines, nets, crew 2 7-3-1933, E.W. Garbut, 15, Town Wall, H/pool 13-11-1939, J.R. Burton, West H/pool 22-11-1947, J.T. Reay, West H/pool, scrapped 1953 Ex-*Sea Nymph*, ex-*Samaritan*
MARGARET wood						Whitby coble, based in Marina ? H/pool
MARGARET ANN wood	HL 331		72'	sail	63t	yawl, fished lines, nets, crew 5 19-4-1883, J. Hogarth, H/pool, vessel missing Feb. 1885
MARGARET BURGON wood	HL 271		23'	sail	4t	coble, fished lines, crew 4 28-8-1876, James Burgon, H/pool 1881, re-reg. Berwick
MARGARET JOYCE	HL 193		9x2x1m		3.1t	10-5-1982, T.J. Horsley, Flamborough Walk, H/pool
MARGARET & ALICE wood	HL 49		29'x6'x2.9'	sail	2.1t	coble, fished lines, crew 3 7-2-1896, George Moore, 2, John St, H/pool, scrapped 1924
MARGARET & ANN wood	HL 81		33'	sail	12t	keel boat, fished nets, crew 5 1-3-1869, James Burgon, H/pool 1875 re-reg. Berwick, when family moved north
MARGARET & ANN wood	HL 279		35'	sail	12t	keel boat, fished nets, crew 5 31-1-1877, James Burgon, sold to Berwick 1881
MARGARET & ELIZABETH wood	HL 113		33'	sail	12t	keel boat, fished nets, crew 4 1-3-1869, Margaret & John Johnson, H/pool 1874, sold
MARGARET & ISABELLA wood	HL 117		22'	sail	5t	coble, fished lines, crew 4 1-3-1869, David Burgon, boat lost & owner drowned 1876 14-9-1876, Lifeboat records show Seaton Carew Lifeboat *Job Hindley* saved 3 men from West H/pool fishing boat
MARGARET & WILLIAM wood	HL 40	1932	45'x13'x4'		13t	built Findochty, fished trawl, crew 2 8-10-1971, David Kent, M/boro 1-7-1976, John Roberts, 1, Havelock St, H/pool, r/n *Lady Grace*
MARGIT wood ON 182629	GY 580	1945	17.43m	120hp	32t	built Frederikshavn, Denmark, oak on oak, fished seine, trawl engine, Hunterstead 2 cylinder, 2-stroke, air start, one of the last in use 1945, built as *Winston*, Danish owners 1949, Ove Langesen, Grimsby 1964, Margit Seiners, Grimsby 1983, Tom Slight, Grimsby 1984, Alan Cook, Durham St, H/pool 1993, Mrs Florence Bramwell, North Shields
MARIA	HL 88		22'x7'x2'		1.6t	fished lines, trawl, crew 2 7-4-1975, W. Mathwin, 12, Mapleton Rd, H/pool 15-6-1978, W. Pearson, 8, Lambert Rd, H/pool
MARIAN steel ON 106969	HL 52	1897	105'x21'x11'	steam	148t	built Edwards Bros. N. Shields, yard No.571, launched 27-10-1897 ketch rig, crew 9, trawler 16-11-1897 H/pools S.F. Co. Victoria Tce, West H/pool 1899, sold to Denmark
MARIE M. grp	HL 35	1988	5.6m	11kw	1.2t	 11-3-1992, H/pool
MARINA wood	HL 126	1946	26'x8'x3'		4.5t	keel boat, fished lines, pots, 11-11-1960, Ivor Walker, Egerton Rd, West H/pool
MARINETTA	HL 154	1970	8.5m	60kw	4.44t	 11-6-1991, H/pool

J. J. (2)

Janoras

Janet Jenson

Joanne

Judeann

Julante

Kathleen

Kristiona

Kudos

Lady Patricia

Lindisfarne

Loch Blair

NAME & MATERIAL	NO.	YEAR	LENGTH	POWER	WEIGHT	DETAILS
MARK	HL 11		27'x8'x2'		2.3t	fished lines, pots
						3-7-1970, Cedric Williams, 12, Gladstone St, H/pool
						29-3-1974, Peter Wallis & ? Northey, H/pool
						10-3-1975, Clark & Jones, H/pool
MARK & ELIZABETH wood	HL 169		24'	sail	8t	coble, fished lines, crew 3
						19-5-1869, Mark Davidson, H/pool
MARLIN	HL 58	1982	5.9x2.2x0.6m		1.1t	
						2-11-1987, T.C. Kitching, Tristram Ave, H/pool
MARLSTON grp	FH 473	1978	9.27mx	89kw Ford	6.3t	built Cornwall, inshore stern trawler
						1978, Derek Harrison, Northgate, H/pool, sold 2007
MARLYNE - EM wood	HL 43	1972	7.15x2.5x1m	37kw	2.9	built Whitby, coble
						16-2-1987, Paul Watson & L. Peacock, H/pool
MARNY GEMMA wood	WY 205	1988	31.5'	128hp Ford		built Whitby by Steve Cook, fished nets, lines, trawl
						6-9-1988, E. & M. Westcough, M/boro
						2009, decommissioned Amble
MARSHA JANE wood	HL 288		19'	sail	3t	coble, fished lines, crew 3
						29-11-1877, Daniel Moor, H/pool
MARTHA JANE wood	HL 36		27'x4'x2'	sail	1.0t	coble fished lines, ex-pilot boat
						1-4-1893, David Moore, 3, Pratts Passage, H/pool & Francis Coulson, 17, Wells Yard, H/pool
						1909, sold for use as pilot boat
MARTHA L. wood	HL 124		21'x7'x2'		2.5t	fished lines pots, crew 2
						6-2-1961, Gordon Abbott, 220, York Rd, H/pool
MARTIN LUTHER wood	HL 93		30'	sail	9t	coble, fished nets, crew 4
						1-3-1869, Robert Davidson, H/pool
						12-1-1877, Ann Davison, H/pool
MARTY wood	HL 121	1943	27'x8'x3'	sail & motor	7.4t	fished lines, pots
						17-9-1959, Geo. Metcalf, 35, Plevna St West H/pool
						28-5-1967, Charles Dutton, 15, Spring Garden Rd, West H/pool
MARUEL wood ON 182029	HL 71	1947	51'x16'x5'	114hp	24t	built Portavogie, fished seine & trawl, crew 4
						24-6-1957, Joseph Edward Picknet, 4, Friarage Gdns, H/pool & Phillip Picknet, 17, South Tce, Redcar
						12-12-1967, Margaret Evans, Llanelli (married woman)
MARY wood	HL 75		31'	sail	10t	coble, fished nets, crew 4
						1-3-1869, William Hodgson, H/pool
						2-10-1875, Mathew Hastings, & Cuthbert Coulson, H/pool
						11-6-1880, Mathew Hastings, H/pool
MARY wood	HL 110		29'	sail	9t	coble fished nets, crew 4
						1-3-1869, Thomas Pounder, H/pool, lost 26-9-1869
MARY wood	HL 150		20'	sail	5t	coble, fished lines, pots, crew 3
						13-4-1869, Robin Crummley, H/pool
						1870, boat found to be unfit for sea
MARY wood	HL 184		18'	sail	2.5t	coble, fished lines, crew 2
						14-8-1869, George Horsley, H/pool
MARY wood	HL 238		19'	sail	3t	coble, fished lines, crew 3
						22-1-1874, James Moore, H/pool
						12-3-1879, Thomas Rowntree, H/pool
						9-7-1887, John Hunter,16, Cliff Tce, H/pool
MARY wood	HL 255		18'	sail	3t	coble, fished lines, crew 3
						25-9-1875, John Hodgson, H/pool
MARY wood	HL 16		23'	sail	3t	coble, fished nets, crew 2
						17-8-1889, James Burgon, 15, Pimlico St, West H/pool
MARY wood	HL 14		27'x6'x2'	sail	3.6t	coble, fished lines, crew 3, built H/pool .
						15-5-1906, Richard Pounder,14, Sussex St, H/pool
						13-4-1921, Robert Cambridge & others, H/pool

NAME & MATERIAL	NO.	YEAR	LENGTH	POWER	WEIGHT	DETAILS
						1924, boat condemned
MARY wood	HL 58	1931	17'x6'x2'	motor	1.0t	coble fished lines, nets, crew 2
						15-9-1936, Joseph Victor Foster, Brunswick Hotel, West H/pool
						10-1939, scrapped
MARY wood	HL 103		16'x5'x2'	motor	1.0t	fished lines, pots, crew 2
						28-1-1948, John Powell, 25, Commercial St, Middleton, H/pool
						3-2-1948, Wm. Gordon Collitt, 19, Arch St, Central Estate, H/pool
MARY & ANN wood	HL 85		23'	sail	6t	coble, fished lines, crew 4
						1-3-1869, Peter Robertson, H/pool
						6-8-1874, Henry Waite, H/pool
MARY & HANNAH wood	HL 311		27'x5.5'x2.5'	sail	3t	coble, fished nets, crew 3
						24-4-1880, Mark Davison, Chapel St, H/pool
						27-10-1888, John Moore, 14, Baptist St, H/pool & Robert Horsley, 8, Wells Yard, H/pool
MARY & ISABELLA wood	HL 276		18.5'	sail	3t	coble fished lines crew 3
						12-12-1876, Thomas Ovington, H/pool
						13-10-1887, Wm. Horsley, 6, Chapel St, H/pool
MARY ALICE wood	HL 70		18.5'	sail	3t	coble, fished lines, crew 3
						1-3-1869, William Hunter, H/pool
						13-2-1875, John French, H/pool
MARY ALICE wood	HL 85		23'	sail	6t	coble, fished lines, crew 4
						2-10-1872, Mary Robertson, H/pool
MARY ANN wood	HL 97		18.5'	sail	3t	coble, fished lines, crew 3
						1-3-1869, James Pounder, H/pool, sold 1883
MARY ANN wood	HL 101		18.5'	sail	3t	coble, fished lines, crew 3
						1-3-1869, Robert Rowntree, H/pool,
MARY ANN wood	HL 133		30'	sail	5t	coble, fished nets, crew 4
						3-3-1869, John Forset & Wm. Clark, H/pool
						1869, lost at Runswick Bay
MARY ANN wood	HL 322		19' keel 25.5'x5.5'x2.5'	sail – lug, jib & oars	3t	coble fished lines, crew 3
						24-3-1882, John Hodgson, H/pool
						14-1-1892, Robert Hodgson, 2, Sandside, H/pool
						1892, William Burgon, Berwick
MARY ANN wood	HL 37		34.5'x12.5'x 5'	sail – lug rig		decked boat, fished lines, nets, ex-Montrose (ME 693)
						2-6-1893, Hugh Lowrie, 37, Durham St, H/pool
MARY ANN wood	HL 43		24'x7'x3'		3t	fished lines, pots, crew 2
						14-1-1957, T. Lilly, 64, West View Rd, H/pool
						5-6-1961, Leslie Murcott, West View, H/pool
						30-3-1962, West & Muir, West H/pool
						6-3-1968, A. Jackson, Blackhall
						29-10-1969, Leo. Judge, 3, Avondale Gdns, H/pool
MARY ANN 11 grp	H 1101		7.45m	18.6kw	1.59t	inshore open boat
						? H/pool
MARY ANN WHITE	HL 310		61'	steam	16t	screw steamer, fished lines, drift, trawl, crew 7
						16-3-1880, Robert White, H/pool
MARY ANNA	HL 33		27'x8'x3'		5.4t	fished lines, crew 3
						20-5-1971, A.W. Fryer, Willington
MARY B wood	HL 96	1974	9.24m	59kw	4.06t	built Whitby
						17-7-1989, Mary B (HL 96), H/pool
						12-8-1998, Louisa Jane (SSS 676), South Shields
MARY COULSON wood	HL 224		19'	sail	3t	coble, fished lines, crew 3
						5-2-1873, Thomas Reid, H/pool
						25-1-1877, John Bulmer, H/pool
						13-2-1882, Robert Rowntree, H/pool
MARY JANE	HL 59		18'	sail	3t	coble, fished lines, crew 3

NAME & MATERIAL	NO.	YEAR	LENGTH	POWER	WEIGHT	DETAILS
wood						1-3-1869, William Davidson, H/pool, scrapped 1869
MARY JANE wood	HL157		29'	sail	10t	coble, fished nets, crew 4 29-4-1869, Henry Albert Wardell, H/pool 1-8-1872, re-reg. Whitby
MARY JANE wood	HL 282		18.5'	sail	3t	coble, fished lines, crew 3 24-2-1877, George Moore, H/pool
MARY JANE wood	HL 46	1895	29'x5'x3'	sail	4.3t	built Hartlepool, coble, fished lines, pots, crew 3 20-12-1895, Robert Stewart, Sussex St, H/pool 19-5-1920, J.S. Leighton, 34, Lily St, scrapped 1931
MARY ZILLAH	HL 101		14'x 5'x 2'		1.0t	fished lines, pots, crew 1 man 4-5-1948, James Edward White, 6, Brougham St, H/pool 1950, wrecked
MAUREEN wood	HL 144	1957	35'x10'x4'	53kw	5.3t	built Whitby, fished lines, pots, crew 2 (ex-MH 42) 18-4-1963, Ian Smith, 22, Pert Rd, H/pool 16-12-1970, F. & W. Golightly, 29, Dowson Rd, H/pool 13-4-1972, Samuel Taylor, Sunderland, scrapped 1995
MAUREEN	HL 81	1948	59'x18'x8'		40t	built Macduff, fished nets lines, trawl 20-5-1974, Peter Coull, 14, Langdon Ave, Billingham 5-8-1975, Elenor Laws, Oxford
MAUREEN NOBLE wood	HL 71	1977	35'x10'x6'	60kw	11t	built Whitby, fished pots, nets, crew 2 26-6-1978, H. & A. Noble, Peterlee 20-3-1987, Maureen Noble, Easington Coll. 26-10-1990, *Toiler* (SD 71), Sunderland
MAVERICK			30'			inshore stern trawler ? John Grand
MAVIS wood	HL 4		21'x6'x2.5'	sail & motor	1.7t	fished nets, lines, crew 2 18-6-1934, John Henry Robinson, 4, Freeman St, H/pool
MAYFLOWER wood	HL 145		40'	sail	9t	smack, fished nets, trawl, crew 3 19-3-1869, Robinson Pounder, H/pool 23-9-1871, Thomas Henderson, H/pool
MAYFLOWER	HL 145		41'	steam & sail	9t	screw steam smack, fished trawl, lines, crew 5 31-8-1885, Thos. King, Whitby St, West H/pool 17-12-1886, J.H. Burnstone, 13, Granger St, West, Newcastle 15-11-1887, J. Nicholson, Buoy House Quay Coble Landing, South Shields
MAYFLY iron ON 110745	HL 2	1899	113'x21'x11'	steam 58hp	191t	built Cook, Weldon & Gammel, yard No.246, launched 7-10-1899 engine, 3cyl. by C.D. Holmes, Hull, trawler, 12 crew 1899 (H 477) 1912, J. Graham, H/pool 31-10-1914, steamed in full gale to Whitby to tow the rowing Lifeboat out to the wreck of the *Rohilla* to rescue survivors 1916, sold to Grimsby 24-4-1917, sunk by gunfire from sub 75m NE by N Scarboro', 3 crew lost
MErGANSER grp	WY 156	1979	9.45m	63kw	6.86t	built Worcester, inshore stern trawler (ex-CO 434) ? H/pool 17-12-1986, Whitby ? Sunderland, decommissioned 2009
MELISA wood	HL 23		30'	sail	10t	coble, fished nets, crew 4 1-3-1869, George Horsley, H/pool, sold to Whitby, 1877
MERCY wood	HL 136		28'	sail	8t	coble, fished nets, crew 4 3-3-1869, Jane Robinson, H/pool, sold to Whitby, 1871

NAME & MATERIAL	NO.	YEAR	LENGTH	POWER	WEIGHT	DETAILS
MICHAEL wood	HL 100	1940	17'x6'x2'	motor	1.0t	fished lines, pots, crew 2 22-9-1947, Thomas William Pounder, 20, St Hilda St, H/pool 5-7-1950, Thomas Boagey, 6, Town Wall, H/pool
MICHEL-DE-AL wood ON 301554	HL 29	1970	34'x9'x3'	59kw	6.1t	built Seahouses 18-1-1971, A. & H. Noble, Peterlee 8-4- 1987, A. Noble, Peterlee 11-4-1987, J. Bourne, Blackhall Col 26-11-1988, T.M. English, Seaham
MICHELLE	HL 60		20'x7'x2'		1.2t	fished lines, pots, crew 1 man 6-9-1972, C.S. Havelock, Blackhall
MICHELLE wood	HL 119		30'x8'x4'	40kw	4.9t	built Hartlepool, fished nets, lines, pots, crew 2 8-5-1979, Alan Evans, Graythorpe 25-1-1988, T. Heatherington, Jedborough Rd, H/pool
MICK wood	HL 34	1910	28'x 6'x 2'	sail	2t	built Hartlepool, lugger, fished lines, nets, crew 3 17-12-1928, James Andrews, 15, Prissick St, H/pool 25-6-1929, J. McGee, & B. Johnson, H/pool
MICKEVEL wood	HL 86	1954	49'x16'x6'		21.8t	built St Malo, France, fished trawl Ex-Docteur Bombard (inventor of the inflatable liferaft) 2-9-1974, Marjorie Brookbanks, Stockton, based H/pool 13-4-1976, Michael Watson, Portsmouth 17-12-1979, D. Morris, Ramsgate 11-2-1980, G.S. McIntosh, Aberdeen 1986, Peel, I.O.M. r/n Cardea 2001, sank after collision with Ocean Hunter (PL 96)
MIDNIGHT MOON wood	HL 1058	1973	13.6m	157kw	17.9t	23-9-1996, Jackie D (LH 519), Leith 27-10-2004, Midnight Moon, H/pool
MINERS FRIEND	HL 22		17'x5'x2'	sail	1.4t	coble, fished nets, lines, crew 3 11-11-1921, Thos. Gibson, 28, East St, Blackhall 9-10-1928, Charles Sharp, Blackhall, motor added before 1928
MIRIAM STEWART steel ON 137101	HL 10	1914	115'x22'x12'	steam 78hp	197t	built Hall Russell A/deen, yard No.550, launched 31-3-1914 ketch rig, trawler, crew 9 16-5-1914, Robert & Mary Stewart, 6, York Place, H/pool 1914–1919, Navy, m/s, 1x3pdr (A.461) 6-9 -1919, Ellis S.T. Co., Scarboro' (SH 256) 1926, North Star F. Co, A/deen, r/n Avondon (A 56) 27-2-1933, lost off Milgoe, Orkney, crew saved
MISS BLANCHE	HL 36		13'x5'x1.0'		0.6t	fished lines, crew 2 10-11-1955, Henry Curell? 47, Sandsend Cres., H/pool
MIZPAH	HL 60		22'x7'x3'		2.5t	fished lines, trawl, crew 2 20-3-1957, V. Wilson, Blackhall, 3-9-59, T. Kennedy, Northgate, H/pool
MIZPAH steel	BCK 627		9.95m	115kw	20t	inshore stern trawler ? Stead Bros Northallerton
MONA - DOR wood	HL 34	1929	28'x6'x3'		2.6t	fished lines, nets, pots, crew 2 17-5-1972, Keith Fletcher, 15, Cliff Tce, H/pool 3-1994, sold to North Shields
MONARCH wood	HL 119		36'	sail	12t	keel boat, fished nets, crew 4 1-3-1869, Robert Tait, H/pool, sold to M/boro' 1871
MONARCH wood	HL 200		18.5'	sail	3t	coble, fished lines, crew 2 1-11-1870, Benjamin Robson, H/pool
MONTBRETIA wood ON 162464	HL 66	1946	47'x16'x6'		32t	built Pwllheli, fished nets, lines 9-10-1947, Leighton, Winspear & Leighton, H/pool 18-9-1951, sold to Filey, reg. trans. to Scarboro'

Longscar

Loyal Friend

Lucia

M.K. Noer

Madame Sands

Margaret

Margaret (2)

Marlston

Maureen

Margit

Maruel

Merganser

NAME & MATERIAL	NO.	YEAR	LENGTH	POWER	WEIGHT	DETAILS
MOORHEN wood	FD 306	1956	45'x16'x6'		22t	built Fraserburgh, Danish-style seiner/trawler 1970, Harry Franklin, Grimsby 1972, Allard Hewson & Co. Grimsby 1975, sold to Fleetwood ? Stan & Raymond Eastwood, H/pool
MORAY GEM wood	A 248	1955	40'	76hp	17t	built Macduff, fished seine/trawl 1955, J.C. Green, Buckie (BCK 28) 1977, F. Paterson, Aberdeen 1882, Stephen & George Horsley, H/pool 8-7-1982, collided with and sank *Nordheim*, 6m off H/pool 1986, Jane Reid, East Lothian (LH 255) 1995, Denholm Fish Selling, Edinburgh 1997, George Bruce, Port Seton 2001, decommissioned
MORAY LASS wood	WK 167					keel boat, fished seine, trawl ? Kenny Johnson, H/pool
MORELEIGH wood ON166925	HL 160	1946	92'x22'x11'	300hp	112t	built Rowhenge, Wivenhoe, Admirality MFV, yard No.47 original engine 3cyl., by W.H. Podd 1946, Admirality -M.F.V. 1545 1946, Fleetwood Drifters (BM 20) as *Iago* 1951, Torbay Trawlers, Brixham 1958, Putford Enterprises, Lowestoft, re-engined – Ruston 335hp 1959, r/n *Moreleigh* (LT 170) 21-5-1965, Albert F. Co. H/pool 18-2-1972, Edith Ann Szlukovinyi, Darlington 24-1-1973, A.B. Adamson, Bolton 16-1-1974, Brackenbury & Salthouse, Fleetwood 1978, sank Morecambe Bay
MORMOND HILL steel ON 125941	HL 36	1908	84'	steam	97t	built Duthie, A/deen, ketch rig, yard No.317, crew 10 1908, Baird & Co., Peterhead, as *Kate Baird* ? r/n *Mormond Hill* (FR 584) 20-3-1923, R.H. Davison, & F. Ray, H/pool 11-1923, James Bowie, Gordonburgh, Buckie r/n *Helen Bowie* (BCK 432)
MORNING STAR steel	HL 81	1988	9.9x4.3x1.8m		16t	built H/pool 9-8-1988, Eric Reeve, Runciman Rd, H/pool 12-7-1994, *Jessie Alice*
MORNING STAR wood	SD 8	1968	9.2m	11kw	3.3t	coble ?, H/pool
MOTTO wood ON 60209	HL 335		68'	sail	61t	smack, fished trawl, crew 5, transferred from Hull 23-5-1883, H/pools Fishery Co.
MOY wood	HL 39		37'x12'x5'	sail & motor	11t	built Lossiemouth, lugger, fished lines, trawl, crew 4 11-12-1930, Robert Hood 12, Sussex St, H/pool
MURIEL wood	HL 102	1944	14'x5'x2'	motor	1.0t	built Southampton, fished pots 12-9-1947, Geo. Sanderson, 12, Town Wall, H/pool
MYSTERY wood	HL 32		18.5'	sail	3t	coble, fished lines, crew 3 1-3-1869, Mark Davidson, H/pool
NANCY wood	HL 162		33'	sail	13t	smack, fished trawl, crew 3 12-5-1869, Thomas Hathuly?, H/pool 16-11-1871, lost near Whitby
NANCY wood	HL 48	1932	18'x5'x2'	sail	1.1t	built Hartlepool, lugger, fished lines, pots, crew 2 15-8-1940, Robert Henry Winspear, 13, Commercial St, Middleton

NAME & MATERIAL	NO.	YEAR	LENGTH	POWER	WEIGHT	DETAILS
NANCY MAY wood	HL 196	1953	9.2x2.7x1.2m		4.9t	18-5-1982, Douggie Veart, Town Wall, H/pool
NAOMI wood	HL 7		20' keel 27'x5.5'x2.5'	sail	3t	coble, fished lines, nets, crew 3 26-9-1887, T.W. Rowntree, 8, Pump St, H/pool 8-7-1892, Wm. Rowntree, 15, Croft Tce, H/pool, sold to Whitby 1898
NAOMI wood	HL 69	1902	26'x6'x2'	sail & motor	3t	built Hartlepool, fished lines pots, ex-Blyth 29-1-1949, Geo. Bulmer 56, Northgate, H/pool, & Major John Townsend, 54, Southgate, H/pool
NARCISSUS wood	HL 92		18.5'	sail	3t	coble, fished lines, crew 3 1-3-1869, Thomas Davidson, H/pool, sold 1874
NATALIE B grp	HL 62	1983	5.35m		0.86t	10-4-1990, H/pool 8-6-1999, Ebins (FR 917), Fraserburgh
NATHAN & ELLEN wood	HL 23		26'	lug sail & 4 oars	3t	coble, fished nets, lines, crew 3 18-11-1890 Wm. Allen, 12, Croft Tce, H/pool, sold to Whitby
NELL wood	HL 202		20'	sail	3.5t	coble, fished lines, nets, crew 3 29-3-1871, Edward Hutton, H/pool
NEL wood	HL 343		22.5'	sail	3t	coble, fished nets, crew 2 22-8-1883, Robert Horsley, H/pool
NELLIE wood	HL 8	1935	31'x7'x3'	sail & motor	3.6t	built Scarbrough, fished nets, lines, crew 2 25-7-1936, Francis Elenor Watkinson, 84, Durham St, H/pool 9-1957, sold to Scarboro'
NELLY AGNES wood	HL 77		34'	sail		keel boat, fished nets, crew 5 1-3-1869, George Robinson, H/pool, sold to Grimsby 1871
NELLY BURGON wood	HL 79		36.5'	sail	14t	keel boat, fished nets, crew 5 1-3-1869, Henry Burgon, H/pool 15-6-1874, Henry Burgon, re-reg. in Berwick 1881
NEMESIS grp	HL 706	1986	6.19m	11kw	1.41t	built Yorkshire 1989, Harry Sevvy (BH159), Blyth 26-10-2004, Nemesis (HL 706), H/pool
NESMAR wood ON 130019	LT 1112	1911	84'x19'x9'	steam 20hp		built John Chambers, Lowestoft, drifter launched 6-5-1911 1911 Helway & Flowers, Lowestoft 1914–1919 Navy, temp. r/n Nesmar 2, 1x3pdr gun chartered by Navy for £52 9s 9d/month (£52.48) 1919, Stranton Drifters, H/pool, scrapped 1936
NICOLA JANE wood	HL 49	1971	20'x6'x2'		1.5t	built Middlesbrough, fished lines, crew 2 15-9-1972, Bell & Fishburn, Billingham 15-11-1988, R. Fishburn, Billingham
NIGHT WATCH wood	HL 170		18.5	sail	3t	coble, fished nets, crew 2 20-5-1869, Francis Hedley, scrapped 1870
NIMBUS	HL 153		23'x7'x2'		1.7t	fished trawl, pots, lines, crew 2 28-6-1968, F. Evans, 68, Milbank Road, H/pool 15-12-1976, Peter Waller, 110, Bruce Cres. H/pool 24-7-1978, Todd & Harrison, M/boro
NIMROD grp	MH 6	2006	6.7m	22kw	1.1t	?, H/pool
NIMROD wood	HL 323		19'	sail	2.5t	boat, fished nets, lines, crew 2 29-3-1882, John Wood, H/pool
NINA	HL 172		26'x8'x3'		6.3t	fished lines, crew 2 30-7-1966, Lesley Best, Easington Lane 24-6-1968, J. Ryan & K. McIver, H/pool 21-11-1968, M.R. Carson, 7, Calder Grove, H/pool 3-7-1970, T.A. Armstrong, Blackhall Rocks

NAME & MATERIAL	NO.	YEAR	LENGTH	POWER	WEIGHT	DETAILS
NORAH	HL 168		28'x8'x3'		4t	fished lines, pots
						14-6-1966, Francis W. Fleetham, 55, Bruce Cres., H/pool
NORDHEIM wood	HL 199	1969	12x4x2m		12.7t	built Thyborn, Denmark, fished trawl
						10-5-1982, Matty McCelland, Rowel St, H/pool
						8-7-1982, sank after collision with *Moray Gem*
NORDIC STAR steel	HL 47	1984	8.7x2.9x0.8m	75kw	3.4t	built H/pool
						2-11-1987, R. Gardner, Milbank Rd, H/pool
NORDIC WAY	HL 36		24'x7'x3'		4.7t	fished lines, crew 2
						4-10-1972, Peter Weegram, 31, Bede Grove, H/pool
NORDLAND wood ON 162079	HL 19		42'x13'x5'	45hp	21t	built Esbjerg, Denmark, fished seine, trawl
						8-3-1955, Thomas Horsman, 21, Scarboro' St, West H/pool
						29-6-1964, John King, Kirkcudbright
						5-12-1966, A.D. Rudd, Kirkcudbright
						1973, Allard Hewson, Grimsby
						1978, Christian Brown, Cleethorpes
NORMAN wood	HL 77	1939	20'x7'x3'	sail & motor	2t	fished lines, nets, pots, crew 3,
						22-5-1942, Gilmore & Tempest, Easington Coll.
NORTH STAR wood	B 392	1982	8.3m	37kw	5.2t	
						?H/pool
NORTH STAR wood	HL 64		29.5'	sail	10t	coble, fished nets, crew 4
						1-3-1869, John Pounder, H/pool, sold to Staithes, 1871
NORTH STAR wood	HL 206		31'	sail	8t	herring coble, fished nets, crew 4
						12-6-1871, Robert Pounder, H/pool, sold to Whitby, 1874
NORTH STAR wood	HL 23	1927	30'x11'x5'	sail & motor	11t	built Anstruther, lugger, fished lines, crew 3
						30-9-1927, Robert Pounder, 1, Sussex St, H/pool
						4-9-1940, sold to Filey, reg. trans. to Whitby 1942
NORTH STAR wood	HL 83	1935	29'x8'x3'		3.4t	fished lines, pots, crew 2
						2-8-1950, Wm. Graham Charlton (Bunny), 16, Burke Place, H/pool
						14-6-1974, Robert Holman, 16, South Cres, H/pool, & Alan Cook, 132, Durham St, H/pool
						6-7-1978, Peter Buckle, 1, Rowell St, H/pool
NORTHERN STAR	HL 116		37'x12'x2'		8.6t	fished lines, pots, nets, crew 2
						21-4-1977, Eric Reeve, & J. Stoddart, H/pool
						6-11-1981, Eric Reeve, H/pool
						16-11-1984, David Simpson, Newcastle
						6-12-1984, Eric Reeve, H/pool
						27-11-1985, J. H. Lee, Colwyn Bay
NORTHMOOR steel ON 109725	HL 59	1900	95'x20'x11'	steam	133t	built Smiths Dock N. Shields, ketch rig, trawler, crew 8
						launched 28-2-1900, yard No.624
						4-4-1900, The Moor S.T. Co., 20, Fish Quay, H/pool
						16-8-1902, sold to Italy, r/n 1903, *St George*
						1915, *Churchsit*, 1916, *Churchsin*, 1920, *Banks o'Dee*, scrap, 1937
NORWOOD wood	LH 347	1970	48'x17'x6'	Volvo 240hp	20t	built Eyemouth Boat Building Co, fished trawl, crew 2
						1970, W.J. Easingwood Eyemouth
						12-4-2005 Alan Hogson, H/pool
						2006, sank H/pool, near port entrance, raised, scrapped
OCTOROON steel ON 137105	HL 68	1914	115'x22'x12'	steam 78hp	195t	built Hall Russell, ketch rig, trawler, yard No.561, crew 9
						launched 20-11-1914
						1914, Sutton S.T. Co. H/pool
						1915–1919, Navy, m/s,1x6pdr AA (A.1431)
						1929, W. Buchan,194, Victoria Rd, A/deen as *Wilson Buchan* (A 268)
						1938, T. Walker, A/deen, as *Star of Dee*
						1943, J.C. Robertson, A/deen
						1945, Walker S.T. Co. A/deen

NAME & MATERIAL	NO.	YEAR	LENGTH	POWER	WEIGHT	DETAILS
						1946, J.W. Johnstone, A/deen, as *River Dee* (A 562)
OCEAN BRIDGE wood	HL 44		30'x8.5'x2.5'	sail	3.1t	coble, fished lines, nets (ex-BK 1079)
						3-7-1895, A.E. Pickard, 2, Bell St, West H/pool
						1897, sold to Berwick
OCEAN QUEEN wood	HL 229		37'	sail	9t	herring boat, fished nets, crew 5
						27-6-1873, Charles Merritt, H/pool, sold to Sunderland, 1876
OCEAN WAVE wood	HL 254		18.5'	sail	3t	coble, fished lines, crew 3
						30-8-1875, Thomas Coulson, H/pool
ODIN	HL 174		17'x6'x2'		1.1t	fished lines, pots
						20-9-1966, G.S. Havelock, Blackhall Coll.
						8-4-1970, Brian Newton, Peterlee
OLGA wood	HL 110	1935	16'x6'x3'		1.5t	fished lines, pots
						18-11-1954, J. Kidson, 14, Sydenam Rd, H/pool
						24-10-1956, M.W. Sanderson, 25, Watt St, H/pool
						12-12-1956, J.R. Waterman, 3, Turnbull St, H/pool
						21-5-1958, Mathews & Kingston, Newton Aycliffe
OLIVE BRANCH wood	HL 32		40'x15'x4'	sail	11t	decked boat, fished nets, crew 6 (ex-SD 40)
						27-9-1892, John Wm. Holman, 7, Brougham St, H/pool
						1900, sold to Sunderland
OLIVE BRANCH wood	HL 8		29.5'	sail	12t	coble, fished nets, crew 4
						1-3-1869, Mark Davidson, H/pool, sold 1877
OLIVE BRANCH wood	HL 120	1920	33'x9'x3'		4.5t	fished lines, crew 3 (ex-BK 300)
						9-9-1959, James Graham, Easington Coll.
						7-2-1967, W.P. Anderson, Blackhall
OLIVE LEAF wood	HL 221		20'	sail	3t	coble, fished nets, crew 2
						28-8-1872, Mathew Hunter, H/pool, sold for use as pilot boat
OLIVE LEAF wood	HL 185		20'	sail	3t	coble, fished nets, crew 2
						19-8-1869, Mathew Hunter, H/pool
ORION	HL 209	1987	8.5x3.5x1.1m	48kw	5.6t	built H/pool
						23-6-1987, Richard Longstaff, Elwick Gardens, H/pool
						10-4-1992, *Brenda Lynne* (SD 386), Sunderland
OSPREY	HL 25	1958	35'x8'x3'		6.3t	built Rhyl, fished lines, pots, nets
						3-8-1970, Kennith Maddison, Peterlee
OSPREY	HL 50	1987	9.3x3.2x1.1m		5.4t	fished pots, nets
						8-7-1987, Stan Weegram, Amberton Rd, H/pool
OSPREY grp	HL 1077	2005	9.95m	95kw		built Cornwall, inshore stern trawler
						4-5-2005, T. Greenwood, H/pool
						2007 sold to Norway
OSPREY 11 wood	LH 113	1961	10.6m	94kw	10t	
OSTRICH iron ON 95801	HL 61	1889	100'x21'x11'	steam 45hp	148t	built Cook, Weldon & Gammel, screw ketch rig, trawler, crew 8, yard No.41, engine, 2cyl. by C.D. Holmes, Hull
						1899, Hull (H 74)
						10-11-1900, F.W. Mason, 53, High St, H/pool, & T.H. Peverill, Northgate, H/pool
						8-2-1917 sunk by gunfire from sub, 135m NE Longstone
OTTO wood	HL 71		18.5'	sail	3t	coble, fished lines, crew 3
						1-3-1869, Maddison Horsley, H/pool
OUR ANN	HL 137	1944	31'x7'x3'		3.9t	built Amble, fished lines, nets, pots, ex-*Pride of the Wear* (SD224)
wood						25-6-1962, Sidney Bradshaw, 84, Howard St, H/pool
						4-12-1972, Stan. Vasey, 31, St Oswald St, H/pool
OUR EMMA wood	HL 232	1964	6.4m		1.92t	built Whitby
						4-4-1991, H/pool
OUR KATIE	HL 191	1954	15.3x5x2.1m	176kw	27t	built St Monance, fished trawl

Mickevel

Milano

Mizpah

Moorhen

Moray Gem

Moreleigh

NAME & MATERIAL	NO.	YEAR	LENGTH	POWER	WEIGHT	DETAILS
wood						?, ex-*Morning Star* (WK 155) 29-9-1982, Cedric Williams, Hart Village
OUR NORAS steel	HL 82	1988	11.8x5.3x3.2m	198kw	40t	built H/pool 14-11-1988, Jo. Gilmore, Blackhall 27-10-1989, *Misty Isle* (DS 4) Dumfries
OUR NORMA steel	HL 2	1989	9.07m	90kw	5.02t	built North Shields 9-11-1989, H/pool 16-5-1991, (OB 132) Oban
OUR PAT	HL 75		23'x7'x2'			fished lines 17-7-1957, Derek Short, Peterlee 3-9-1959, Frank & John Murray, H/pool 18-10-1960, Derek Wilson, 189, Wynyard Rd, H/pool
OUR RITA wood	HL 36	1946	8.6m	26kw	2.4t	built Amble 10-4-1992, H/pool
OUR THELMA wood	HL 87	1943	27'x8'x3'	31kw	3.4t	fished lines, pots 19-9-1951, Fred Train, 2, Tempest Rd, H/pool
OUR TRACY	HL 28		25'x7'x3'		2.9t	fished lines, pots 29-12-1970, Edward Gibbon, 22, Redworth Walk, H/pool
OUR TRACY JANE wood ON 182577	HL 95	1947	47'x15'x6'		23.5t	built Peterhead, fished seine, trawl 15-11-1978, Cedric & Keith Williams, H/pool 10-11-1986, H. Wilson, Morpeth 25-11-1986, Small & Co., Lowestoft
PAM wood	HL 39		16'x6'x2'		1.0t	motor dinghy 21-6-1956, Pyith & Shadforth & Pyith, H/pool 5-5-1959, T. Cornwell, 47, Sandsend Cres. H/pool
PAM	HL 64		16'x4'x2'		0.8t	fished lines 7-9-1972, J.B. Wilson, Seaton Carew, H/pool
PAMELA wood	HL 68		19'x6'x2'	sail	1.4t	fished lines, pots, crew 3 22-5-1942, Benjamin Thomas Hood, 45, Southgate, H/pool
PAMELA E. wood	HL 15	1982	10m	89kw	5.7t	built Kilkeel, ex-*Boy Andrew* ? H/pool
PANTRY BOY wood	HL 99		19'x6'x2'		1.4t	fished lines, pots, trawl, crew 2 29-9-1958, Cecil Leighton, 3, Talbot Place, H/pool 13-2-1967, H.M. Bousfield, 9, Pounder Place, H/pool 29-10-1975, K. Cadwallender, 45, Perth St, H/pool
PARKMORE steel ON 137107	HL 76	1915	115'x22'x12'	steam 80hp	199t	built Hall Russell, A/deen, ketch rig, yard No.582, launched 7-9-1915 engine 3cyl. by Abernethie, A/deen 16-10-1915, R.H. Davison & others, H/pool 1915–1919, Navy, m/s, 1x6pdr (A.164) 10-2-1925, D. Dow, Granton (GN 66), r/n *Ocean Nymph* in 1935 1936, R. Irvine, N. Shields, r/n *Ben Torc* (SN 99) 1939–1945, Navy m/s (FY 807) 1956, scrapped by Dorkin, Gateshead
PATRICIA wood	HL 65		25'x7'x2'	sail & motor	2.2t	lugger, fished lines, crew 3 30-11-1936, Mrs Alice Smith, 51, Hermit St, H/pool 3-11-1937, Herbert Vernon Merrick, 24, Alderson St, West H/pool 20-4-1938, Frederick King, Dock House, Harbour Tce, West H/pool
PATRICIA wood	HL 95	1959	27'x8'x3'		2.9t	coble, fished lines, nets, pots, crew 2 17-3-1959, W.K. Grigg, 39, Wansbeck Gdns, West H/pool 17-3-1960, Victor Deer, 30, Cobden St, West H/pool 28-9-1962, Matty McClelland & Danny Cole, Rowell St, H/pool 9-1964, reg. trans. to Sunderland (ex-*Eileen*)

NAME & MATERIAL	NO.	YEAR	LENGTH	POWER	WEIGHT	DETAILS
PATRICIA A. wood	WY 35	1971	8.7m	35kw	3.8t	? H/pool
PAUL DONNA	HL 25		10.9x2.7x0.5m		2.7t	built Rhyl
						21-4-1988, M.A. Sennett, Seaham
PAVONIA wood	HL 114	1955	50'x16'x5'		22t	built Macduff Eng. Co. fished trawl, seine
						1955, P. Simpson, Thurso (WK 53)
						1969, D. Simpson & others, Thurso (WK 53)
						6-9-1977, Eric Picknet, H/pool (HL 114)
						2004, Calum Miller, private use (40+FBA member)
PEARL wood	HL 85		16'x5'x2'	sail	1.0t	coble lug rig, fished lines, crew 2
						17-8-1941, James Booth Robson, H/pool
						25-6-1947, K. Richardson, 50, Elwick Rd, West H/pool, scrap 1949
PEGGY wood	HL 2		27'x8'x4'	sail & motor	4.3t	lugger, fished lines, nets, pots, crew 3
						15-5-1934, Francis Pounder, 89, Hutton Ave, West H/pool
						1936, sold to Sunderland
						? Tug Wilson, H/pool
						2001, Mick Dawson S. Shields, restored, afloat on Tyne
PEGGY POUNDER wood	HL 81		34'x8'x3'	sail & motor	7.8t	lugger, fished nets, lines, crew 5 (ex-lifeboat)
						5-8-1916, Francis Pounder, Ashbrooke, Park Rd, West H/pool
PERO ? wood	HL 126		31'	sail	10t	coble, fished nets, crew 4
						1-3-1869, William Barnard, H/pool, wrecked 1887
PERSEVERANCE wood	HL 74		33'x11'x6'		11.6t	fished lines, pots, crew 3, ex-Hallmark
						22-9-1947, Wilfred Earnest Cook, 26, Hart Lane, West H/pool
						29-9-1949, Davis & Moore, H/pool
						8-3-1954, K.O. Airey, M/boro
PETERBOROUGH	HL 41	1896	104'x20'x10'	steam	161t	built Mackie & Thompson, Govan, launched 29-1-1897, yard No.136
steel ON 108451				45hp		engine 3cyl. by Muir & Houston, Glasgow
						1896, Hagerup & Doughty (GY 244)
						1906, Consolidated Fisheries
						1914–1919, Navy m/s, 1x6pdr (A.631)
						15-1-1923, Geo. Whammond, 127, Durham St, H/pool, & others
						13-7-1927, H & B. Trawlers, 37, King St, South Shields
						31-12-1927, Waterloo S.T. Co., 3, Victoria Rd, Milford Haven
						28-5-1934, scrapped, Wards, Castle Pill
PHAETON steel	SN 59	1985	13.4m	149kw	19.4t	inshore stern trawler
						? H/pool,
PHOENIX wood	HL 251		19'	sail	3t	coble, fished nets, lines, crew 3
						5-3-1875, Charles Grange, H/pool
						19-2-1876, John Graham, H/pool
PHOENIX wood	HL 99	1978	6.2x2.4x2.2m	13kw	5.4t	
						16-11-1988, Stephen Holroyd, Penarth Walk, H/pool
PSYCHEDELIC	HL 56		26'x8'x6'		5t	fished lines, pots
						3-8-1972, Colin Roberts, 7, Hartness Rd, H/pool
PIENNEL ? wood	HL 55		27'	sail	11t	coble, fished nets, crew 3
						1-3-1869, Thomas Coulson, H/pool
PILGRIM wood	HL 83		27'	sail	8t	coble, fished nets, crew 4
						1-3-1869, Mathew Hunter, H/pool
						10-7-1872, Reed, Trentholme & Wilson, H/pool
PILGRIM wood	HL 291		19' keel 27'x5'x2' oa	sail -lug & jib	3t	coble, fished nets, lines, crew 3
						1-4-1878, Thomas Coulson, H/pool
						13-10-1891, Geo. Sothern, 10, Wells Yard, H/pool, sold1895
PILOT ME	HL 161		27x7'x3'		3t	fished pots, trawl (ex-BH 186)
						14-2-1967, Wm. Blackwell, Staithes

NAME & MATERIAL	NO.	YEAR	LENGTH	POWER	WEIGHT	DETAILS
						13-4-1976, A.F. McBurney, Redcar, sold to Sunderland, 1978
PIONEER	HL 59					
PODEROZA	HL 125		20'x7'x2'		2.2t	fished lines
						21-10-1960, Arthur Harren, Horden
POLLY wood	HL 293		16'	sail	1.0t	coble, fished trawl, crew 1
						20-5-1878, William Peart, H/pool
PREMIER wood	HL 2	1930	32'x8'x4'		5t	built Scarboro', fished lines, pots
						15-7-1969, Brian Graves, 18, Baker Close, H/pool
						16-7-1969, R.E. Strickland, H/pool, & E. Kent, Norton
						26-1-1973, Joseph Mathwin, 28, Bruce Cres, H/pool
						3-4-1973, Clayton & Douglas H/pool
PRESS ON wood	BF 65	1956	55'	317kw?	46t?	built Macduff Boatbuilding Co., fished seine, trawl
						1956, W. Watt, Gardenstown
						1969, Hartlepool Seiners (W.K. Grigg) H/pool
						1986, A. McDougal, Tarbet (AH 94)
						? Smith, Arbroath
						? J. Bruce Fraserburgh, no trace after 1997
PRIDE OF REDCAR wood ON 162466	HL 70	1950	47'	60hp Ruston	25t	built Slater & Barnard, Lossiemouth, cost £6,500
						1950, Picknet family, Redcar (fished from H/pool)
						24-4-1968, Thos, Creswell, Hadleigh, Suffolk
						25-2-1977, R.W. Tuck, Seaham
						4-12-1980, J. Ramsey, Wokingham
						25-6-1986, Kennith Johnson, 13, Lumley Sq.
						19-1-1987, Tom Whitehead, Maryport
						27-7-1988, J. Cully, & W. McClements, Portavogie
						2-9-1988, J. Cully, Portavogie
						1969, Thomas Creswell, Hadleigh, Suffolk
PRIMITIVE wood	HL 67		30'	sail	10t	coble, fished nets, crew 4
						1-3-1869, Thornton Bulmer, H/pool
						4-2-1873, Ann Bulmer, H/pool, sold to Sunderland
PRIMROSE wood	HL 30		29'x6'x2.5'	sail -lug & jib		coble, fished lines, nets, crew 3
						2-5-1892, Robert Hodgson, 1, Cambridge Bldg, Sandside H/pool
						? sold for pilot boat at West H/pool
PRIMROSE wood	HL 86	1930	39'x14'x5'		14t	built Cockenzie, fished lines, pots
						23-9-1958, Ewart Parsons Ltd, 42, Park Rd, West H/pool
PRIMROSE II wood	BF 87	1980	17.5m	231kw Cat		built Herd & Mackenzie, fished trawl, seine, & stand-by work
						1980, Joseph Kay Whalsay, as *Flourish II* (LK450)
						1988, J. Innes & J. Watt, Fraserburgh, as *Heather Brae* (BF 87)
						1999, A. Kenning, Mallaig, as *Leander K*
						2000, Ian Smith, Tarbet, as *Primrose II*
						2007, Major Hartley, H/pool
						2007, sold to Barra,
PRINCE IGOR wood ON 167491	HL 61	1888	56'x17'x6'	105hp	31t	built Frederickhaven, as sailing cutter *Mary*, fished trawl/seine
						oak on oak, engine installed before WW2
						23-5-1952, Wm. Edward West Craske, 41, Town Wall, H/pool
						23-7-1969, Henry Edward Craske, 2, Lumley Sq, H/pool
						29-6-1972, S. Robinson, Wallsend, & R. Casson, Monkseaton
						19-9-1977, Wm. Thos. Sanderson, Whitby
						25-8-1978, G. Dutton, London SW10
PRINCE OF WALES iron, ON98733	HL 8	1891	106'x20'x11'	steam 50hp	158t	built Cook, Weldon & Gammel, trawler, dandy rig
						engine 3cyl., by C.D. Holmes, Hull, 9 crew (ex-H 136)
						16-1-1914, J. Pattison, St Hilda's Cres., H/pool
						25-3-1917, sunk by sub 17m E by S Girdleness
PROGRESS	HL 45		42.5'x14'x10'	sail		ketch, fished nets, crew 5 (ex-SN 143 North Shields)

NAME & MATERIAL	NO.	YEAR	LENGTH	POWER	WEIGHT	DETAILS
wood				lug rig		15-8-1895, Walter Cook, H/pool Hotel, Duke St, West H/pool
						1900, scrapped
PROGRESS grp ON 378895	HL 189	1981	33'x15'x5'	240hp DAF	15.6t	inshore trawler, fished trawl
						17-6-1981, Keith Stead, Northallerton
						2000, sold to Jersey
PROGRESS grp	HL 189	1989	11.8m	179kw.	23t	inshore stern trawler
						12-2-1991, *Puffins Pride*, Leith (LH 105)
						5-4-2000, Keith Stead, r/n *Progress*, H/pool
PROSPECTION wood	BF 14	1954	45'	82kw	20t	built Macduff Eng Co., fished seine, trawl, re-engined 1970
						?, F. Laurence, Whitehills
						?, Fred Pearson, Marine Drive, Hartlepool
						? , D.B. Ewan, & H. Findlay, Whitehills, Banff
						1993, Thomas Lillco, Morpeth
						1996, fishing Amble
						2007, derelict on beach Newburgh, Fife, burnt on beach clean up
PROSPERITY wood	HL 27		30'	sail	10t	coble, fished nets, crew 4
						1-3-1869, Thomas Pounder, H/pool, sold to Sunderland 1876
PROTECT US wood	HL 14	1926	47'x15'x5'		17t	built St Monans, fished trawl
						20-7-1970, Derek Fowler, M/boro
PROTECTOR wood	HL 162	1914	26'x7'x2'		3.2t	built H/pool, fished lines, pots
						5-8-1965, Alfred Watt, Spennymoor
						18-12-1969, John Grand, Blackhall Coll.
PROUDFOOT wood	HL 151		36'	sail	12t	keel boat, fished nets
						20-4-1869, Wm. Middlemiss & Alexander Comb, H/pool
						31-1-1870, Francis Headley, West H/pool
PROVIDENCE	SD 262	1948	9m	23kw	3.3t	
						? H/pool
PROVIDENCE wood	HL 4	1937	44'x14'x7'		20.8t	built Cockenzie, fished lines, pots, nets, ex-*Euphrates*(LH 80)
						21-1-1955, L. & J. Robinson, 5, Frarage Gdns, H/pool
						20-12-1955, Geo. Craig, Eyemouth, re-reg. Berwick 1958
PROVIDENCE wood	HL 80	1926	35'x10'x3'		11.3t	built Eyemouth, fished nets, lines, crew 2
						27-5-1958, W. Musgrove, Easington Coll. wrecked 1958
PROVIDER wood	BH 57					coble
						? H/pool
PROVIDER wood	HL 14	1923	31'x11'x4'	sail & motor	6.8t	built St Monance, fished lines, pots, trawl, crew 4 (ex-KY 211)
						19-11-1934, J.W. Horsley, 6 Baptist St, H/pool &
						Geo. Horsley, 21, Marine Drive, H/pool
						4-9-1947, H.D. Horsley, 45, Earl St, & W.G. Bloomfield, Seaview Tce, Hartlepool
						7-2-1952, H.D. Horsley, 25, Earl St, H/pool, sold to S/land 1953
PROVIDER wood	HL 46		31'x11'x4'		6.8t	fished lines, pots, trawl
						24-8-1954, Edward Deer, 36, Town Wall, sold to Sunderland, 1955
PROVIDER II wood	WA 44	1958	7.83m	63kw	5.7t	inshore stern trawler, worked from Marina
						? H/pool, decommissioned 2008
PRUDENT wood	HL 274		18.5'	sail	2t	coble fished lines, crew 2
						6-10-1876, Johnson Pounder, H/pool
						23-8-1877, George Corner, H/pool
R.H. DAVISON steel ON 137110	HL 79	1916	115'x22'x12,'	steam 78hp	210t	built Hall Russell, ketch rig, trawler. Launched 18-4-1916
						yard No.583 crew 9, engine 3cyl. by builder
						15-5-1916, Hartlepool S.T. Co.
						1916-1919, Navy, APV1x6pdr (A.3296)
						6-4-1933, D. Wood, A/deen, as *Trielia* (A 260)
RACHEL wood	HL 22		27'x6'x2'	sail	2t	coble, fished lines, crew 3
						29-5-1890, Alexander Johnstone, 24, Slake Tce, Middleton

Nesmar

North Star

Norwood

Osprey

Our Ann

Our Kate

NAME & MATERIAL	NO.	YEAR	LENGTH	POWER	WEIGHT	DETAILS
RADIANT MORN wood	HL 19	1954	8.4x2.2x1m	42kw	2.9t	built Amble
						2-5-1985, Alan Smith, Stockton
RAE? wood	HL 37		31'	sail	12t	coble, fished nets, crew 4
						12-9-1882, Mary Hastings, H/pool
RAINBOW wood	HL 347		20' keel 27'x6'x2.5'	sail lug & jib	3t	lugger, open boat, fished nets, lines, crew 3
						10-3-1884, Robert Cambridge, H/pool
						26-3-1891, John Lowrie, 20, Clayton St, H/pool
						31-7-1893, Robert Carver, 9, Dovecote Yard, H/pool
RANGER steel	SR 82		9.92kw	69kw		inshore stern trawler, works from Marina
						? H/pool
RAPID	HL 63		30'x7'x3'		3.2t	fished lines
						2-11-1972, H.& K. Wilson, Blackhall Coll.
REACH OUT wood	HL 64	1973	9.9x2.9x1.1m	59kw	4.9t	built Whitby
						13-1-1988, R. Powell, Horden
						1-8-2006, Rachell (BF 3), Banff
REAPER wood	HL 11	1922	32'x11'x 5'	sail & motor	8.8t	built Peterhead, fished lines, trawl, nets, crew 3 (ex-LH 31)
						25-10-1934, Alfred Davison, 3, Sussex St, H/pool
						29-9-1937, Edward Sidney Gardner, 71, Commercial St, Middleton
REBECCA wood	HL 46		26'x5'x3'		2.6t	built on the Tyne, fished lines
						22-7-1940, reg. to local group, sold to Blackpool 1940
REBECCA JANE grp	HL 239	1991	8.1m	90kw	5.6t	built Silloth, inshore stern trawler
						31-7-1991, H/pool
						14-6-2006, (GU 37) Guernsey
						18-6-2008, (W 37), Waterford
RECLAIMED wood	HL 137		31'	sail	11t	coble, fished nets, crew 4
						3-3-1869, Maurice Harber, & Geo. Loughborough
						21-10-1873, Rowntree, Robson & Horsley, H/pool
						1876, sold to Whitby
REGNAULT steel ON 133315	H 156	1913	115'	steam 80hp	208t	built J.T. Eltringham, Stone Quay, S. Shields, launched 3-7-1913
						yard No.294, engine by Shields Engineering Co.
						1913, R. Irvine, N. Shields, as Northern Queen (SN 246)
						1914–1919 Navy, m/s (No.52)
						1920, F. & T. Ross, Hull
						? Sutton S.T. Co. Hull
						1937, W.J. Cook (Hull or Hartlepool?)
						1938, Sedgewick S.T. Co,(Hull or Hartlepool?)
						1939, Active F. Co. (J. Marr) Hull
						1940, J. Bennet Ltd, Hull
						1945, Anglo Steam F. Co. Grimsby (GY 46) as Inganes
						Feb 1953, scrapped
RELIANCE wood	BF 80	1988	18.1m	328kw		built Macduff
						4-2009, Major Hartley
RELIANT grp	HL 126	1989	7.24m	14kw	3.93t	
						6-10-1989, H/pool
RENOWN wood	HL 24		31'x9'x4'	sail & motor	9t	lugger, fished lines, crew 3
						30-9-1927, Wm. Cuthbert Snowden, 4, Lumley Sq. H/pool
						7-2-1928, foundered
RESCUE ON 68969	HL 355		83'	steam	78t	built Eltringham, Stone Quay, S. Shields, yard No.32, fished lines crew 7, screw steamer
						20-8-1884, John Pattison, H/pool, sold to Plymouth 1898
RESPONDO iron ON 121601	HL 63	1905	115'x21'x11'	steam 60hp	209t	built Cochranes, Selby, ketch rig, trawler, launched 8-4-1905, yard No.341, engine 3cyl. by C.D. Holmes Hull, crew 9
						1905, Cole, Carter & Galvin, Milford Haven (M 37) as Emerald

NAME & MATERIAL	NO.	YEAR	LENGTH	POWER	WEIGHT	DETAILS
						1906, insured for £6,000
						1911, fished off Munros Bay, Spain, landed in Milford for £158
						19-1-1917, Sleight, Grimsby, as *Respondo* (GY1019)
						1917–1919, Navy, Fishery Reserve
						22-11-1933, Doris Burton S.T. Co. H/pool (HL 63)
						1934, insured for £2,500
						23-1-1939, R.H. Davison, LNER Bldg, High St, H/pool
						10-5-1940, Yolland & Llewellin, Milford Haven
						9-1940, lost off the Old Head of Kinsale (enemy aircraft?)
RES----? wood	HL 226		19'	sail	3t	coble, fished lines, crew 3
						16-4-1873, Cuthbert Snowdon, H/pool
RHODA wood	HL 94		18'	sail	3t	coble, fished lines, crew 3
						1-3-1869, Robert Davidson, H/pool
						15-10-1875, Thomas Pounder, H/pool
RIPPLE wood? ON 102701	HL 38	1893	39'x9'x5'	steam main & 2 jibs	14t	screw steamer, fished trawl, lines, crew 4
						25-7-1893, Michael Burke & Hugh Melvin, West H/pool
						1896, sold out of fishing
RISLINGTON wood	HL 56		18'	sail	2t	coble, fished lines, crew 3
						1-3-1869, John Cambridge, H/pool
RITA wood	HL 36		22'x7'x2'		1.9t	fished lines, crew 3
						8-7-1940, reg. to local group, H/pool
RITA AILEEN wood	HL 99		17'x6'x2'		1.3t	built Abedeen, fished lines, pots, crew 2
						22-9-1947, Robert Ryder, 4, Lumley St, H/pool
ROBERT wood	HL 17		28'x6'x2'	sail	3.4t	built Hartlepool, coble, fished nets, crew 3
						13-6-1906, Wm. Horsley, 13, George St, H/pool
ROBERT wood	HL 37		27'x6'x2'	sail	3.2t	coble, fished nets, crew 2
						17-6-1909, James Hick, 22, Town Wall, H/pool, wrecked 1911
ROBIN	HL 3		19'x5'x1.5'	sail	1.7t	coble, fished lines, crew 2, r/n *Lavinia* 1929
						4-4-1924, Geo. Horsley, & Frank Sotheran, King St, H/pool
ROBIN HOOD wood	HL 166		30'	sail	11.5t	coble, fished nets, crew 4
						19-5-1869, Robert Hood, H/pool
ROBIN HOOD wood	SD 43					Whitby coble
						? H/pool
ROBIN HOOD II wood	HL 129	1960	30'x9'x3'		4.5t	built Whitby, coble, fished lines, pots, trawl (ex-WY 156)
						26-7-1961, Frank Sutheran, 1, Darlington St, H/pool
						15-10-1962, Frank Reed, & Thos. Noble, Gibb Sq. H/pool
						21-6-1968, Frank Reed, 4, Frier Tce, H/pool, sold to S/land, 1972
ROCKET wood	HL 102		26'	sail	8t	coble, fished nets, lines, crew 4
						1-3-1869, Robert Rowntree, H/pool
						9-6-1876, Johnson Pounder, H/pool
						23-11-1876, Jonathan Nicholson, H/pool
ROMY-JAY steel	HL 1086	2008	9.82m	143kw	11.9t	built Hartlepool, inshore stern trawler, built H/pool
						30-5-2008, H/pool
RONNIE	HL 48		15'x5'x2'		0.6t	fished nets
						24-7-1972, R. Maddison, Peterlee
RONSUS wood	GY 1359				23t	built Denmark, fished seine, trawl
						? Sleight, Grimsby
						1982, Lola, H/pool & Wm. Taylor, H/pool
ROSE wood	HL 37		31'	sail	12t	coble, fished nets, crew 4
						1-3-1869, George Horsley, H/pool
						24-2-1876, Thos. Reed & Mathew Hunter, H/pool
ROSE wood	HL 128		13.5'	sail	0.5t	small boat, fished draw net, crew 2
						3-3-1869, Wm. Blenkinsop, H/pool
ROSE	HL 273		25'	sail	5t	coble, fished nets, lines, crew 3

NAME & MATERIAL	NO.	YEAR	LENGTH	POWER	WEIGHT	DETAILS
wood						20-9-1876, Harvey Peak, H/pool
ROSE	HL 286		21'	sail	3.5t	coble, fished nets, lines, crew 3
wood						31-10-1877, Robinson Pounder, H/pool
ROSE	HL 73		20'x5'x2'	sail	1.0t	lugger, fished lines, nets, pots,
wood						8-10-1938, Robert Wilford, 22, Bowser St, West H/pool
ROSE MARY	HL 57	1913	31'x10'x3'		6t	fished pots, lines, nets, trawl, crew 3, ex-Sunderland
wood						21-6-1946, Thos. Forsyth, 46, Southgate, H/pool
ROSE OF ENGLAND	HL 95		27'x7'x2'		2.4t	fished lines, pots, nets, crew 3
						24-12-1947, J.W. Beresford, 82, Wilson St, West H/pool
						30-7-1948, F. Sutheran, 66, Hart Rd, sold to S/land 1950,
ROSE OF SHARON	HL 31		22'	sail	3t	coble, fished lines, nets, crew 3, scrapped 1916
wood						7-9-1892, Thos. Wm. Rowntree, Beacon House York Place, H/pool
ROSEWOOD	HL 114		18.5'	sail	3t	coble, fished lines, crew 3
wood						1-3-1869, Robert Pounder, H/pool
						17-5-1873, Robert Yeal, H/pool
ROVER	HL 6		26'x8'x2'	sail & motor	5.3t	lugger fished lines, crew 4
wood						17-11-1924, Gustav Groth, High St, H/pool, scrapped 1929
ROVER	HL 62		17'x6'x2'		1.3t	
						13-3-1957, J.R. Temple, 59, Miers Ave, H/pool
						20-7-1959, B., J.W. & J.V. Snowden, H/pool
ROYAL HUSSAR	HL 138		28'x10'x0.5'		2.9t	fished lines, nets
						? H/pool
						13-1-1980, R.E. James, Whitby
ROZ-E.	HL 146	1977	31'x11'x4'	104kw	7t	built Southampton, fished lines, nets, pots
grp						17-7-1979, J.T. Newton, M/boro
RUGBY	HL 5	1889	88'x20'x10'	steam 44nhp	107t	built Earl's, Hull, launched 7-3-1889, yard No.323
iron						screw, trawler, ketch rigged, ex-Grimsby (GY 201)
ON 96194						engine 2cyl. by Earls, boilers by F. Sudden, Stockton
						1889, Wm. Grant, Cleethorpes
						1892, G.F. Sleight, Grimsby
						3-1899, Wm. Grant, Grimsby
						12-4-1899, J.C. Graham, Fish Quay, H/pool
						8-1899, sold to Grimsby (GY 201)
						1913, The Rugby Wreaking Co. (salvage vessel) reg. H/pool
						1917, J. Doig, Grimsby
						2-1924, Grimsby Trawler Owners Direct Supply Co.
						11-1924, Bertha Backcomb, Grimsby, scrapped 1935
RUTH	HL 32		22'x6'x2'		1.4t	fished lines, nets, pots
						23-3-1971, H. Robinson, Billingham
RUTH LESLIE	HL 8	1983	9.6x3.8x1.0m		6.7t	built Middlesbrough
						30-9-1983, F.J. Evans, Hunter St, H/pool
						14-3-1988, Brian Ramsey, Howden Rd, H/pool
SABRE TOOTH	HL 86	1989	9.93m	246kw	7.13t	built Port Isaac
grp						27-9-1989, (E 111) Exeter
						19-7-1990, (HL 86) H/pool
						28-11-1991, (M 558) Milford Haven
SAGITTARIUS	LH 77	2000	9.8m	186kw	15t	inshore stern trawler
steel						1-5-2008, based Leith
						2009, Alan Greenwood, H/pool
ST CHRISTOPHER	HL 39	1969	16x5.3x2.1m	179kw	27.3t	built St Etable, France, fished trawl
wood						6-11-1986, Brian Harvey, Bolden Coll (BN 19)
						21-4-1987, Brian Harvey & Peter Coull, Billingham
						19-10-1987, Brian Harvey & A.G. Wiseman, Fraserboro'
SAINT CLAIR	HL 301		22'	sail	5t	coble, fished lines, crew 4

NAME & MATERIAL	NO.	YEAR	LENGTH	POWER	WEIGHT	DETAILS
wood						14-10-1878, James Borthwick, H/pool, re-reg. Berwick 1880
SALLIARITAU ? wood	HL 358		28'x6'x2'	sail	3.4t	coble, fished nets, lines, crew 3
SALMON LASS wood	HL 352		20'	sail	3t	15-9-1914, John Pounder, 1, Sussex St, H/pool coble, fished nets, crew 2
						8-7-1884, Robinson Pounder, H/pool
						6-5-1891, Robert Cambridge, 13, Wells Yard, H/pool
						1894, sold to Whitburn
SALT WINDS wood	HL 90	1987	8.9x2.9x1.3m	29kw	5.3t	
						8-7-1987, Kenneth Pearson, Throston, H/pool, reg. closed 3-1989
SAMARITAN wood	HL 66		30'	sail	10t	coble, fished nets, crew 4
						1-3-1869, Thomas Pounder, H/pool
						29-3-1886, Thos. Coulson, 12, Wells Yard, H/pool
SAMARITAN wood	HL 358		20'	sail	2t	lugger, fished lines, crew 3
						16-10-1884, William Morris, H/pool
SAMARITAN wood	HL 21		20'x6'x2'	sail	2t	built Hartlepool, coble, fished drift net, crew 2
						30-5-1906, Robert Pounder, 1, Sussex St, H/pool, sold 1908
SAMARITAN wood	HL 29		21'x5'x2'	sail	2t	built Hartlepool, coble, fished nets, lines, crew 2
						25-11-1921, Robert Pounder, 1, Sussex St, H/pool,
						28-6-1927, A. & R. Davison, York Place, H/pool
						1928, r/n *Sea Nymph*
SAM'S wood	SSS 3	1976	8.6m	9kw	3.3t	
						? H/pool
SAMUEL wood	HL 14		18.5'	sail	3t	coble, fished lines, crew 3
						1-3-1869, Thomas Marshall, sold to Seaham, 1881
SANDRA	HL 167		20'x7'x2'		2.3t	fished lines, pots
						14-6-1966, Ronald Pounder, 44, Winterbottom Ave, H/pool
						26-8-1971, Frederick Smith, 24, Mulgrave Rd, H/pool
SANRENE wood ON 333969	GY 152	1969	18m	150hp Gardner	34t	built by Jans Vester, Genna Havn, Denmark fished seine/trawl-stand by duties
						1969, W.E. Sanderson, Cleethorpes
						1993, Ian Boagey, H/pool
SARAH wood	HL 4		18.5'	sail	3t	coble, fished lines, crew 3
						1-3-1869, Robert Hood, H/pool
						1885, Cambridge (boatbuilder), H/pool
SARAH wood	HL 192		19'	sail	3t	coble, fished lines, crew 3
						9-3-1870, Richard Pounder, H/pool
SARAH wood	HL 265		19'	sail	3t	coble, fished lines, crew 3
						16-3-1876, Charles Cambridge, H/pool, scrapped 1883
SARAH wood	HL 287		18'	sail	3t	coble, fished lines, crew 3
						12-11-1877, James Rowntree, H/pool
SARAH wood	HL 10		22'x5'x2'	sail	1.2t	canoe, fished nets, lines, crew 2
						18-10-1929, Geo. H. Horsley, 6, King St, H/pool, sold to M/boro, 1932
SARAH ANN wood	HL 6		18'	sail	3t	coble, fished lines, crew 3
						1-3-1869, Pounder Davidson, H/pool
SARAH ANN wood	HL 298		20'	sail	1.0t	fishing boat, fished trawl, lines, crew 2
						16-8-1878, William Chapple, H/pool
SARAH ANN wood	HL 24	1967	9.84m	90kw	4.07t	built Whitby
						13-11-1990, *Chelcie Ann* (HL 24)
						18-12-2002, *Sarah Ann* (HL 24)
SARAH JANE wood	HL 10		22'	sail	3.5t	square stemmed boat, fished lines, crew 2
						15-2-1888, James Tipp, 25, Durham St, H/pool
						15-4-1888, lost at sea

Our Tracy Jane

Pavonia

Phaeton

Pot Luck

Press On

Pride of Redcar

Primrose

Prince Igor

Progress

Progress (2)

Prospection

Provider

NAME & MATERIAL	NO.	YEAR	LENGTH	POWER	WEIGHT	DETAILS
SARAH LYNN grp	HL 122	1994	6.57m	37kw	2.2t	built Little Neston, West Sussex 24-11-1994, *Hilbre* (CH 522), Chester 24-1-2001, *Sarah Lynn*, H/pool
SARAH LYNN II grp	HL 2	2000	7.52m	23kw	1.2t	small coble 10-8-2004, H/pool
SAUCY LASS wood	HL 193		18.5'	sail	3t	coble, fished lines, crew 3 15-3-1870, Thomas Davidson, H/pool, wrecked 20-11-1875
SAUCY NELL wood	HL 299		18'	sail	1.0t	keel boat, fished trawl, crew 2 19-8-1878, Frederick Smithson, H/pool
SAVARIA steel ON 145053	HL 36	1917	120'x22'x12'	steam 72hp	247t	built Cochranes, Selby, trawler, crew 9, yard No.692 engine, 3cyl. by Earls of Hull 1917, built as Admirality non-standard Mersey class trawler m/s *Cornelius Buckley* No.3581, 1x12pdr gun 1922, H.C. Baker, Grimsby (GY1341) r/n *Savaria* 1923, Baker & Green, Grimsby 1927, H.C. Baker, Grimsby 1928, Croft F. Co, Ayton House, Brougham St, H/pool 1931, R.H. Davison, L&NER Buildings, High St, H/pool (HL 36) 1932, A. Brown, N. Shields, r/n *L.H. Rutherford* (SN reg) 1937, A/S Raagan, Norway, r/n *Raagan* (R-161-H) 1940, German Navy, r/n *Eber*, guardboat NS21, sunk by Allied planes 17-2-1942, 59.07N 05.17E, south of Austboen
SCANBOY wood ON 166673	GY 579	1948	16.5m	80hp Ruston	23t	built Clarkson, Barton-on-Humber, Danish seiner/trawler On Register of Historic Vessels, Cert No.889 1948, Scania F. Co. Grimsby 1952, Scanboy F. Co. Grimsby 1968, Delga F. Co., Grimsby 1982, Delga F. Co. & J.J. Collins Grimsby 1983, Ton Sleight, Grimsby 1993, Major Hartley, H/pool ? Newry (N62)
SCEMA wood ON 187225	HL 79	1957	47'x15'x6'	88hp Kelvin	24t	built Thompson, Buckie fished seine, trawl, sister to *Dunelm* 23-10-1957, Lola Fishing Co, H/pool 8-6-1984, A.S. Lee, Sunderland 1993, Derek Rutherford, Morpeth
SCORPION grp	HL 183	1980	30'x11'x5'	150hp	8.24t	built Worcester, inshore trawler, fished trawl, nets, 21-9-1980, Keith Fletcher, Raby St, H/pool 2008, based in Eyemouth
SCORTON wood	AH 37	1973	15m	177kw		built Garrard Bros. Arbroath, fished trawl/seine 1973, Frank Reed & others, H/pool 1988, Mallaig Boatbuilding Co. r/n *Minch Harvester* (OB 441) 2002, D. MacNiel Castlebay, based Barra (CY 812) 2008, G. Askell, Carradale
SCOTCHMAN wood	HL 159		14'	sail	1.0t	small boat, fished lines, crew 1 1-5-1869, William Fowler, H/pool
SCOTIA wood	HL 316		37'	sail	9t	coble, fished nets, crew 5, ex-Whitby 17-5-1881, Webster & Graham, H/pool
SCOTTY	HL 194	1982	10x3x2m	90kw	6.6t	built Whitby 10-5-1982, K. & H. Wilson, Blackhall Coll. 15-4-1987, J. & E. Griffin, Blackhall Coll.
SEABIRD grp	HL 30	1989	7.32m	37kw	2.47t	8-12-1989, H/pool
SEA BREEZE wood	HL 7	1991	9.96m	90kw	15t	built Toms Poulran, inshore stern trawler 25-3-1991, Aberystwyth, as *Seren Y Don* (AB 54)

NAME & MATERIAL	NO.	YEAR	LENGTH	POWER	WEIGHT	DETAILS
						28-9-2001, Kirkcaldy (KY 1) 12-5-2009, H/pool, as *Sea Breeze* (HL 7)
SEA FISHER wood	WY 76	1972				Whitby coble, based in marina ? H/pool, decommissioned
SEA FLOWER wood	HL 262		37'	sail	12t	keel boat, fished nets, crew 6, ex-Anstruther 14-2-1876, J.G. Grieveson & J. Frampton, H/pool
SEA FLOWER wood	HL 21		23'x9'x3'	sail	2.5	keel boat, fished lines, crew 3 15-3-1890, John Young Purvis, Whitburn (ex-563 ME)
SEA JADE steel	HL 208	1980	9.1x3.6x1m	44kw	5.5t	built Graythorpe, H/pool 15-5-1987, Raymond Browne, Spearman Walk, H/pool
SEA NYMPH wood	HL 29		21'x5'x2'	sail	1.3t	lugger, fished nets, lines, pots, crew 3, ex-*Samaritan* 26-11-1928, Edward William Garbut, 18, Town Wall, H/pool 1933 motor added, re-reg.
SEA QUEST	HL 20		7.8x2.3x0.5m		1.1t	 18-5-1984, Winston Pearson, Lamberd Rd, H/pool, to Blyth 1988
SEA QUEST grp	HL 31	1985	7.87m	45kw	2.4t	built Cornwall 19-6-1990, H/pool 19-10-2007, *Grouse III* (KY 61), Kirkcaldy
SEA ROAMER grp	HL 120	1974	8.35t	37kw	1.4t	built Harrogate 9-2-1989, H/pool
SEA SHARK wood	HL 92	1989	29'x8'x4'	89kw	6.7t	fished nets, lines, pots 17-7-1978, D. Bousfield, Pounder Place, H/pool
SEA SPRAY	HL 139		24'x8'x3'		3.6t	fished lines, crew 2 25-7-1962, Percy Hughes, 193, Hart Lane, H/pool 27-10-1983, J.W. Hughes, Hart Lane, H/pool
SEA SPRAY wood	HL 18	1976	10.6x3.5x1.7m	62kw	9.7t	built Thornaby 17-4-1984, Robert Flannery, Moor Tce, H/pool
SEA SPRITE	HL 26		22'x8'x3'		2.9t	fished lines, pots, crew 2 29-12-1970, G. Smith & D. Olds, Peterlee, 15-11-1971, H. Dent, Peterlee, r/n *Tek-Naaf* in1971
SEA VENTURE	HL 56	1981	7.8x2.7x0.6m	29kw	1.9t	built Scarboro' 2-11-1987, J. Walsh, St Hilda's Chare, H/pool 11-7-1995, *Donna Anne* (BCK 369),
SEA WITCH	HL 61		8.2x2.5x0.9m		3t	 26-5-1988, W.A. Hall, Catherine Grove, H/pool
SEAGULL wood	HL 100	1908	21'x6'x2'	sail	2.2t	built Hartlepool, lugger, fished lines, crew 3 30-9-1918, John Pounder, 15, Croft Tce, H/pool
SEAHAWK wood	HL 154		22'x6'x2'	sail & motor	2t	lugger, fished nets, lines, crew 3 20-9-1932, J.R. Pugh, 7, Raby Rd South, West H/pool 2-12-1932, C. Straughton, 33, Corporation Rd, H/pool 16-11-1933, Stanley Steels, 30, Tristram Ave, West H/pool
SELINA wood	HL 65	1901	28'x5'x2'	sail	1.9t	lugger, fished lines, nets 11-12-1901, J. Hastings, 8, St Mary St, H/pool & Margaret Swales, 1, Croft Tce, H/pool 28-9-1905, James Hastings, Pier House, Sandgate, H/pool 24-8-1910, John Cambridge, 7, John St, H/pool, sold 1917
SEMNOS steel ON 133644	HL 91	1914	115'x22'x12'	steam 70hp	216t	built Duthie, A/deen, ketch rig, yard No.396, launched 24-1-1914 trawler, engine 3cyl. by Lingerwood, Glasgow, crew 9 1914, National S.F. Co. A/deen (A 18) 1914–1919, Navy, m/s, 1x3pdr (A. 1195) 1-5-1918, Grahams, H/pool 16-5-1919, Friarage S.T. Co. H/pool 1924, W. Carnie, Granton (GN 25) 1938, Silver Star F. Co., A/deen (A 423)

NAME & MATERIAL	NO.	YEAR	LENGTH	POWER	WEIGHT	DETAILS
						1939–1945, Navy, D/L, APV. (FY 726)
						1943, Regent F. Co., A/deen (A 18)
						1953, Iver F. Co., A/deen
						1958, scrapped Hamburg
SEVEN SONS wood	HL 98		21'	sail	3.5t	coble, fished lines, crew 3
						1-3-1869, Joseph Robinson, H/pool
						8-11-1873, William & Pounder Robinson, H/pool, scrapped 1875
SEVEN SONS wood	HL 62		18.5'	sail	3t	coble, fished lines, crew 3
						1-3-1869, Francis Bulmer, H/pool
SHABRI grp	HL 1070	2001	5.67m	12.7kw	1.7t	built Yorkshire
						5-4-2001, H/pool
SHAKESPEARE wood	HL 160		42'	sail	30t	smack, fished nets, crew 5
						5-5-1869, Wm. Bartlett, H/pool, lost, reg. closed 10-5-1870
SHAMROCK	HL 72		27'x8'x2'		2.8t	fished lines, nets, pots
						4-7-1975, Stanley Grills, 172, Seaton Lane, H/pool
						25-6-1979, G.L. Brown, 45, Bilsdale Rd, H/pool
SHANKLIN wood? ON 68558	HL 42		99'x16'x7'	steam fore & aft rig		screw steamer, schooner rig, fished lines, trawl
						19-4-1895, A.E. Pickard, 2, Bell St, West H/pool, sold1901
SHARON wood	SD 385		5.3m	9kw	1.3t	
						? H/pool
SHARON ANN wood	HL 162	1992	12.9m	152kw	19.7t	built Polruan
						11-3-1993, Alan Greenwood, H/pool
SHAUN DAWN	HL 106	1988	8.5x3.1x2.1m		9.2t	built Liverpool
						16-11-1988, L.H. Pearce, Bournmouth Drive, H/pool
SHEENA	HL 31		22'x7'x3'		22t	built Stockholm, fished pots
						1-6-1971, Joseph Ward, 66, Wansbeck Gdns, H/pool
						3-2-1975, M. Garthwaithe, Darlington
SHEENA MACKAY wood	HL 177	1932	41'x 14'x 5'		13.9t	built Macduff, fished lines, nets, pots
						15-2-1979, P.J. Ferguson, Blaydon
						10-11-1980, D.G. Rhodes, Blyth
						10-3-1981, M.P. Sedgewick, Seaburn
						25-7-1984, C.E. Eckersley, Buckie
						20-9-1984, M.P. Sedgewick, Sunderland, reg. closed 7-1984
SHIAN	HL 23		17'x7'x1'		2t	fished lines, pots, crew 2, ex-*Zaca*
						11-7-1953, Herbert Martin, 51, Welldeck Rd, H/pool
						9-6-1954, Thos. Raymond Truman, 23, Baptist St, H/pool
						16-4-1957, Milburn & Lamplough, H/pool
						14-6-1957, Grylls, & Jemmett, H/pool
						15-7-1959, Keith Fleetham, 18, Duke St, H/pool
SHEILA wood	HL 81	1940	23'x7'x3'		2.2t	built Norway, fished lines, pots, crew 2
						12-9-1947, Geo. Hogg, 64, Sandsend Cres. H/pool scrap 1956
SHIRLEY ANN	HL 141	1950	24'x7'x3'		2.8t	fished lines
						2-8-1962, Ronald Heartherington, Thirsk
SIL	HL 24		21'x 6'x2'		1.8t	fished lines, pots, ex-*Thomas David*
						2-9-1954, Thos. & David Lilly, West View, H/pool
						15-2-1955, Flounders, Walker, & Grainger, H/pool
SILVER DARLING	HL 40	1977	8x2.8x1.0m	43kw	3.8t	built Maldon
						16-9-1986, Sidney P. Davison, Regency Drive, H/pool
SILVER LINE wood	WY 146	1959	10.4m	63kw	6.1t	
						? H/pool
SILVER STAR wood	HL 78	1931	21'x6'x2'		1.6t	built Middleton, fished lines, pots, crew 2
						22-5-1942, Simeon Reay, 11, Sea Tce, Middleton, H/pool
						25-6-1947, Wm. Graham Charlton, 5, Sea View Tce, H/pool

NAME & MATERIAL	NO.	YEAR	LENGTH	POWER	WEIGHT	DETAILS
						21-9-1956, James Potts, 3, Croft Tce, H/pool
						18-9-1961, John Atkinson, 43, Brougham Tce, H/pool
SILVER JUBILEE wood	HL 90	1977	9.8m	89kw	5t	fished lines, pots, ex-*Hera* (WY 268)?
						13-12-1976, R. A. Robinson, 40, Marine Drive, H/pool
SILVER MOON OF TEES – grp ON 397708	HL 192	1981	10x4x1.5m	132kw	14.9t	built Worcester, inshore stern trawler
						28-6-1982, Clive Marrison, Stockton
						20-3-1987, N.K. Prentice, Tarbert
SINQUINA ? wood	HL 20		32'	sail	10t	coble, fished nets, crew 4
						1-3-1869, Robert Scott Pounder, H/pool, lost 16-6-1869
SIX BROTHERS wood	HL 42		18.5'	sail	3t	coble, fished lines, crew 3
						1-3-1869, Mathew Hastings, H/pool
SIX BROTHERS wood	HL 48		27'x5'x2'	sail	1.5t	coble, fished lines, nets, crew 3
						7-3-1900, George Whammond, 4, Lily St, H/pool, scrap 1933
SLIPSTREAM wood	HL 240	1965	8.1m	60kw	5.4t	
						14-2-1992, H/pool
SMILING MORN steel ON 106535	HL 27	1896	95'x19'x11'	steam 48hp	126t	built Hall Russell, A/deen, screw schooner rig, launched 3-3-1896, yard No.300, trawler, crew 8, engine 2cyl. by builder
						1869, Foyers S.F. Co. A/deen
						4-5-1908, T.H. Peverill, Northgate, H/pool & F.W. Measor, High St, H/pool
						12-12-1910, Wm. Cappleman, 6, Cliff Tce, H/pool
						14-7-1916, Wm. Barton, 15, Esk Tce, Whitby
						2-8-1916, sunk by sub 10m E of Coquet Island (time bomb)
SMILING MORN wood	HL 242		18.5'	sail	3t	coble, fished lines, crew 3
						30-3-1874, Pounder Davison, H/pool
SNOWGOOSE wood	HL 54	1965	21'x7'x2'		1.8t	built Whitby
						20-4-1972, British Railway Staff Assn Darlington
SONNDERBORGE wood ON 337308	HL 6	1969	62'	172kw	43t	Built Denmark, fished seine, trawl
						1982, Consolidated Fish, Grimsby
						1993, Richardson Seiners, Grimsby (H 63)
						11-1-2001, Major Hartley, H/pool, scrapped 2003
SOPHIE grp	HL 1060	1989	5.6m	7kw	1.6t	built Beverley
						5-11-1996, *Sarah Lynn II*
						5-1-2001, *Sophie*
SOUTHMOOR ON 109724 steel	HL 58	1900	95'x20'x11'	steam	133t	built Smiths Dock, N. Shields, ketch rig, launched 28-2-1900, yard No.625, trawler, crew 9
						27-3-1900, The Moor S.T. Co. Fish Quay, H/pool
						19-9-1902, Evan Mackenzie, Genoa, Italy as *Salvor*
SOVEREIGN wood	HL 165	1936	43'x15'x6'	62kw Gardner	18t	built Noble, Fraserburgh, fished, trawl, pots (ex-LH 368)
						listed in the Register of Historic Ships, Cert. No.164
						1936, Tom Hall, Newhaven
						? Navy?
						1946, Dawson, Seahouses
						? Port Seaton?
						22-10-1965, Victor Deer, 30, Cobden St, H/pool
						26-2-1969, D. Alexander, & E. Wood, Whitburn
						2010, under restoration, based North Shields
SOVEREIGN II wood	HL 45	1908	29'x10'x3'	sail & motor	5.6t	built Cockenzie, lugger, fished lines, pots, nets, crew 4
						15-4-1936, Henry Davis Horsley, 45, Earl St, H/pool
						25-6-1947, Joseph Victor Foster, 7, Cliff Tce, H/pool
SPARROW HAWK wood	HL 179		30'	sail	10t	coble, fished nets, crew 4
						7-7-1869, John Shepard, H/pool
SPRAY wood	HL 300		22'	sail	2t	coble, fished lines, crew 2
						3-10-1878, Henry Arnold & Wm. Aspinel, H/pool
						12-6-1879, Robert Robertson, H/pool, scrapped 1882

Provider II

Ranger

Rebbeca Jane

Regnault

Respondo

Romy-Jay

Ronsus

Rugby

Sagittarius

Sanrene

Sarah Lynn

Sarah Lynn II

NAME & MATERIAL	NO.	YEAR	LENGTH	POWER	WEIGHT	DETAILS
SPECTRON wood ON 378890	HL 77	1973	28'x8'x2'	60kw	4.2t	built Whitby, coble, fished pots, lines, nets, crew 2 10-3-1975, Keith Fletcher, Clavering, H/pool 1-7-1980, John Rowntree, 37, Percy St, H/pool ? sold r/n *Else Riley*, scrap 2007
SPINDRIFT grp	HL 59	1986	9.8m	261kw	5.3t	built Cornwall 29-10-1990, H/pool
SQUIRREL? wood ON 86387	HL 330		62'	sail	66t	ketch, fished lines, crew 9 10-4-1883, F. Pounder, H/pool, vessel lost
ST. AIDEN	HL 89	1946	54'x16'x6'		24.8t	built Zwolle, Holland, reg. trans. to Montrose, 1974 15-3-1971, one season scalloping from Kirkcudbright 12-2-1973, T.H. Jones, Hoylake, Cheshire 1974, reg. trans. to (ME 69) to Cockenzie, Fife, laid up
ST. IVES	HL 31		18'x6'x2'		1.3t	fished lines, ex-*Isabell* 14-8-1948, Sidney Bradshaw, 84, Howard St, H/pool 23-1-1956, M.H. Porritt, 17, Town Wall, H/pool
ST. JOHN wood	HL 1		22'	sail	3t	coble, fished lines, crew 3 29-9-1886, Wm. Pounder, 23, Sussex St, H/pool 1909, Wm. Simple, Sunderland
ST. JOHN wood	HL 99	1905	18'x5'x2'	sail	1.7t	built Hartlepool, lugger, fished lines, crew 2 30-9-1918, Thos. Pounder Metcalf, 4, Sussex St, H/pool, sold 1923
ST. MARY steel ON 99499	HL 54	1898	91'x19'x9'	steam	99t	built Wood Skinner, Bill Quay on Tyne screw, ketch rig, trawler, crew 8 21-3-1898, St Hilda's S.F. Co., 4, Town Wall, H/pool J.B.Graham (managers) shareholders Samuel Thos. King, J.T. Graham, John James Lister, Samuel Francis, J.B. Graham 17-4-1916, sold to Milburn, Whitby
ST. HILDA steel ON 99495	HL 50	1897	91'x19'x9'	steam	93t	built Wood Skinner & Co., Newcastle screw, ketch rig, fished trawl, crew 8 26-1-1897, St Hilda S.F. Co., 4, Town Wall, H/pool 17-4-1915, Milburn, Whitby 25-9-1916, captured by sub sunk by gunfire, 20m NE Scarboro'
ST. HILDA steel ON 187221	HL 25	1955	102'x22'x12'	2SA-6cyl Crossley	182t	built H. Scarr, Hessle, trawler, launched 6-4-1955, yard No.725 22-6-1955, Friarage S.F. Co., H/pool 11-7-1963, Boston Deep Sea, Fleetwood, reg. trans. to Lowestoft
ST. HILDA	HL 177		23'x7'x2'		2.3t	fished lines, pots, crew 2 14-2-1967, Alan Vale, 33, Davison Drive, H/pool 28-5-1970, John Hardy, 28, Greta Ave, H/pool
ST. HILDA	HL 703	1999	5.09m	11kw	0.66t	4-1-1999 H/pool
STAR wood	HL 36		18.5'	sail	3t	coble, fished lines, crew 3 1-3-1869, George Horsley, H/pool, sold 1876
STAR wood	HL 65		18'	sail/oar	3t	coble, fished lines, crew 3 1-3-1869, John Pounder, H/pool 11-5-1872, Mark Davison, H/pool 12-6-1876, George Corner, sold to M/boro1877
STAR wood	HL 129		14'	sail	0.75t	small boat, fished draw nets, pots, crew 2 3-3-1869, James Westhill, Seaton Carew
STAR wood	HL 237		18.5'	sail	3t	coble, fished lines, crew 3 15-12-1873, Thomas Pounder, H/pool, sold to Seaham 1875
STAR wood	HL 264		18.5'	sail	3t	coble, fished lines, crew 3 16-3-1876, Charles Cambridge, H/pool, scrapped 1883
STAR OF HOPE	HL 165		40'	sail	14t	coble, fished nets, crew 5

NAME & MATERIAL	NO.	YEAR	LENGTH	POWER	WEIGHT	DETAILS
wood						19-5-1869, Robert Sheldon, H/pool 2-10-1872, Geo. Greveson, H/pool, lost off Yarmouth, Oct. 1873
STAR OF HOPE wood	HL 165		40'	sail	14t	coble, fished nets, crew 6 30-7-1870, Thomas Pattison, H/pool
STAR OF HOPE wood	HL 28			sail & motor		coble, double ender, possibly one of the first fitted with engine 1871, Geo. Horsley?
STAR OF HOPE wood	HL 28	1908	45'x12'x4'	sail & motor	21.7t	built Hartlepool, motor lugger, fished lines, nets, crew 6 29-4-1908, Ralf Cole, 174, Sherriff St, West H/pool 22-1-1919, Leonard Hodgson, 56, Church St, West H/pool 6-5-1911, R.W. Milburn Whitby
STAR OF HOPE wood	HL 49	1923	35'x7'x3'	sail	4.5t	built Hartlepool, lugger, fished lines, pots, trawl, crew 3 9-4-1936, Lawrence & Melvin Carter, Church St, Seaton Carew 1939, sold to Scarboro'
STAR OF THE EAST wood	HL 333		46'	sail	14t	lugger, fished trawl, nets, crew 6, ex-Berwick 19-5-1883, Thomas Hogarth, H/pool 4-12-1885, Nicholas Dyer, Coltmans Passage, H/pool 19-5-1886, Alex. Whitford, 38, High St, H/pool
STAR O'TAY wood ON 60798	HL 290	1870	92'x19'x9.3'	steam - rig fore & aft 50hp.	29t	built Rennoldson, North Shields, fished lines, trawl, crew 5 engine, side lever, single-cylinder, ex-paddle tug 1874/1875, Dundee 4-3-1878, Isaac Sharp, H/pool, sold, 7-1878 (from register) 1878, North Shields 1881, Scarbrough 21-5-1888, sprang leak, sank, Lyndsway Rocks, Milford Haven
STATLEY wood	HL 168		18'	sail	3t	coble, fished lines, crew 3 19-5-1869, Mark Davidson, H/pool, scrapped 1875
STATLEY wood	HL 177		30'	sail	12t	coble, fished nets, crew 4 29-6-1869, Charles Cambridge, H/pool, sold to Seaham 1870
STELLA MARIS grp	HL 705	1999	33'	116kw Daewoo	12t	built Penryn, inshore stern trawler 28-3-2000, Martin Walsh, H/pool
STEPHANOTOS wood	HL 84	1882	40'x15'x2'	sail & motor	24t	built Eyemouth, lugger, fished lines, nets, crew 5 15-8-1916, Francis Pounder, Ashbrooke, Park Rd, West H/pool 12-3-1922, wrecked
STORMY C steel	WY 818	2003	9.96m	119kw Volvo	15.9t	built Barton-on-Humber, inshore trawler ? Bridlington, crab fishing 2008, Tony Greenwood, H/pool
STRANDBY wood	HL 7	1941	46'x 14'x 6'	62hp	24t	built Faborg, Denmark, as Lola, oak on oak, fished seine/ trawl original engine, single-cylinder, re- engined 1967 with Cummins 6cyl. pre-1948, Whitehaven (WA 14) 12-4-1948, J. Graham & Son, Albert Pugh, Wm. Thomas & Martinus Carlson, all H/pool 6-4-1964, Carlson & Lola F. Co., H/pool 1-2-1957, Lola F. Co., H/pool 18-7-1963, Arthur Fenwick, Brierton Lane, H/pool 27-4-1965, Geo. Smith, Banff, & Simon Smith, West H/pool 15-3-1966, S.J. Stevenson, Whitley Bay 25-10-1966, S.J. Stevenson & J.A. Lyon, North Shields 7-2-1975, J.A. Lyon, North Shields 12-11-1976, E.H. Hanson, North Shields 1977, B.E. Porrit, Ramsgate ? Ramsgate Maritime Museum, scrapped 2007
SUCCESS wood	HL 199		18.5'	sail	2.5t	coble, fished lines, crew 3 18-10-1870, Robert Spence, H/pool

NAME & MATERIAL	NO.	YEAR	LENGTH	POWER	WEIGHT	DETAILS
SUCCESS wood	HL 9	1948	31'x7'x3'		3.7t	30-10-1871, Thomas Coulson, H/pool fished lines, nets, pots
SUCCESS wood	HL 45	1992	9.74m	26kw	3.8t	5-5-1948, George & John Hogg, H/pool built Amble
SUE CHRISTINE	HL 143		25'x9'x4'		5.3t	22-4-1992, H/pool fished lines, pots, trawl, crew 2, scrapped 1974
SUMMER CLOUD wood	HL 112		36'	sail	13t	16-10-1962, Raymond Edward James, 3, York Place, H/pool keel boat, fished nets, crew 5
SUNBEAM wood	HL 186		21'	sail	3t	1-3-1869, David Borthwick, H/pool 18-6-1872, Mary Borthwick, H/pool 12-2-1877, James & David Borthwick, H/pool coble, fished nets, crew 2
SUNBRITE wood	HL 38	1971	9.5m	61kw	4.3t	30-8-1869, Thomas Watt, H/pool, sold 1871 built Whitby, coble, ex-Sunderland?
SUNRISE wood	HL 60	1950	8.8m	27kw	2.53t	? Alec Johnstone, H/pool built Amble, coble
SUPERB wood						22-5-1992, H/pool keel boat
SUPREME wood	HL 45		53'x18'x6'	sail & motor	25t	? H/pool built Eyemouth, fished lines, nets, crew 7 4-4-1910, Thomas Hood, 4, John St South, H/pool 17-3-1913, Thomas Hood & others, H/pool, motor added 1914 11-9-1918, Francis Hastings, Rockhurst, South Crescent, H/pool 1920, wrecked
SUPREME wood	HL 42	1965	15.9m	238kw	39t	built Anstruther, fished seine/trawl 1989, Supreme, H/pool 15-11-1989, Numora III (BA 42) Ballantrae
SUPREME wood	HL 1073	1973	16.77m	172kw	48t	built Fraserbrugh, fished trawl, seine 1-1-1989, Five Sisters, Oban 22-3-1995, Aurora, Castlebay 14-4-1998, Primrose, Fraserburgh 2-7-1999, Primrose, Castlebay 17-7-2002, Supreme, H/pool, Kenny Johnson
SUPREME ENDEAVOUR wood ON 162465	HL 109	1950	41'x16'x6'	60hp Kelvin	23t	built Slater & Barnard, Lossiemouth, cost £6,500 fished trawl, seine, first trawl net cost £17 10s (£17.50) 16-5-1949, Joseph Edward Picknett, 66, Marine Dr., H/pool Phillip Picknet, 17, South Tce, Redcar 4-11-1975, Terry Clapp, 8, Spalding Rd & Barry Clapp, 42, Southbrook Ave, H/pool
SUPREME ENDEAVOUR II wood ON 706157	HL 42	1965	15.9x5.2x1.9m		41t	built Anstruther, fished trawl 18-12-1986, Kennith Johnson, Lumley Sq., H/pool 5-5-1987, r/n Supreme
SUSAN wood	HL 45	1929	23'x7'x2'	sail & motor	2.1t	fished lines, pots 4-10-1956, Stanley Leviet, 8, Westbourne Rd, H/pool
SUSAN ANN wood	HL 22	1948	26'x7'x3'		3t	built Mevagissey, fished lines, pots 1-7-1970, C.W. Maddison, Rotherham 5-8-1970, Wm. Mathwin, 12, Mapleton Rd, H/pool
SUSAN LOUISE wood	HL 44	1969	8.9x3.2x1.2m	53kw	5.3t	built Middlesbrough 14-7-1987, C. Robbins, & R. Nesbitt, H/pool
SUSANNE	HL 102		27'x8'x3'		3.3t	fished lines, pots, ex-Freda, ex-Madge 18-6-1954, Garland & Duffy, H/pool 19-8-1955, Sidney Bradshaw, 84, Howard St, H/pool

NAME & MATERIAL	NO.	YEAR	LENGTH	POWER	WEIGHT	DETAILS
						2-8-1962, B.B. Shaw, 5, Union Rd, H/pool
						8-10-1970, Robert Kelly, 12, Lumley Sq., H/pool
						1-12-1980, David Owens, Wiltshire Way, H/pool
SUVERA grp	HL 1054	1992	9.8m	101kw	11.3t	built Middlesbrough 21-2-1992, H/pool
SUVERA wood	MH 276	1978	7.9m	37kw	3.4t	 ? H/pool
SVEN KNUD wood ON 167501	HL 72	1911	53'x15'x4'		20.8t	built Svendborg, Denmark, motor cutter, fished seine, crew 4 ex-Buckie (BCK 200) 17-7-1950, Wm. Craske, 41, Town Wall, H/pool 16-10-1952, Wm. & Henry Craske, 21, St Hilda St, H/pool 10-11-1960, Richard Newton, Sunderland
SWEET HOME wood	HL 348		27.5' keel 29'x11'x2.5'oa	sail	9t	lugger, fished nets, lines, crew 4, ex-Montrose 19-3-1884, John Shaw & Wm. Watt Jnr, H/pool 24-6-1890, J.C. & J. T. Graham, H/pool, sold to Kirkcaldy 1893
SWIFT wood	HL 232		19'	sail	3t	coble, fished lines, crew 3 19-8-1873, James Bond, H/pool, sold to Middlesbrough 1874
SWIFT wood	HL 313		18'	sail	2t	boat, fished trawl lines, crew 3 1-7-1880, Edward Jobson, H/pool
SWIFT wood	HL 314		36'	sail	8t	smack, fished trawl, lines, crew 4 16-8-1880, Simeon Wray, H/pool, sold to Yarmouth 1882
SWIFTWING steel ON 145827	HL 147	1925	86'x18'x7'	240hp Ruston	99t	built Cochrane, Selby as steam drifter 1925, Seagull F. Co. Lowestoft, as *Sternus* (LT 238) 1954, steam replaced by diesel, r/n *Swiftwing* 20-2-1964, Lola F. Co. scrapped 1970
SYBIL iron ON 86390	HL 53	1883	98'x21'x10'	steam,45hp & sail	127t	built Baltic Iron Works, Hull, screw ketch rig, fished trawl, crew 8, engine 2cyl., by Wood Bros. Sowerby Bridge, built as fish carrier 13-10-1883, H/pool Fishing Co. (reg. in Stockton as fish carrier) ?-8-1884, Craddock, & Brocklebank, London 12-2-1885 refitted for trawling, re-reg. (LT 77) ?-3-1885, Brocklebank, London (manager, Jones, Lowestoft) 19-2-1890, London Trawlers Ltd (LO 37) fishing Milford Haven 3-10-1895, sold to Germany
SYLVIA T. grp	HL 1076	2004	6.4m	24kw	1.93t	built Cambourne 24-2-2005, H/pool
TALLY O. wood	HL 156		30'	sail	10t	coble, fished nets, crew 4 26-4-1869, Thomas Hodgson, H/pool 7-6-1871 Geo. Gales, Staithes
TANTALLON wood ON 91080	LH 1131	1885	65'x17'	steam 50hp	125t	built Hawthorns, Leith, dandy rigged trawler, launched 6-1885 engine 2cyl. by builder, possibly first steam trawler in H/pool 1885, L. Kendal, North Berwick 1897, J.T. Graham, H/pool 12-9-1910, sank 20m SE H/pool
TAURUS grp	CO 6	1989	11.6m	240hp Cummins	24t	inshore trawler, based H/pool 1989, Stead Bros. Northallerton
TEESSEAL	HL 131		50'x11'x5'		16t	fished lines 5-7-1978, D.A. Wallis, Castleton Rd, Seaton Carew
TERN wood	HL 8		33'x9'x2'		4.0t	built Whitby, fished lines, pots 5-2-1970, Alfred Watt, Spennymoor 29-3-1974, L. Giddy, Stockton 14-7-1976, J. McGahern, Stockton, r/n *Shawnie Boy* 1976
TERRI LOUISE steel	HL 34	1988	9.99m	131kw	10.7t	built Barry, inshore stern trawler 6-11-1996, *Oyster Hound* (CF 40), Cardiff 17-10-2002, *Terri Louise* (HL 34) H/pool 29-8-2007, *Terri Louise* (WD 246), Wexford

Scema

Scorton

Scotty

Sea Breeze

Sharon Ann

Sonderborg

Sovereign

Spectrum

St Hilda

St Hilda

Stormy C

Strandby

NAME & MATERIAL	NO.	YEAR	LENGTH	POWER	WEIGHT	DETAILS
TERRI LOUISE wood	HL 6					built Denmark, fished seine/trawl
						2007, Major Hartley
TETSUKO steel	HL 179	1979	27'x10'x3'	89kw	6t	fished lines, nets, pots, inshore stern trawler
						21-6-1979, Peter Waller, Bruce Cres., H/pool
THANKFULL wood	HL 40		21'x6'x2'	sail	1.3t	built Hartlepool, lugger, fished lines, nets, crew 3
						4-2-1929, L.W. Carter, 12, Church St, Seaton Carew
						3-10-1932, J.B. Robson, Jnr, 15, Ashburn St, Seaton Carew
						28-7-1933, A. Stevenson, 28, Dalton St, West H/pool
THANKFULL wood	HL 5	1916	30'x10'x4'	sail & motor	9t	built Yarmouth, lugger, fished lines, nets, crew 5
						29-1-1919, A.R. Sutton, Fish Quay, H/pool
						1919 sold to Scarboro'
THE BOYS wood	HL 83		20'x6'x2'		1.5t	fished pots, lines, crew 3
						28-5-1942, Thos. Forsythe, 46, Southgate, H/pool
						24-6-1942, Geo. Whammond, 4, Friarage Gdns, H/pool
						24-9-1946, Robert Winspear, 2, Prospect Place, Whitby
THE DOGGER	HL 128		25'x7'x3'		2.8t	fished nets
						25-7-1978, K. Pearson, Throston Grange Lane, H/pool
THE BROTHERS wood	HL 73	1927	28'x7'x4'		4t	fished trawl, lines
						4-11-1975, T.M. & B.M. Clapp, H/pool
THE FIVE BROTHERS wood	HL 60		18.5'	sail	3t	coble, fished lines, crew 3
						1-3-1869, James Moor, H/pool
						12-8-1875, James Bond, H/pool
						25-10-1876, Jonathan Nicholson, H/pool
THE MICHELLE	HL 110	1960	9.5x2x1.1m		3.5t	
						16-11-1988, Ron Stead, Sandsend Cres., H/pool
THE ROVERS wood	HL 19		24'	sail	3t	coble, fished lines, crew 3
						31-1-1890 James Hastings, John St, H/pool
THISTLE wood	HL 2		30'	sail	6.5t	Scotch yawl, fished lines, crew 4
						27-4-1887, Wm. Riddle, 28, Bank St, Middleton, H/pool
THISTLE steel ON 120944	LL 64	1906		steam 67hp	228t	built Cochranes, Selby, launched 12-3-1906, yard No.362
						screw, ketch rig, engine, 3cyl. by C.D. Holmes, Hull
						1906, J. Duncan & Co. Liverpool
						? W. Wray, H/pool
THISTLE wood	HL 10		26'x6'x2'		2.4t	fished lines, pots, trawl, crew 3
						30-11-1944, J.H. Leighton, 39, Lily St, H/pool
						13-12-1944, Francis Osbourne, 1, Dock Gate Cottage, West H/pool
THOMAS wood	HL 9		29'	sail	11.5t	coble, fished nets, crew 4
						1-3-1869, Mark Davidson, H/pool, scrapped 1877
THOMAS wood	HL 182		20'	sail	3t	coble, fished nets, crew 2
						13-8-1869, Thomas Horsley, H/pool
THOMAS wood	HL 101		22'x5'x2'	sail	2.2t	built Hartlepool, lugger, fished lines, crew 2
						1-10-1918, Robert Horsley, 8, Wells Yard, H/pool
THOMAS DAVISON wood	HL 315		42'	sail	12t	keel boat, fished nets, crew 6
						6-1-1881, J.W. Holman, & Geo. Griveson, H/pool
						22-5-1890, J.W. Holman, 7, Brougham St, H/pool
THOMAS SUTTON steel ON 137109	HL 80	1916	115'x22'x12'	steam 78hp	211t	built Alex. Hall, A/deen, ketch rig, trawler, yard No.519,
						launched 16-3-1916, crew 9, engine by builders
						1916, Sutton S.T. Co. 19, Fish Quay, H/pool
						1916–1919, Navy, m/s, 1x6pdr, AA (A 3276)
						23-12-1921, G. Robb, A/deen, r/n Craiglea (A 822)
						1957, scrapped
THOMAS & JAMES	HL 143		18.5'	sail	3t	coble, fished nets, crew 4

NAME & MATERIAL	NO.	YEAR	LENGTH	POWER	WEIGHT	DETAILS
wood						15-3-1869, Johnathan Nicholson, H/pool
						30-7-1870, Robert Sheldon, H/pool, sold to Whitby 1876
THOMAS & MARY wood	HL 18		30'x7'x2'	sail	4.7t	built Hartlepool, coble, fished nets, lines, crew 3
						15-6-1906, Thomas Sayer, 16, Sussex St, H/pool
						1912, James Young, Sunderland,
THOMAS YOUNG steel ON 137357	HL 15	1914	115'x22'x13'	steam 83hp	194t	built Eltringham, Willington Quay, launched 7-7-1914, yard No.303 ketch rig, trawler, engine 3cyl. by Shields Engineering Co. 1914, (SN 67)
						1915–1919, Navy, 1x12pdr, 1x6pdr (A 1143)
						11-4-1919, T.H. Peverill, 13, Albion Tce, H/pool
						24-1-1924, stranded and abandoned
THORA wood	HL 55		24'x7'x3'	sail & motor	2.6t	lugger, fished lines, crew 3
						8-2-1933, J.R. Graham, 15, Cliff Tce, H/pool, wrecked 1934
THREE J'S	HL 131		19'x6'x2'		1.5t	fished lines, pots, ex-*Mag* (SD 73)
						15-9-1961, T. Cummel, 47, Sandsend Cres. H/pool
						29-10-1962, J.W. Jarps?, Owton Manor, H/pool
THREE LADS wood ON 182660	GY 137	1950	50'	132hp	41t	built Buckie, fished pots
						1950, F.C. & A.J. Sutherland, Grimsby
						1967, Wm. Lewis, 85, Marine Drive, H/pool & Walter Lewis Grimsby
						1969, W. & F. Lewis, Bridlington
						1976, Bonser & Tonkin, Penzance
						1993, G.K. Tonkin, Penzance, Cornwall
THREE PALS wood	HL 50		17'x5'x2'	sail	1.0t	lugger, fished lines, pots, crew 3
						3-10-1931, John Southern, 12, Third St, Blackhall, scrap, 1935
THREE SONS wood	HL 43		18.5t	sail	3t	coble, fished lines, crew 3
						1-3-1869, Mathew Hastings, H/pool, sold to Whitby, 1874
THRIVE wood	HL 89	1896	57'x18'x6'	sail & motor	54t	built Eyemouth, lugger, fished nets, lines, crew 7
						10-10-1917, F. Pounder, Ashvale, Park Rd, H/pool, scrapped 1925
TIKI	HL 67		27'x6'x2'		1.9t	
						23-1-1973, R.P. Thwaite, Blackhall
TINE ANDERSON wood	HL 170		48'x15'x6'		21t	built Aarhus, Denmark, fished seine/trawl
						20-7-1966, Barbara Hetherington, Llanethly, based H/pool
						11-1974, reg. closed
TOILER	HL 62	1972	36'x12'x2'		12.3t	fished lines, pots, trawl
						14-8-1972, Clive Morrison, Stockton
TO ME wood	HL 269		18'	sail	2.5t	coble, fished lines, crew 3
						8-8-1876, James Bond, sold to Whitby, 1880
TOP O' THE MORN wood	HL 14		21'	sail	3t	coble, fished lines, crew 3
						26-1-1889, Anthony Davison, 14, Chapel St, H/pool
TORNI	HL 2		24'x7'x2'		2.8t	fished lines, pots, ex-ship's lifeboat from *Torni*
						11-8-1948, W.K. Blair, Wolviston
TORS iron ON 98728	HL 59	1891	104'x21'x11'	steam 50hp	187t	built Cochrane, Beverley, ketch rig, trawler engine 3cyl. by C.D. Holmes Hull ex-*Golden Hope* (H 131) ex-*Olga*
						7-5-1911, Charles Hall, Cleadon, Sunderland
						1914, C. Hall, H/pool
						13-7-1915, Harry Wood, & Niels Schorn, Grimsby
						28-7-1915, mined, 43m E of Spurn Point. 8 crew lost
TOTTY	HL 148		16'x4'x2'		1.0t	fished trawl lines
						17-8-1965. Hunter Boagey, 54, Keswick St, West H/pool
TRACY JANE wood	HL 82	1936	47'x15'x5'		18t	built Clyde, fished trawl
						16-5-1974, Cedric Williams, 12, Gladstone St, H/pool
TRACY MICHELLE	HL 21		8.3x2.7x1.2m		4.3t	built Whitby

NAME & MATERIAL	NO.	YEAR	LENGTH	POWER	WEIGHT	DETAILS
TRADE WINDS	HL 118		25'x7'x4'		4t	10-9-1984, David Horsley, York Rd, H/pool built Germany 4-9-1959, F. Bain, 35, Carlton St, H/pool 15-10-1962, W.O. White, Eaglescliffe 28-7-1967, S.E.D. Johnson, 20, Patterdale St, H/pool 28-10-1969, Daniel Cummins, 6, Snowden Grove, H/pool
TRAWLER wood	HL 303		14.5'	sail	2t	boat, fished trawl, crew 1 21-7-1879, Frank Pringle, H/pool
TRES AMIGOS	HL 154		29'x7'x3'		4.3t	fished pots, lines 6-5-1965, J.W. Snowden, 43, Wharton Tce, H/pool
TRIUMPH iron ON 49728	HL 18	1867	95'x18'x10'	steam 50hp	102t	built T. Hepple & Co, Low Walker, yard No.215, crew 7 engine 1cyl., lever, by builder, ex-paddle tug Wonder fished trawl 15-1-1890, J.K. & J.C. Graham, 9, Union St, H/pool 1894, F. Goodwill, Scarboro'
TRIUMPH wood	HL 150	1949	27'x8'x2'		3.8t	26-6-1968, W. Wilkinson, Haswell 2-9-1971, Joseph Mathwin, 28, Bruce Cres., H/pool 10-8-1972, P.R. Hare, Billingham
TRIX wood	HL 56	1933	30'x9'x3'	sail & motor	4.7t	built Hartlepool, lugger, fished lines, nets, crew 4 26-6-1933, W.H. Whelpton, 12, Mill St, H/pool 23-8-1941, J.M. Ross, 440, Clethorpe Rd, Grimsby
TRIX	HL 104		28'x6'x2'		2.4t	fished lines, nets, pots 22-11-1978, T.J. Horsley, Alfred St
TRIX wood	HL 256	1994	6.8m	10kw	2.9t	6-12-1994, H/pool
TRUDI grp	HL 127	1978	9.98m	85kw	3.49t	built Penryn, inshore stern trawler 18-4-1989, H/pool 2008, based at North Shields, decommissioned
TRUDY MAY wood		1965	12m	113kw	16.5t	? H/pool
TRUDY MAY grp	HL 1068	1990	32'	127kw Cat.	23.7t	built Penryn, inshore stern trawler 6-12-1990, *Cygnus Altratus* (HL 26) 21-3-1997, *Altratus* (UL 369), Ullapool 7-9-2000, *Trudie May* (HL 1068), H/pool
TRUE LOVE	HL 125		17'x6'x2'		1.1t	fished nets, pots 6-4-1978, J.R. Phillips, Sandsend Cres., H/pool
TRUSTY wood	HL 32	1923	31'x11'x5'	sail & motor	8.5t	built Cockenzie, yawl, fished nets, lines, pots, crew 2 29-6-1939, Lawrance Carter, 4, St Hilda St, H/pool 1953, sold to Stornoway, ex-*James Ann* (ML 55)
TRUSTY II wood	HL 13	1955	24'x7'x3'		2.3t	built Stockton, fished lines, nets, pots 18-4-1955, L.W. Carter, 4, St Hilda St, H/pool 20-6-1958, Leonard Robinson, 10, Victoria Place, H/pool 4-9-1959, Evans & Barnfather, West H/pool 17-9-1959, Evans, Barnfather, & Southeran, H/pool 27-11-1968, James Flounders Potts, 3, Croft Tce, H/pool
TWEED wood	HL 58		30'	sail	10t	coble, fished nets, crew 4 1-3-1869, William Davidson, H/pool, lost 1869
TWIN SISTERS wood	HL 4		28'x10'x4'	sail & motor	8.7t	lugger, fished nets, lines, crew 4 10-6-1925, Geo. Davidson, 7, York Place, H/pool, wrecked 1926
TWO BROTHERS wood	HL 98	1900	30'x6'x2'	sail	4t	built Hartlepool, lugger fished lines, crew 2 18-9-1918, Frank Southeran, St Mary St, H/pool
TWO PALS wood	HL 97	1914	21'x5'x2'	sail & motor	1.3t	built Hartlepool, lugger, fished lines, pots, crew 2 31-10-1938, Robert Nolan Maiden, 16, Sea Tce, Middleton

NAME & MATERIAL	NO.	YEAR	LENGTH	POWER	WEIGHT	DETAILS
						1958 scrapped, ex-*Brotherly Love*
TWO SISTERS wood	HL 34		29'	sail	10t	coble, fished nets, crew 4 1-3-1869, George Coulson, H/pool,
TWO SISTERS wood	HL 304		19.5'	sail	3t	coble, fished lines, crew 3 6-8-1879, John Shepherd, H/pool, 1898, used for piloting
TWO SISTERS wood	HL 2	1920	29'x9'x3'		6t	built Filey, motor ketch, fished lines, crew 1 15-10-1954, L. Breward, 17, Clarendon Rd, H/pool
UBIQUE wood	HL 66	1946	48'x16'x8'		31t	built Pwllheli, fished nets, lines, crew 5 2-8-1946, Leighton, Winspear & Leighton, H/pool (r/n *Monbreha*)
UNITY wood	HL 64		29'x7'x2'	sail	2.5t	coble, fished nets, lines, pots, crew 3, ex-Whitby 14-5-1901, Elizabeth Ann Major, 96, Brougham Tce, West H/pool 1905 sold to T.E. Reynolds, Seaham
VALDEE grp	HL 701	1981	10.9m	98kw	14.9t	built Worcester, inshore stern trawler 1989, S. Hale, Whitby (WY12) 1-9-1997, Derek Harrison, H/pool (HL 701) 5-8-1999, Kirkcaldy as *Sea Spray II* (KY 11)
VALDER wood	HL 87		38'x11'x5'		12.5t	fished lines, seine, crew 3 11-4-1942, A.R. Sutton, Foggy Furze H/pool, & S. Walker, N. Shields 9-1-1945, R.S. McDougal, Rye, reg. trans. to Rye 1945
VENTURE grp	CK 925	1998	9.97m	112kw	17t	inshore stern trawler
VENTURE	HL 141		29'x7'x3'		2.7t	built Amble, fished nets 21-5-1978, T. Elliot, Easington Coll. & R. Powell, Horden
VENTURER wood	HL 1063	1986	8.05m	40kw	2.1t	built Newcastle, inshore stern trawler 2-2-1999, H/pool
VENUS wood	HL 123	1992	7.67m	85kw	1.82t	built Amble 22-5-1992, H/pool
VIC wood	HL 67		22'x6'x2'	sail & motor	1.4t	built Hartlepool, lugger, fished lines, pots, crew 2 1-3-1937, Richard Stevenson, 46, Commercial St, Middleton 24-6-1940, Herbert Bell, 25, St Oswald St, West H/pool 29-4-1942, J.E. Archbold, 70, Ormsby Rd, West H/pool
VICTORY wood	HL 52		26'	sail	7t	coble, fished nets, crew 4 1-3-1869, Thomason Pounder, H/pool, sold to Staithes 1871
VICTORY wood	HL 51		28'x6'x2'	sail & motor	2t	lugger, fished lines, nets, pots, crew 3 13-11-1931, Lawrance Carter, 12, Church St, Seaton Carew
VIE	HL 111		26'x8'x3'		3t	fished lines pots 12-9-1947, Wm. Marshall, 5, Oakley Gdns, H/pool 9-8-1949, C.C. Smith, 173, Park Rd, West H/pool
VITAL SPARK wood	HL 32	1930	9.5m	30kw	6.54t	built Scarboro' 13-3-1991, H/pool
VIKING	HL 113		31'x8'x3'		4t	line, nets, pots 22-2-1977, W. P. Anderson, Jesmond Rd, H/pool
VIKING II	HL 58		20'x6'x2'		1.4t	built Whitby 25-9-1972, D. Newton, Darlington
VIN wood	HL 22		20'x6'x2'		1.5t	fished lines, pots 27-6-1956, Y.C. Leighton, 39, Lily St, H/pool 24-3-1961, Geo. Horsley Leighton, 181 Bruce Cres., H/pool
VIOLA	HL 18	1890	27'x7'x2'	sail	4t	built Filey, coble, fished nets, pots 25-7-1919, Amos Major, 6, Topcliffe St, West H/pool, scrap 1921
VIOLET wood	HL 8		41'	sail	13t	decked boat, fished nets, crew 5 1-10-1887, Peter & Henry Burgon, 18 Commercial St, H/pool
VIOLET wood	HL 38	1905	18'x5'x2'	sail	1.5t	built Sunderland, coble, fished lines, crew 2, also foy-boat 27-9-1909, Robert Ward, 9, Armstrong St, Castle Eden
VULCAN	HL 156		28'x8'x3'		3.6t	fished lines, nets, pots

Supreme

Supreme Endeavour

Swiftwing

Sybil

Tantallon

Taurus

Terri Louise

Tetsuko

Thistle

Three Lads

Tine Anderson

Trudi

NAME & MATERIAL	NO.	YEAR	LENGTH	POWER	WEIGHT	DETAILS
W. S. BURTON steel ON 139831	HL 86	1917	122'x22'x13'	steam	234t	18-5-1967, T. Noble, & P. Holroyd. H/pool 13-5-1971, R. Pounder, & K. Trotter, H/pool built Hall Russell, A/deen, yard No.596, 9 crew 13-3-1917, R.H. Davison, H/pool 1917–1919, Navy, m/s, 1x6pdrAA (A.3036) 23-9-1929, Walker, Aberdeen, as *Star of the Wave* (A 60) 1940–1946, Navy, m/s (FY 1590) 1943, Purdy, N. Shields, r/n *Lynne Purdy* 1947
WANDERER wood	HL 3	1920	26'x6'x3'		3.5t	fished lines, pots, ex-*Nellie* 2-11-1954, S.M. Gowler, Seaton Lane, West H/pool 8-9-1956, Francis Barnfather, 5, Nelson St, West H/pool
WANDERER grp	HL 235	1991	6m	36kw	2.48t	built Falmouth 27- 9-1991, H/pool 13-5-1992, (LK 234), Lerwick
WATER LILY wood	HL 161		31'	sail	10t	coble, fished nets, crew 4 6-5-1869, Ralph Curry, H/pool, sold to Staithes 1870
WATER LILY wood	HL 256		33'	sail	5t	coble, fished nets, crew 4 16-10-1875, Joseph Turner, H/pool
WATER LILY wood	HL 11		27'x6'x2'	sail	3.4t	lugger, fished lines, nets, crew 3 3-3-1925, Charles Jones, East St, Blackhall
WATERWITCH wood	HL 1		26'x5'x2'	sail	1.4t	lugger, fished lines, pots, crew 3 27-1-1930, Daniel Hogg, 9, Wells Yard, H/pool 10-9-1930, G.W. Wardropp, Pratts Passage, H/pool
WAVECREST wood	HL 198	1980	9.1x2.1x1.0m	50kw	4.7t	built Whitby, coble, fished lines, pots 18-3-1983, Frank Allen, Howbeck Lane, H/pool
WAYFINDER steel	SH 76	1998	13.1m	229kw	31t	built Grimsby, fished trawl ?, W. Hodgson, Whitby St, H/pool, sold 2008
WAYSIDE FLOWER wood	HL 4	1910	43'x12'x6'	sail & motor	21t	built Filey, coble fished nets, lines, crew 5 (ex-SH 32) Scarboro' 15-1-1914, local group, inc. Coulsons & Horsleys, H/pool 16-12-1914, destroyed in bombardment
WAYSIDE FLOWER wood ON 186569	BH 5	1954		95hp	17t	built Eyemouth, fished trawl 1969, R. Robinson, Amble 1982, Frank Burgan, H/pool
WELFARE wood	HL 33		43'x15'x4'	sail	14t	decked boat, fished nets, crew 7, ex-965 BK 27-9-1892, John Wm. Holman, 7, Brougham St, H/pool, sold 1905
WELCOME wood	HL 138		18.5'	sail	3t	coble, fished lines, crew 3 3-3-1869, Robert Pounder, H/pool, sold 1883
WELCOME wood	HL 139		28'	sail	8t	coble, fished lines, crew 4 3-3-1869, Robert Pounder, H/pool
WELCOME wood	HL 58	1906	21'x6'x2'	sail	2.2t	built Hartlepool, coble, fished drift net, crew 2 3-5-1911, John Cambridge, 7, John St, H/pool
WELLSPRING wood	BA 337	1960	12.1m	56kw	15.7t	built Fraserburgh, fished trawl 1969, Donald McLean & others, Maidens, Ayrshire 1993, A. Young, Redcar, based H/pool
WEST WIND	HL 58		22'x7'x2'		2t	fished pots, lines 13-5-1953, Joseph Pringle, M/boro 4-8-1955, John Wm. Machin, 23, Hart Lane, H/pool
WESTBOURNE wood	HL 49	1943	25'x7'x3'		2.8t	fished lines, pots 12-12-1956, Stanley Levill, 8, Westbourne Rd, West H/pool
WESTBURN wood	HL 47	1929	22'x7'x2'		1.9t	fished lines, pots 27-10-1956, John Edward Pearson, 40, Powlett Rd & Stanley Maiden, 38, Powlett Rd, West H/pool
WHITE HEATHER wood	HL 116	1926	35'x14'x6'		14.6t	built Eyemouth, fished seine (ex-BK 13) 23-3-1959, A. Fenwick, Westmoreland St Garage, West H/pool

NAME & MATERIAL	NO.	YEAR	LENGTH	POWER	WEIGHT	DETAILS
WHITE HEATHER wood	HL 124	1989	8.59m		2.24t	built Amble 28-11-1995, H/pool
WHITE HEATHER IV steel	LH 1	1981	20.8m	375kw	86t	built Cambeltown Shipyards, fished trawl seine 1981, Jim Aitchison, Eyemouth 2007, Major Hartley, H/pool, sold 2008
WHITE STAR wood	HL 187		20'	sail	2t	coble, herring coble, crew 2 3-9-1869, Eden Pounder, sold to Sunderland 1871
WHITE STAR	HL 65		20'x7'x2'		2.3t	fished lines pots, ex-*Maggie* 13-10-1950, Mathew Hastings Porritt, 17, Town Wall, H/pool 28-5-1953, James Edward White, 6, Brougham St, H/pool
WHY NOT wood	HL 210		32'		12t	keel boat, fished nets, crew 2 2-8-1871, Alfred Smith, H/pool, re-reg. at Whitby 1871
WILDFIRE ON 88149	HL 357		70'	steam & sail	19t	sloop rigged steamer, fished lines, crew 7 1-10-1884, John Pattison, H/pool (skipper John Farrell)
WILD ROVER wood	HL 707	1970	7.78m	40kw	4t	built Whitby 1990, (HL 10) 2002, (HL 707)
WILLIAM wood	HL 25		18.5'	sail	3t	coble, fished lines, crew 3 1-3-1869, Robert Yeal, H/pool
WILLIAM wood	HL 13		26'	sail	10t	coble, fished nets, crew 4 1-3-1869, Thomas Marshall, H/pool sold 1872
WILLIAM wood	HL 257		18.5' keel 26'x6'x2' oa	sail	3t	coble, fished lines, crew 3 26-10-1875, Robert Allen, H/pool 19-2-1890, Cuthbert Coulson, 9, John St, West H/pool
WILLIAMS wood	HL 219		19'	sail	3t	coble, fished lines, crew 3 25-7-1872, William Heron, H/pool
WILLIAMS wood	HL 324		39'	sail	12t	keel boat, fished nets, lines, crew 5, ex-Berwick 6-4-1882, W. & F. Hastings, H/pool 22-2-1884, William Hastings, H/pool 11-10-1887, James & John Graham, & James Holtom, H/pool 1889, transferred to Grimsby
WILLIAM & ALICE wood	HL 285		21'	sail	3t	coble fished lines, crew 3 23-10-1877, William Winspear, H/pool
WILLIAM & ANN wood	HL 294		21'	sail	1.5t	smack, fished lines, crew 2 20-5-1878, William Seymore, H/pool, scrapped 1879
WILLIAM & ANN wood	HL 294		18'	sail	1.0t	boat, fished lines, nets, crew 2 4-1-1879, William Seymore, H/pool
WILLIAM & ANN wood	HL 306		19'	sail	3t	coble, fished lines, crew 3 27-9-1879, John Horsley, H/pool
WILLIAM ALICE wood	HL 88		29'	sail	7t	coble, fished nets, crew 4 1-3-1869, William Harper, H/pool, sold to Staithes 1871
WILLIAM NICOLAS wood	HL 69		29'	sail	11t	coble. fished nets, crew 4 1-3-1869, William Hunter, H/pool
WINDFALL wood	HL 59	1943	26'x8'x3'		3.4t	fished lines, pots 5-2-1957, John Stewart, 27, Warren Rd, H/pool
WINDSONG wood	SH 82	1977	10.3m	52kw	7.7t	coble, fished nets, pots ? , Peter Rolf, Redcar, based H/pool
WINDWARD	HL 136					
WINIFRED wood	HL 155	1935	48'x15'x6'		23t	built Anstruther, keel boat, fished lines, pots 1969, George Leighton, H/pool 11-12-1972, Joseph Oswold Rennie, 63, Turnbull St, H/pool
WOODROSE wood	HL 106	1939	31'x8'x3'		3.7t	built Newcastle, fished lines, trawl 22-11-1950, G.F. Whitfield, 158, Stockton Rd, H/pool
XMAS DAISY	LT 765	1911		steam		built Lowestoft, launched 29-4-1911, drifter

Trudy May

Trusty

Venture

Venturer

W.S. Burton

Wavecrest

Wayfinder

Wayside Flower

Wayside Flower II

White Heather IV

Wild Rover

Windsong

NAME & MATERIAL	NO.	YEAR	LENGTH	POWER	WEIGHT	DETAILS
wood ON 130008				25hp		engine by Elliot & Garrord 1911, L.R. Tripp, Lowestoft 5-1914, towed SS *Caroline* into Tyne from position 40m SE 1914–1918, Navy 1918, Stranton Drifters, H/pool, scrapped 1936
YORKSHIRE ROSE wood	HL 12	1978	9.9x3x1m	48kw	4.9t	built Whitby, coble, fished nets, pots 23-5-1984, Kevin Race, Lime Cres, H/pool
YOUNG WILLIAM wood	HL 124		30'	sail/oar	10t	coble, fished nets, crew 5 1-3-1869, Ann Davidson, H/pool 14-6-1872, Joseph Ransen, H/pool 7-10-1878, Mark Davison, H/pool
YVONNE MARIE	HL 14		11.9x4.2x1.7m	70kw	13.4t	built in France, fished trawl 16-3-1984, J.O. Rennie, Turnbull St, H/pool 1993, K.J. Connolly, Lowestoft

Xmas Daisy

Yvonne Marie

BIBLIOGRAPHY

Maritime Hartlepool, Bert Spaldin (Printability Publishing on behalf of Bert Spaldin, 2005)
Royal Navy Trawlers, parts 1 and 2, Gerald Toghill (Maritime Books, 2003)
Lloyds War Losses WW1 (Lloyds of London Press Ltd, 1990)
The Railway Gazette, December 1910
The Hartlepools and the Great War (Chas. A. Sage, 1920)
The Trawlermen, David Butcher (Tops'l Books, 1980)
The Driftermen, David Butcher (Tops'l Books, 1979)
Sailing Fishermen, Colin Elliot (Tops'l Books, 1978)
Sailing Trawlers, Edgar J. March (Percival Marshall & Co. Ltd, 1953)
Beyond the Piers, Ron Wright (The People's History Ltd, 2002)
The Real Price of Fish, George F. Richie (Hutton Press Ltd, 1991)
Olsens Fisherman's Almanac (E.T.W. Dennis & Son Ltd)
Last of the Hunters, Peter Mortimer (North Tyneside Libraries & Arts Dept, 1987)
History of Hartlepool, Sir Cuthbert Sharp (John Procter, 1851, reprinted H/pool Council 1978)
Following the Fishing, David Butcher (Tops'l Books, 1987)
Swept Channels, Taffrail (Hodder & Stoughton Ltd, 1935)
Fishing Ports Served by the LNER (LNER, 1923)

Additional information:

www.aberdeenships.com
www.milfordtrawlers.org.uk
www.miramarshipindex.org.nz
Teesside Archives, Middlesbrough
The Scottish Fisheries Museum, Anstruther
North East Lincolnshire Archives, Grimsby
Hartlepool Libraries Reference Section
Hartlepool Maritime Archaeology Dept
Port of Lowestoft Research Society
Alan Cook
Stephen Horsley
Keith Williams
Sonny Ray
Tony Pearson
Derek Bradley
Robbie Wray
Jenny Hillier

Above: The abbey church of St Hilda overlooks the fleet.

Below: Hauling in the trawl net on board the *Norwood*.

Above: A line of modern inshore vessels which have replaced many of the traditional cobles.

Below: A line of traditional cobles moored up between trips.

Visit our website and discover thousands of other History Press books.
www.thehistorypress.co.uk